THE GOOD ASSASSIN

By

Judy Lucas

ISBN: 1-4033-0398-3 (Electronic)
ISBN: 1-4033-0399-1 (Softcover)
ISBN: 1-4033-0400-9 (Hardcover)
ISBN: 1-4033-0401-7 (Rocket Book)

Library of Congress Control Number: 2002103598

This book is printed on acid free paper.

Printed in the United States of America
Bloomington, IN

1st Books - rev. 05/21/02

This book is dedicated to
two of the least handicapped people I know.

Darryl Harrington, who lost his leg and hip, but has never stopped
living a full and happy life.

Sarah Cripps, sightless at birth, but never let that stop her from being
the best lawyer in town.

With thanks to my daughter, Jane.
Her gift of a computer made it possible.

Judy Lucas

PROLOGUE

THE NATIONAL LABORATORY
Oak Ridge, Tennessee USA
September 1999

The receptionist handed him the visitor's pass. He clipped the tag to his coat lapel and opened the heavy steel door when she buzzed him through. He knew his way without an escort and proceeded down the immaculate hallway, fluorescent lights gleaming on the highly polished vinyl floors. A couple of corners to turn, then through swinging double doors to the lab.

A white-coated technician stood to the side of the large, dimly lighted room. Various cabinets and equipment were moved to the side and space left open in the middle of the floor. The woman put down a clipboard and looked up.

"Jeff, I'm glad you could make it."

"You know I'll come every time you call me." The visitor let a cynical smile flow over the woman. She came to him and he pecked a kiss on the cheek of her long narrow face. "What have you got for me?"

She looked disappointed with the greeting, but moved to the center of the room. He followed to what looked like a miniature race track laid out in the cleared space on the floor. An object that might have been a tiny moon buggy, or maybe the Mars rover, sat to the side. Twenty feet long and ten feet wide, the banked oval track looked like a kid's toy setup.

"What's this? You run out of funding or something? No new projects to save or destroy the planet? Now you're playing with toys?"

The woman gave him a condescending look and turned her attention to a complicated control panel. She hit a series of switches and several green lights glowed around the track, then with a smug look she pushed a toggle switch and the little moon buggy took off with astonishing speed. It raced around the track in a blur. There was no sound, none at all except the soft whirl of the wheels.

With a control that looked somewhat like the hybrid offspring of a computer mouse and joystick, she slowed the speed and stopped the car in front of her visitor. He started to reach for it, but she quickly backed it away from his hand. Her voice was sharp when she commanded, "Stay back. Do not reach inside the painted circle. Don't touch anything."

With the control, she made the car perform several maneuvers, backwards, forwards, side to side and around in circles. He stood back and watched. She increased the speed of the vehicle again until it seemed to blend in with the track, moving so fast he could not keep eye contact. She slowed the car to a sedate pace and stopped it when it reached her side of the track.

"Some toy you got here. You're pretty good with that radio control. Every kid I know will want one."

The woman snapped switches and the glowing green lights went out. "It's not a toy," she said, "no antennas, no radio control, no batteries." She continued to shut down the control board, but left the little vehicle untouched on the floor. She pulled off the lab coat, placed it on a plastic hanger and hung it on the rack with several more of the white coats. "Now you can buy me supper."

"Aw, come on, I'm a reporter, remember?"

"It's not for publication yet. I'd be in trouble if they knew I let you in here." She reached a hand to touch his cheek.

He grabbed the hand, squeezing a little harder than necessary. "You can be a real tease," he said, gritting his teeth behind the smile. "Maybe I won't be so anxious to come, next time you call."

He could see the threat hit home before she lowered her eyes. She flexed her hand when he released it, then picked up her purse. When she turned to face him she arched an eyebrow with a confident smile.

"Oh, you'll come. This is big, really big. Maybe it will save or destroy the planet. That 'toy' is the automobile of the future."

CHAPTER ONE

Nashville, Tennessee USA
September 1999

His flight from New York was late arriving at the Nashville International Airport. Vanderbilt University Hospital should have sent a car to meet him. No one in the crowded concourse approached him or materialized with his name on a sign. If they waited at all, there was no one here now.

Dr. Ahmed Faziz, a stocky man of average height with a full neat beard and graying brown hair, made his way down the long ramp from the deplaning area to a bank of pay telephones. Only his clothing set him apart from the other passengers leaving the terminal. Fishing in the pocket of his wrinkled suit of thin cotton for American change, he telephoned the hospital information number.

Several minutes on hold, and two transfers from the Hospital to the University, he was told Dr. Faziz was not expected until the next Friday. The woman was quite apologetic, but Dr. Lowell who made the arrangements for the seminar was not in today. Reservations on the correct date were made for Dr. Faziz at the Vanderbilt Plaza Hotel. If he would take a taxi, perhaps he could check in a few days early.

Ahmed was beginning to regret his decision to come here. A phone call to the hotel confirmed his reservation for the following Friday. The desk clerk politely informed him nothing was available until then. The confusion left him feeling angry and increased the misgivings he had from the beginning for this engagement.

He went to the lower level of the airport terminal carrying a badly worn satchel, his only luggage. A long line of newly arrived passengers waited at the taxi cab stand. Signs on minibuses offered transportation between the airport and the downtown area, but it had been years since he was in the United States and he had no idea what, if any, hotels with rooms available were close to the University.

Grudgingly, he waited in line for a taxi. When it was finally his turn, Ahmed gave the driver the address of an acquaintance from whom he had recently received a letter. The cabby, with an East-Indian accent informed him he knew the area. A small Arab and Indian community flourished in an older neighborhood near Vanderbilt University.

At the second story apartment of a rundown house his welcome was anything but cordial. The boy who answered the door offered no apology or excuses. "My father is not here. I did not know you were expected." The youth shrugged his narrow shoulders into a clean shirt. "I have to go to class. You can stay here or go, as you want."

"I will wait," Ahmed nodded curtly. In his homeland a discourteous youth would not be tolerated.

The boy again gave a disinterested shrug. "No problem."

After the youth left, Ahmed turned on the television and found an all news channel. He left the announcer giving day old news and went to the kitchen. Donuts and stale potato chips were the mainstays, along with a freshly opened can of ground coffee. A carton of milk, bread, and a few eggs rounded out the supplies, making it obvious guests were not expected.

The kitchen table held several newspapers. From Nashville, Knoxville, Chattanooga and Atlanta, he scanned the headlines. The articles and by-lines had nothing of interest for him, though someone had highlighted several of the items concerning the current U. S. Presidential election race.

Ahmed was sorry he had come to visit his friend. Not really a friend, someone he had worked with off and on at least fifteen years ago. The letter had arrived with an invitation to visit when in the States or Ahmed would never have presumed to renew the acquaintance. When he was contacted by the University to speak at the seminar, a certain amount of curiosity about the reason for the letter prompted him to accept the engagement.

Ahmed looked at his watch, trying to decide whether to stay or find a hotel when he heard the apartment door open. He half stepped forward to see who entered. A shadow crossed the door between the rooms. A man followed, walking slowly into the kitchen. Ahmed blanched, then sat heavily on a chair as his knees gave way.

"Abbey," using a friendly greeting, the tall, slender man seated himself opposite Ahmed and spoke in Arabic, "you do not see a ghost. I am indeed alive."

Ahmed recovered his voice. He could feel his pulse racing with the shock. "Ibrahim, I thought never to see you again. There was word of your execution at the hands of the Israelis.

"It was Yuseff." The man smiled sadly, but offered no further explanation.

"The boy?" Ahmed made a gesture toward the door.

"Yuseff's son. He now calls me father. A good boy, he will do as I ask. It was I who sent the letter, and suggested to the University to invite you to participate in the seminar on AIDS. You have come far in your medical career, my friend."

Ahmed smiled ruefully, feeling a little more at ease. "And you have not changed at all. It was you who made arrangements for the airline ticket. I am here a week early. Why?"

"There is something you can do for me. A favor I will collect for the times I have helped you. Ah, now, do not look so surprised. It is a small thing; one a man of your experience will not hesitate to perform."

Ahmed stiffened. "I no longer accept those assignments. I am a doctor now, nothing more. It has been ten years since I was active."

The eyes of the man across from him narrowed. "Your mother, is she well? You have made a home for her, have you not? Someone of her advanced years deserves comfort in her old age. Then there is the child you call your own, even if he is a foundling. What age is he now? Twelve, thirteen? Ah, you sent him to be schooled in England. Yes, I believe I have heard he is doing quite well."

The voice paused, then hardened. "You will do this. If you refuse, certain individuals will know where to find you. Everything you have worked for will be gone. The man once known as the best can no longer hide." The speaker's dark eyes glittered. "I may decide to visit your son myself. Do you understand what I say?"

Ahmed stared back at the man who had managed to escape death at the hands of the Mossaad. He had no doubt he was trapped. His breath rushed out with the words. "What is this favor you ask of me?"

* * * * *

David Middleton, flat on his back, pulled in his stomach muscles and tightened his grip on the iron bar. His arms felt like putty, muscles burning with the effort. He blew out his breath and pressed upward. The bar moved another inch.

"Come on..., come on..., you can do it!" the voice wheedled from beyond his field of vision. "One more time! A little higher! That's it. Higher, take it easy now. Up..., up..., that's it, that's it. Okay, we got it now, you can let go." It took an effort to loosen his fingers. The bar with weighted ends moved from over his head as two men attached it to hooks. He sat up, holding still for a moment while his breathing quieted, then grabbed the towel that was thrown over his face.

"You did it, you did it. See, what did I tell you? You're one strong son of a bitch." David balled up the towel and threw it at the man in front of him. Jim Ed's enthusiasm wasn't in the least dampened. He continued to grin, teeth white in his dark face. "Man, you just bench pressed two fifty, flat on your back. Pretty remarkable for a man who..."

David allowed himself to smile at his friend. "Yeah, I guess it is. You can say it. For a one-legged man. My personal best, isn't it?"

Not just my leg, David thought. That whole side is gone. No hip, no leg, no anything below the rib cage. I left it in the Persian Gulf with the remains of a land mine.

Jim Ed was telling everyone within earshot what he had accomplished. It was an accomplishment, David guessed. Without a left hip, balance was difficult on the narrow bench, even flat on his back. "Hey, loud mouth, hand me those sticks before I try it with you next."

Jim Ed, whose own physique looked like it belonged in a body building magazine, was still grinning. "I'm proud of you, man. Now I'm going to set you up another twenty pounds."

"Not today," David shook his head, "I'm due in court. I'll call you later."

"Okay, counselor. Go knock 'em dead over at the courthouse." He handed David his crutches. "Need any help in the shower?"

David fastened the metal cuffs at his wrists, took hold of the handles on the hip high metal rods, and swung his six foot two frame upright. He shook his head. "You know better than that."

Jim Ed moved on to his next customer. "That's a real man." He nodded in David's direction. "I'd sure hate to be the poor slob who calls him handicapped."

David took a quick shower. He was pretty good at hopping and balancing on his one leg, but the gym shower floor tended to be slippery. All that chlorine and commercial cleaner Jim Ed used, he thought. Most of the time he waited until he was home where a series of built in bars and handholds helped. And privacy. The army surgeons had done a good job patching him up. Even the scars weren't too bad, what with all the skin grafts to cover the exposed muscle and flesh. Still, it was a sight he would just as soon no one else would see. He could do without the pity he got from most strangers.

David toweled himself dry without having to share the locker room. He dressed, got his crutches and left by the rear door without disturbing Jim Ed again. A short walk around the corner of the square saw him to his office.

He was surprised to see his Girl Friday and paralegal, Ellen Taggert, already at her desk. It was still early, another two hours before the court appearance. She looked up as he came in. "Ellen," he said affectionately, "you know I can't pay overtime. What brought you in so early?"

The silver haired woman at the desk answered his grin with one of her own. One of the reasons he had hired her was her sense of humor. She didn't need money, so the reference to overtime was a private joke between them. David had given up trying to govern the hours she put in, though he tried not to take advantage of her. She was passionate about every case they took on, no matter how big or small.

Not that anything big ever happened in this small town. Good thing I've got my army stipend, he thought. Not much work for a lawyer here in Smithville. He had been appointed public defender for the county and that made up the bulk of his practice. The case today was a local man, accused of killing and eating a neighbor's cow.

Ellen didn't bother to explain or defend her early hours. "Look who's up early," she said, as she handed him the morning mail. "Mr. Snead is due to come in at nine-thirty, court at ten. Mr. and Mrs. Martin at one-thirty for their will, and unless you bring something back from the courthouse, that's it for today."

David knew his schedule as well as she did, but never interrupted when she went over it. It was her job, and she took pleasure in being efficient and businesslike about everything. Like always calling the clients by the formal address. She knew three-fourth of the population of the county on a first name basis; here at the office it was business. Mr. Snead was the defendant for today, even though she had known him, the missus and their passel of kids for years.

David took the mail, bestowing one of his more engaging smiles on Ellen, and headed for his office. The ground floor of the old building was divided into three rooms. The front was the reception area with the street side glass windows and Ellen's desk; behind was a side hall with a staircase to the upper floors. A rather spacious conference room that doubled as his law library opened off the hall. David's office ran the width of the building to the rear, with a door opening to the outside alley.

David had bought the rundown structure with a VA loan when he came back home. He had taken pleasure in doing most of the work of restoration himself. The offices were finished, old wood wainscoting sanded, polished and gleaming; the walls above painted a light winter wheat tan. Oriental rugs and mahogany furniture loaned a quality of elegance to the large rooms. It had taken a chunk out of his savings, but worth it. He enjoyed beautiful things.

The living quarters on the second floor were still under construction, but he made do, enjoying the privacy of his own place. He had no plans at the present for the third floor other than storage. It was full size and could be another apartment if he ever needed the rent money. It had been the talk of the town when he bought the building, even more when he moved in. What did a one-legged man need with a three story house?

David proceeded to his office with the mail tucked under his arm. The decorating style he had chosen for himself could only be called comfortable. While he had his share of rugs and dark wood bookcases, his desk was a huge old rolltop, complete with a massive wooden armchair on springs and wheeled pedestal. It creaked with his weight as he sat down. He propped the crutches against the wall beside the desk and opened the morning's postal offering. Ellen entered through the open door to place a mug of fresh coffee on the desk. He only glanced up at her.

David read the mail carefully, including the junk mail, before disposing of it. Slowly sipping the hot coffee, he reread the letter from his sister. She was, as usual, nagging him to come visit. When he took time, he would write that he was too busy in his successful law practice to visit right now. A bill from the local electric co-op would go to Ellen for payment. He went over a few other papers on his desk to refresh himself for today's court case. He buzzed Ellen, offered to make breakfast which she declined, then levered himself up the stairs to his kitchen.

After a Spartan meal of cereal, toast, orange juice and vitamins, David turned on the spigots in his whirlpool tub. The oversize fiberglass unit was a luxury, along with the specially designed shower, but well worth the investment. He had spent six months in rehab and knew the healing power of hot, swirling water when he over extended his muscles. As the water ran, he brushed his teeth, careful to use mouthwash and shaved with extra care. When the tub filled, he stripped and settled in the relaxing water.

David was not unhappy with his life. When he was wounded, he was devastated at first. You don't lose part of yourself and not notice it. After being patched up in a field hospital, he was quickly airvac'ed to Germany. There was a question as to whether the surgeons could save enough of him to matter, much less let him walk again. They had made the effort, though, and his manhood was scarred but intact. He could father a child they told him, not to worry.

David hadn't worried about sex at that point. He was determined to walk, and not always with crutches either. He amazed the doctors and therapist with his strength and tenacity. He worked with the CPO to design a prosthesis he could wear, then learned to swing his body so the artificial leg and foot moved forward. When he got out of the tub, he dried carefully and used a deodorant powder on his upper body and stomach. The molded plastic of the brace that held the leg to his body made him sweat. An extra long tee shirt helped, too. He always wore the leg when he went to court. No jury or judge should be made to feel sorry for him, and so transfer the feeling to his clients. He was too good a lawyer to take advantage of that situation.

Downstairs again, he had time to go over the wills he had drawn up for the Martins before Ellen escorted Mr. Snead through his door. He invited the spare man to sit down, but was ignored as Cal Snead continued to stand and kept running his dirty finger inside the stiff collar of an obviously new white shirt.

"Please sit down, Cal. We need to go over what's going to happen in court this morning."

"Sorry," the man finally sat. "I know what's going to happen. Been there before."

"I know you have." David had the feeling that maybe he wasn't such a good lawyer after all. "I'm your lawyer and I'll do everything I can to get you off. You know that, but this is the third time. You already admitted to the sheriff you killed the cow. Before that it was chickens and a pig. You ate them, too. Why don't you plead guilty and I can make an arrangement with Mr. Clemmons to let you work off the cost of the livestock?"

Snead's chin was sticking out at a stubborn angle. "Cow come over in my yard. Same as the chickens. Cow got in the garden. Tore up the beans and squash. Corn was 'bout ready to pick. Cow ate the corn, we ate the cow. Seems fair to me."

David gave up with a groan. Maybe he could convince the judge to make the sentence light. Otherwise, the wife and kids would be left for the county and state to support.

****

He was angry. Ibrahim was so sure Ahmed would fall in with his plans that everything was pre-arranged. Gathering information, selecting the equipment and making arrangements was Ahmed's prerogative. Now there was little time for preparations. Ibrahim had been right about one thing. Ahmed was the best. There were no warrants in any part of the world for Dr. Ahmed Faziz. Because of careful planning, no one had ever connected him with any of the services he performed. Ahmed knew what he had to do.

Using directions given him at the apartment, he walked three blocks to catch a city bus. The scant passengers were a mixed lot, mostly blacks and foreign-nationals such as himself. In the back of the bus he heard Spanish spoken. None of them had given him a second look as he boarded. He studied a man across the aisle from his seat, copied the relaxed posture and nodding head. He rode the short distance to an upscale shopping mall, exiting the bus at the main entrance.

Walking the entire mall, he watched to see if he was noticed. The ability to blend into his surroundings had always been an asset. Americans were a different lot since he was here last. The dress was more casual, but they seemed in a hurry to finish their errands. He looked down at the outmoded suit he had thought to wear to the seminar. The virtual isolation of the place he had chosen for his home did not lend itself to a wardrobe other than the loose shirts and cotton pants he wore most of the time. As he window shopped the abundance offered for sale, he thought back to the time when money was reason enough to accept an assignment. No more. He would do what Ibrahim asked, but on his own terms. It would not be difficult. Training and skills from years past surfaced in his mind. Again he studied the people he passed, picking up the English with the southern drawl of this area. A booth in the middle of the concourse offered amber tinted sunglasses, but wearing them was more vanity than necessity. None of the passing shoppers gave him more than a glance. Quickly finding what he needed, he paid cash for everything, money provided by Ibrahim.

He left the mall, his purchases in a new wheeled carry-on bag; a suit, shirt and tie on hangers in a matching garment bag. On the return bus he again studied the passengers, honing skills he never meant to use again. Back in the apartment he settled down to rest. The flight had been long and tiring, the jet lag catching up. Tomorrow would bring memories. Memories Ahmed would as soon leave in the past.

The next day, Ahmed and the boy, in the pickup truck that belonged to the youth, took a main highway into a small suburban town. Used car lots occupied space on both sides of the four lane highway, interspersed between a few stores and a post office set between weed-grown vacant lots. They stopped at one such car lot in the main part of the town. Most of the vehicles offered to purchasers were obviously very well used. Shabby signs advertised instant credit, so much a week in payment. The youth went to look for the manager while Ahmed leaned against the truck surveying the less than desirable line up of vehicles that stocked the front row.

A man came out of a small garage wiping his greasy hands on a shop towel. The boy introduced Ahmed as his uncle and asked if the request had been filled. The man, with a shock of brown hair and bristly beard, nodded and led them behind the building. A green 1999 Bonneville waited, clean and shiny. The boy asked if all the equipment was in place and the man reached in the car to pop the trunk lid.

After looking the car over, Ahmed transferred his belongings from the truck to the car and again checked the special equipment. It was not the best. An automatic hand gun with extra clips and a 30.06 slide-action semiautomatic rifle with a scope, along with several four round magazines, hid under a rough brown wool army blanket. Green and khaki camouflage coveralls, without the orange vest used by hunters, were folded neatly beside rubber boots. A quick inspection of the gun showed it to be in working condition. Ahmed lifted the gun to sight through the scope, but was stopped by the hand of the brown haired man. "Not here," the man shook his head.

Ahmed glanced up to see a police patrol car go down the street. He paid the agreed price from a cache of one thousand dollar bills, money also given him at the apartment. None of this was to his liking, but the boy had been in charge of the arrangements and he let it go.

Ahmed closed the trunk lid, not pleased, but again he had no choice, given little time to prepare. The man with the bushy beard headed to the shop without a backward glance. The boy slammed the truck door and roared out of the lot without the customary farewell. Ahmed got in the green car and drove onto the street.

At a discount station, he fueled the car and bought a map of Tennessee, paying with the change from his mall purchases. Out of town he began to look for the interstate junction. He entered the ramp marked Knoxville and turned on the cruise control. The car was a nice piece of engineering for an American assembly line, with a velvet ride and responsive handling. He had settled down for the drive until he began to wonder why this car was on a lot with vehicles of much lower quality. He decided to take the first opportunity presented to replace the drive out tag the car lot had supplied. If the car was stolen, it might trigger the police to stop him.

He left the interstate at the first exit that advertised lodging. Motels, fast food restaurants, and gas stations with their quick fix markets lined the street leading into the town. Pulling into an older, run down motel, where the faded sign advertised $ 21.99 Single, he paid cash for a room with two double beds.

Disgusted, Ahmed looked at the poor surroundings as he carried his luggage into the room. He did not want this assignment. The past should stay in the past. A cracked mirror drew his attention to the present. He had cut his hair shorter for the seminar, but the full beard he let grow over the last few years would be convenient now. He was not so much worried that someone would recognize him, but later, if needed, he could shave and change his appearance. Ahmed placed his trust in only himself. The boy in Nashville he would not trust, nor the man at the car lot. Ibrahim would use them, the same way he controlled Ahmed.

He turned down the dusty spread on one of the beds, hung the clothes he was wearing neatly away and slept as only one who was used to catching sleep whenever possible can do.

It was full dark when he woke. He showered quickly in the lukewarm water and dressed in one of his new outfits. He saw a restaurant a few doors down and walked there to have his supper. The night was pleasant, and the brief exercise felt good. Back at the motel, he again took note of the drive out tag. He glanced around at the other vehicles in front of the rooms. A couple of Ohio plates, an old pickup truck with a rusty Tennessee tag.

The short nap in the afternoon had revitalized him and the air was cool after the late summer day's sun. He walked to the side of the motel where the small swimming pool had already been drained, or maybe never filled this summer. Noting a driveway continued around the end of the building from the paved parking area, he slowly walked around the corner. The back of the office was evidently a small apartment. A late model Chevrolet Lumina sat in the drive behind the apartment. Ahmed continued to amble along, to all appearances seeming to enjoy the evening walk.

When he was sure no one watched, he again went to the back of the building, this time with a small screw driver from a tool pouch in the green car. He quickly removed the license plate from the Chevy, checking to be sure Tennessee used only one plate. He slipped the thin metal inside his jacket and nonchalantly strolled past the office toward his room.

He put the key in the lock and was about to open the door when he heard the voice. "Hey, honey, maybe you want some company?"

Ahmed turned toward the voice, but the question was not directed to him. The speaker was a young black girl, so small she could hardly reach the window of the old pickup truck. Apparently she was talking to its occupant.

Ahmed shook his head. A whore plying her trade. The dress she wore was too large on the thin body. Too young, Ahmed thought, but it was none of his business. He turned the key and entered his room, closing the door quickly. He took the license plate from his jacket and tossed it on the chair.

He stretched out on the bed before realizing the TV had no remote. For a few moments he willed himself to relax. What he was asked to do did not sit well with his stomach. His mind roamed back to past years, when as a young fanatic he had held the value of human life so casually. Mentally shaking himself, he got to his feet and stepped over to the TV. As he reached for the ON button, he heard voices on the other side of the thin wall. A low growl, answered by high pitched giggles. So she had made a sale. Ahmed sighed as he returned to the bed. A child had just sold her body. What was it that forced her into prostitution? She was thin, but not starving. He had seen too many children dying of starvation. He knew the difference. Drugs, probably, even that young. Nothing he could do about it now. With an effort, he turned his attention to the television.

Ahmed woke up some time later when something slammed into the wall of his room. He looked at the now blank, silent TV screen. The sound had come from the next room where he heard the voices. Shouting now, and screams along with great, wrenching sobs. He sat up, and waited for someone to come from the office. Minutes went by and no one came. He picked up the telephone and dialed 0. No one answered. Surely someone would hear the commotion and report it. Rising, he went to the door in the wall that connected the rooms. His side opened easily, but the other door was locked. He went outside and pounded on the next door. No response, but the screaming stopped. Ahmed ran to the office, only to find it dark and empty.

Returning to his room, he again listened at the door of the next room. Still quiet. Ahmed debated dialing the 911 number. No, he could not call the police; it would seriously endanger his plans. He could not afford to call attention to himself in this situation. He listened again; quiet, except for the squeaking of bed springs. They had started again. Disgusted, he entered his room.

It was only minutes until the screams started again. Short and muffled, this time, barely more than moans. Weak, he thought, she was not fighting now. He went to the inside door this time and pounded with his fists. He yelled that he would call the police. Abruptly, the sounds of violence ended. Then the outside door slammed shut and the truck engine started.

Ahmed ran outside, to see the old truck turning onto the highway. Tires squealed as it sped away. He looked around. The only other car in the parking lot was the Ohio vehicle; the room in front of it dark. No one wants to get involved he snorted, tension snaking along the back of his neck. Nor can I.

In spite of knowing it was impossible for him to call for help, he pushed open the door to the room. The overhead light glared down on the bed. With no further thought Ahmed went to the girl, turning back the tangle of sheets.

She lay still as death, her face swelling from a mass of bruises and abrasions. He could see other marks of the man's violence on her naked body. A soft moan told him she was still alive. She might be a whore, but he knew the signs of rape. The kind where the sadistic pervert achieved his pleasure from pain.

He brought a wet towel from the bathroom and gently wiped the blood from her face. An exclamation escaped his lips when he continued to minister to her body. "By the Holy One..." Small, puncture like wounds covered her abdomen. There was little blood. Seldom injuries bled as profusely as in the movies, he knew. Looking for other signs of injury, he ceased when the movements started blood to seep from the wounds. The girl moaned again, her breathing shallow. "Quiet, little one," he murmured.

There was nothing he could do here. She must have help. Going to the wall, he opened the door into his room. Getting a grip on his screaming nerves, he quickly packed his belongings and took them to the car. Checking again, the motel was quiet and no traffic moved on the highway. His watch glowed 2:00 AM. Back to the girl, he wrapped her in the bed sheets and carried her to the car. Stretching her gently in the back seat, he went back to her room to see if she had a handbag, or anything that would identify her. He would take her to the hospital; they would notify her family. All he found was a garish colored red and pink dress.

It took him half an hour to locate the hospital from the address in the phone book. Neon Emergency Room lights pointed to the side. He moved the car into a parking place where he could watch the door. It seemed quiet for the moment. He wondered if he could take one of the wheelchairs he could see in the hall, and leave the girl just inside, without being seen himself. Finally deciding that was the best he could do for her, he opened the car door, then quickly shut it when an ambulance screamed to a halt at the entrance. A city police car was right behind it.

Ahmed waited again, knowing that every minute was crucial. Again slipping from the car, he reached in the back for the girl. He knew she was dead even before he touched her. No pulse, no breath, no life. He sagged back against the door. The silent Angel of Death had claimed another child while he sat helpless.

A beam of light was coming down the row of cars. A Security Guard checking the parking lot. Ahmed started the car, put it in gear, and drove as sedately as he could manage, away from the hospital.

CHAPTER TWO

Ahmed stood by the late model sedan in the heavy shade of trees and thick brush lining a rough gravel path. The sheet wrapped body of the young girl lay on the back seat of the automobile.

The drivers' side door of the car stood open. He moved slightly until his body blocked any view of the interior. Making an effort to smile, he deliberately appeared in no hurry to go anywhere. Posture relaxed and non-threatening, he kept his hands out in front of him where they could be seen.

Inwardly, he was fuming. He could feel sweat start to trickle between his shoulder blades. The woman in the golf cart wore the uniform of a Park Attendant. She was informing him this campground belonged to the U. S. Army Corp of Engineers. He did not want to be here. A wrong turn of events, and a wrong turn on the road caused this problem. One of many. From the very start there had been nothing but problems.

"Sorry, I have to ask you to leave," the attendant was telling him. "You pay a fee to camp here. If you want, you can picnic in the day use area. No charge for that." She gestured toward the other side of the park.

"That's okay." He used the American slang and made sure his drawl matched the dialect of this area. "Didn't know you had to pay. I'll leave." He continued to stand, smiling at the woman. He watched as the attendant backed the golf cart down the gravel path to a paved road, giving the automobile room to pass. He got behind the wheel and shut the car door. The engine started at the turn of the key. At least the automobile was one thing that had gone right.

* * * * *

"What do you suppose he was doing up there on the service road?" The camper held the leash of her dog, talking to the park attendant. "I saw the car turn in from the campsites before you came around."

"Probably throwing out garbage," the woman in the golf cart answered. "Good thing you saw him, he was pretty well hidden. Guess he wanted a place no one could see him toss out the trash. He's been in here about half an hour. Lots of people don't know the road dead ends at the Park and stop to ask, but he breezed on by the gatehouse. I gave him time to turn around, but he didn't come back out. I better go clean up the litter. Want to ride up with me?"

"Yeah, he had all four doors open, from what I could see before he heard you coming. Was anything inside the car?"

"I couldn't see inside, he was standing in the way. Like I said, probably garbage from lunch. Found a shady place and decided to clean up his car. Believe me, worse has been thrown out in here. Why people can't use the dumpsters...; well, come on, I need to get back to the gatehouse."

The two women drove off in the cart, the dog jogging along side. They turned on a gravel service track that ran behind the campsites on the hill that descended to the lake. The path ran under low tree limbs, providing a canopy of deep green shade.

"Keep an eye out, would you? He was right about here, just before this track comes out on the lakeside road." The park attendant steered the cart over the large rocks and ruts of the little used path.

"After the sun on the lake it sure is dark in here," the woman camper scanned the underbrush for anything that the man in the green car might have discarded.

The dog, a large mongrel, suddenly stopped, jerking on the leash. The attendant braked the golf cart as a low growl came from the dog's throat.

A bright splash of color showed, caught on the lower limb of a small tree. The camper patted the dog and he quieted. "Looks like that is all there is. I didn't see any hamburger wrappers or Styrofoam cups."

"A towel, maybe? Wonder why he threw it out?"

The camper laughed, a nervous sound. It wasn't funny in the dim light beneath the heavy shade. There was something eerie about the sight. "Maybe he's a traveling salesman, picked up a hooker and had sex in the car. Cleaning out the evidence before he goes home to his wife."

The attendant laughed too. "Might be right, but sounds more like you read it in a book. Let's go look."

Both women got out of the cart and stepped into the heavy brush at the side of the path. The tree was about four feet farther into the woods. The attendant picked up a stick and reached over to the bright fabric. The dog let out another low growl.

The stick moved aside the draped material and a pink plastic belt hung by thread loops. The camper let out a gasp. "It's a dress!"

"Or blouse," the stick moved the dress, but didn't pull it off the limb. "Look, it's stuck on those burrs. Cheap rayon it looks like. If I pull it off, it's going to tear. The belt is cheap, too. Look around, shoes or anything else? I wonder if there's a body that belongs in it?"

The camper gave another shudder. "You are kidding, aren't you?"

"Oh sure. This was probably thrown out before the man was here." The park attendant glossed over the discovery.

"No. See here, the leaves beside it are still damp from the dew. It hasn't dried up here in the shade yet. There is not a drop of moisture on that belt.

No leaves or dirt on the dress and we did have some wind and rain yesterday. It was put here just now."

"Well, like you said, maybe he was getting rid of the evidence before he went home to his wife. Looks to me like something a hooker would wear. That color would stand out in the dark."

"And how would you know?" The two women laughed at each other.

"You're right," the park attendant conceded to her friend. "I'm going back to the gatehouse, want to come along? If he hasn't left the park yet, I can get the license plate number even if he won't talk to me."

"No, I'll go back to my campsite. I don't want to run into that man, even with Mutt along." She pulled the dog closer.

The golf cart rounded the curve of the lake road that led to the entrance and the gatehouse. Parking the cart beside the small structure that served as an office, the attendant went inside. "Hey, Johnny, did you get the plate number of that green car when he came into the Park?"

The man at the fee window put down the newspaper he was reading. "Nah, didn't stop. Maybe he wanted to use the restroom. Saw the car go out a few minutes ago. It was a Wilson County plate, but I didn't catch the number. Why?"

"Well, if he used the restroom it wasn't in a bathhouse."

"Why, what's the matter?"

"The car was on the service road back of the campsites. Guess he thought he was hid. I didn't see it until Liz told me it was there. She saw him pull in. He left when I asked him, then I went to check for trash. Guess what? He had thrown out a pink dress!"

"Awe, some kids probably changed clothes in there so they could swim."

A pickup truck pulled up to the gate and the driver rolled down the window. "Hi folks, anything going on?"

The woman attendant walked out to the truck. "Ed, did you see a green Pontiac that just left here? The guy just threw out a pink dress up in the woods behind the campsites."

The man in the fee window winked at the driver. "Maggie's on one of her mystery kicks again. Probably nothing to it."

"Maybe you aren't so way out," he said to the woman through the rolled down window. "You know that old logging road back of the Kinkaid farm? Your Pontiac pulled out just as I passed. Roared out of there like the devil was on his tail."

"Johnny," Maggie yelled. "Come out here."

"I heard," John called back from the open window. "I'll call the Sheriff and the Rangers.

****

Ahmed waited for the pickup truck to pass, then turned the car on the paved road. His mind was not on his driving and he had to slow for the winding curves. Never had his luck been so miserable. He could only hope the driver of the truck took no notice of a vehicle coming from a side road. As the curves smoothed out toward the main highway, Ahmed calmed his nerves and slowed the car to the speed limit as he followed the road signs back to I-40. Even if he could wish he had not come here, he had to admit the scenery was spectacular. The high bridge over the dammed up Caney Fork River afforded a magnificent view of Center Hill Lake. The tree lined shores gave a green tint to the clear water.

He wasn't so much worried by the events of this morning as irritated with himself. It had been too many years since he was active. Instead of keeping his focus on the assignment, he had reacted like the doctor he was. In his hurry, he had taken the wrong road. How was he to know it ended in the campground? It was barely a trace on the map, and in the early morning light showed little signs of civilization. Perhaps not all was lost. They would find the dress, but not the body. The logging road made a much better place for the girl. He regretted the need to hide her, but it should give him a few days until she was found. The woman at the campground could only describe a white male of average height and weight, with a brown beard, yellow sunglasses, and a southern accent.

Reaching the Interstate, he turned west and set the cruise control on the speed limit.

****

The Sheriff's Deputy arrived at the campground first. Maggie stuck her head out of the gatehouse sliding window. "Hi Bobbie. You got our call?"

"Yeah, the dispatcher said it wasn't urgent. What's going on?"

"Something strange, maybe nothing. Just thought you should have a look."

The deputy pulled the cruiser to a parking space, and walked back to the window, her uniform starched and spotless on a trim figure. John came in from the park and nodded to the Deputy. "Yep, it's a dress. You go on, I'll close up. A Ranger should be here by then. I'll bring him down."

The golf cart turned into the service road with the deputy's car behind it. Maggie stopped as the bright colored material showed through the trees. Bobbie joined her at the side of the road. She echoed John's words, "Yep, it's a dress."

Maggie gave her an exasperated look. "Is that all you can say?"

"Well, what do you want me to do, arrest the man for littering?"

"Don't you think it was a little strange? I tell you there was something funny about that man." Maggie actually shivered.

A white Government pickup truck with a Park Ranger and John inside, pulled up behind the patrol car. The man in the Ranger's uniform joined them at the side of the road. "Hello Maggie. Hi there lil' bit. Got this big mystery solved yet?"

The girl cringed at the nickname. "Hello Mac. Maybe I need to be on my way. This looks more like your jurisdiction."

"Now don't get your dander up, girl." He turned to Maggie, "John told me what you said. Now you tell me."

Maggie again told the story. The Ranger listened without interrupting. "Sure you're not just mad that somebody got past you at the gate?"

Maggie glared at the ranger. "Take my word for it, there was something strange about that man."

Bobbie looked a little more sympathetic. "Calm down, Maggie, we believe you. I'll check the missing persons reports. Mac, will you get the dress, or do you want me to get it? It will help if we know the size.

The Ranger chuckled again, but stepped into the brush and retrieved the dress. He handed the garment to Bobbie. "Tell the Sheriff to let me know if he needs any help from Uncle Sam. Want a ride back up the hill, John?"

"No, I'll ride back with Maggie. Thanks for coming, Mac." John looked slightly embarrassed by the whole thing.

"I've got your description of the man and the car, and I'll drive that logging road on my way out," Bobbie told them. "If anything turns up on the reports, I'll let you know."

"Now see what you started," John growled at Maggie as she got in the cart.

"I guess I'm being silly, but something seemed strange when I talked to the man. Can't put my finger on it, just the way he was standing, no…, well, it will come to me. He looked ordinary enough, but there was something familiar about him."

"Did you recognize him from somewhere?" John gave her an incredulous look.

"John," Maggie stopped the golf cart and stared at him, "you're not going to believe what I just remembered."

****

Ahmed punched off the cruise control at the exit he had marked on the map. Several businesses occupied sites close to the interstate. A chain motel looked fairly new and only a few cars sat in the parking lot. A quick stop market with fuel pumps was across the street. He pulled the Bonneville up beside a pump, filled the tank and paid cash to the lanky clerk who was more interested in the football game on TV.

Ahmed dawdled, looking at some of the merchandise. He came back to the counter with cheese crackers and a cold drink. The clerk looked annoyed, but came to the register. "Is this the town the Vice President's from?" He kept his voice slow in a southern drawl.

"Yeah," the man responded. "Thought I saw a Tennessee plate on your car. Anybody from Tennessee should know that."

"Car belongs to my sister, I'm just visiting."

"Oh. You want this bagged or something?" The clerk turned back to the TV as the announcer yelled TOUCHDOWN TENNESSEE. The camera panned as the crowd in Neyland Stadium went wild.

Ahmed picked up his purchases and went out the door. The clerk never looked back. Maybe, just maybe, the man would remember him. It was a ploy he had used in the past. He would establish several identities, knowing witnesses seldom gave the same descriptions. It always helped to have the authorities confused.

He drove the short distance to the bridge over the Cumberland River, then turned left into the main part of town. It was the same as he had memorized from the photos Ibrahim had shown him. Bank on the corner, furniture store, yes, nothing was changed. He drove past the business district and turned on a side road. Through a neighborhood of rundown houses he located the area of trees that had been marked on the aerial photograph. Not good, he thought, not far enough from the main road. He brought the photograph to mind again, concentrated and remembered the dirt road ran for a mile or so behind the main business district. Ah, yes, it would have to do, but he was not happy that the woods did not seem as large as it had looked in the picture.

Stoically, Ahmed knew he would continue. He had no choice. Then a plan began to form in his mind. He would complete the assignment, but on his own terms. American politics meant nothing to him, but he was tired of killing. Things were beginning to fall into place. Things that would allow him an out. He did not know the purpose of the assignment, or why he had been chosen. He did not want to know. When this was over, if he could pull off a deception, with the illusion of earnest effort, perhaps there would be no more contacts. He no longer had the heart for it.

Driving back to the interstate he entered the west ramp, turned on the radio and listened to the country twang of the singer.

****

Halfway between the campground gate and the main highway, Bobbie Foster turned the patrol car from the paved road. An inspection of the old logging road behind the four hundred acre farm that belonged to Evan Kinkaid only brought her to where the Pontiac had turned around. She also had to turn her car around in the tight space. A timbered bridge, long abandoned, was partially collapsed and would not have borne the weight of a bicycle much less an automobile. No wonder the green car had turned around and gone back to the paved road. Lots of people looking for a shortcut tried the side roads. Every time they had to turn around.

Bobbie got out of the car and squatted to look at the tire tracks. Probably nothing at all to the discarded dress. She peered down into the ravine the bridge had once spanned. Moss covered rocks, brush, and a few lush ferns with a trickle of water for a creek revealed nothing unusual. She thought about going down to check behind the big boulders that formed a mini-dam against the main lake, but movement in the brush stopped her. Snakes were out this time of year and there had been a couple of big rattlers reported in the area. She wasn't especially scared of snakes, still it was against the law to kill rattlesnakes. They had been imported to control the mice and rat populations. She shook her head and went back to the car.

Bobbie continued her rounds of the four Army Engineer campgrounds on the lake, finding every thing quiet, and arrived back in town in time for a late lunch. She asked the sisters who owned the restaurant if they had seen a bearded man driving a late model green Bonneville. No, they had answered, too busy to notice much but customers, and every other man in town had a beard. Who was she looking for?

She told them it was just a complaint and the topic turned to an upcoming dance. She fended off questions about her date and listened to the gossip from several other late customers. When she left the restaurant, she had pretty much forgotten the green automobile.

Bobbie pulled the patrol car into the allotted parking space, cut the engine, then sat with clipboard in her hand. She chewed on the eraser end of a well-used pencil before she put her thoughts on the report log. She made a few notes on the report, marked her stops and logged the miles. She did note that a cheap red, pink and black, size small dress had been found at Center Hill in a suspicious location. She would turn the dress in, in case someone wanted to claim it.

****

Ahmed stayed on I-40 until he reached a suburban Nashville exit. He drove several miles in either direction from the interstate, making mental notes of the surroundings. Back at the interchange, he ate chicken and dumplings at a restaurant, and to his surprise found them delicious. He finished his early supper with a cobbler and ice cream. The waitress paid special attention to his needs, filling his coffee cup often. While he would have preferred to stay anonymous, he made sure she would remember a southern gentleman.

Across the highway, he turned the green car into a Park and Ride fenced area. On the last row of parked cars, he pulled the Bonneville beside a battered pickup truck. Quickly checking around him, he took stock of the cars parked in the area. A wide variety presented itself, some newer models included. He could hear the traffic on the heavily used interstate, distinguishing between the rumble of the big semi-trucks and the buzzing of automobiles. No one was in sight. A large interstate billboard behind the parking lot protected the area from view in that direction. He would "borrow" one of the parked vehicles when the time came. It would leave a false trail, then he could go back to the tourist seen driving the Bonneville. Ahmed turned the green car back to the highway and headed for Nashville. This was only a slight change in his plans. He would not chance another motel. It would be all right.

He parked the car in the alley behind the boy's apartment and made sure it was locked and secure, with the blanket thrown over the equipment left in the trunk. The youth was preparing to leave for his job as a waiter, and did not question Ahmed's return. Telling the older man that fresh food was in the refrigerator and he would be back around midnight, the boy let the door slam behind him.

Ahmed had not asked the whereabouts of Ibrahim Hassim. He valued some time alone, but if the man should appear it would give Ahmed the chance to begin his plan for the assignment. For a moment it felt like old times. Honor among thieves, he reminded himself, had never been true.

He turned on the television set just in time to catch the 6:00pm news. Some local stories, then an item that caught his attention. The Vice President of the United States would arrive at the Nashville airport at 2:00pm tomorrow, for a short visit in his home town.

****

Maggie and John were cleaning up the gatehouse office when Liz and Ed Tidwell pulled their camping trailer to the top of the hill from the lakeside campsite. Both of them went outside to say goodbye to their friends.

"Been a great season. Shame you have to close up the place." Ed and John shook hands.

"Don't even know if we will open in the spring. Funding was cut for this area, and they tell me Congress is talking about selling off the dam and the lake."

Liz looked fighting mad. "Don't they know how many people use these campgrounds and how much revenue they bring in to our community? Hey, Maggie, how about coming over to the farm and help me e-mail our esteemed senators and representatives. Maybe we can stop it before they find a buyer.

Maggie looked over at John. "Go on," he told her, "I want to get in a few more days fishing myself before we lock up the place."

"Great," Liz responded. "Give me a day to get this trailer unpacked, then come on out. We're leaving for Florida the end of the week, but I'll have plenty of time."

CHAPTER THREE

The day after his unplanned return to Nashville, Ahmed left the apartment before the boy woke up. He had done a sweep the night before, washing dishes and wiping anything that might hold his fingerprints. He took the dish cloth with him to use on the car. In his usual meticulous way, his neatly packed roll-about case and suit bags were inspected to insure nothing was missing. This time he did not intend to return. The green automobile was where he left it with nothing disturbed. He found his way to the Interstate and headed east, into the morning light.

The main flow of traffic was to the west, commuters heading into Nashville to begin their work day. Ahmed paid attention to his driving. The heavy traffic made him nervous. It had been a long time since he had been required to drive in a city of any size. I am getting too old for this, he thought and breathed a sigh of relief when he reached the downtown split and turned east on I-40

It was late enough into September for the weather to have cooled, but this day promised rain. The air was sultry and the sky reflected the sun's rays with fingers of red tinged clouds. A red dawn, he thought, a good omen. He could go through the woods; rain would help wash out signs of his passage.

He pulled off the Interstate and turned into the Park and Ride he spotted yesterday. Most of the vehicles he had seen before were already parked for the day, including the pickup truck. He glanced at his chronograph watch. Time for breakfast. He needed to eat. Before the day was over, he would need the energy.

Across the street, he ordered breakfast, asking for extra biscuits. Again, he flirted with the waitress, drinking black coffee and asking for refills.

Outside, in the green car he mentally went over his plans. American newspapers were wonderful. Even the itinerary of the Vice President was public information. Today the Vice President would speak at an impromptu town hall meeting, designed to placate the tobacco farmers in this part of Tennessee. Ahmed had no trouble memorizing the line up of routes and times.

A State Police cruiser, with the distinctive Tennessee markings, turned into the restaurant parking lot. Ahmed looked up, but was not disturbed. He pulled out the map of Tennessee he had purchased the day he got the car, again noting alternative routes into and away from the target town. He looked at his watch. He would wait until the troopers left the restaurant.

* * * * *

Maggie and Liz were busy planning their strategy. Having completed and sent e-mail and letters to all of the Tennessee senators and representatives, they wanted to enlist the aid of the President and Vice President.

"Didn't the newspaper say the VP is home for a few days?" Maggie asked.

"Yeah," Liz answered with a grin. "Came for a family visit, the paper said. Good time for a visit, especially since they set up a town hall meeting so he can talk the tobacco farmers into voting for him. Kind of a hard sell, wouldn't you say?"

"I don't know," Maggie replied. "I kind of like his environmental stand. Do you know his family? Maybe we could get in to see him in person."

"Ah, I was thinking the same thing. I met him when he was a Senator, but no, I don't know them personally. I do, however, know someone who does. Ellen Taggert. I think she knows everyone in Tennessee. I'll give her a call."

Ellen had been at her desk for more than an hour when the telephone rang. "This is the office of David Middleton, Attorney at Law, Ellen Taggert speaking. How may I help you?"

"Ellen, Liz Tidwell here. Haven't seen you for a while. How's the daily grind going?"

Slow, Ellen thought, but she wouldn't admit that to Liz Tidwell, of all people. That would be like broadcasting the information over the local radio station. "Great! David's the best. More and more people calling him. What can we do for you today?"

"Actually, it's you I need. I want to ask a favor. Did you know the Vice President is home?"

Not again, Ellen winced. Too many locals knew of her connection to the family. "I do read the newspaper, Liz," she responded acidly.

"You know Maggie from the campground? She and I have a project going. Environment, sort of. We would love to get the VP involved. If we could see him while he's here, it would help a lot. Think you might get us in?"

"Oh, I don't think so. I do hate to bother him when he's here. Even politicians have to rest sometime."

"Ellen, this involves us right here in town. Congress is planning to sell our lakes and dams to private enterprise. We might end up with a lot of foreigners telling us how to run our city and state. Tell you what, when we form a committee, I'll see they select David to represent us in Washington."

Ellen's mouth quirked at the corner. Her answer should be no, but David could use some recognition. She knew what Liz was doing, but Liz always kept her word. "All right, I'll see what I can do. Anytime the VP can make it,

Okay? I won't ask for special favors. I'll call you when I know something."
She hung up the telephone as the front door opened to admit her niece.

"Hi, Aunt Ellen. I came by to see if you can take some time off and go out to lunch."

"Are you on the night shift now, Bobbie?" Ellen gave a wry smile to the girl. "I thought you were working."

"I traded a couple of days for the weekend. Thought we could do some shopping, or maybe a movie. How about it?"

"Sorry, dear. Something has come up and I may go out of town this afternoon. Why don't you ask David?"

Bobbie stepped to the hall and looked to the back. "David's not here, is he?. Besides, he always turns me down."

"David went to the VA Hospital this morning. He should be back around two. No, no, nothing wrong. He needed to get the brace adjusted. Is that why you are going to work this weekend? Because you know he won't be at the dance?"

"That obvious, is it?" Bobbie flopped down in the reception chair with a sigh. "Sometimes I think I should just come right out and propose to him. He knows there is no one else I would consider spending my life with!"

Ellen's smile was generous. Sometimes she felt the same frustrations over the young man's complacent attitude. "Give him some more time, Bobbie. After all…"

"After all, what? He's not the first person to loose a leg. It's already been three years since he came back, and the clocks ticking on me. You want to know why I'm not going to the dance? I don't want to be the oldest old maid there!"

This time Ellen laughed out loud. "You forget I know how old you are. Twenty-seven isn't that old nowadays. Women don't get married at eighteen anymore. And David is only thirty. You've got plenty of time."

"Hah!" Bobbie countered, "Around here, it's still teenage brides. I don't want to end up being a bridesmaid to my sisters' kids!"

Ellen had to laugh, but Bobbie was right. It was past time for David and Bobbie to marry. It wasn't any secret, the whole town knew it. "Why don't you run out and get us some hamburgers. I'm going to make a phone call, and when you get back, we'll have lunch."

****

Jeff Fischer was having a bad morning. Not only was he hung over, Belle Walker was standing in front of his desk. He detested the overweight, foul mouthed gossip columnist. If she were a man, she'd have the biggest balls in town.

"What's the matter, lover boy? You still banging that skinny PHD from Oak Ridge?"

Jeff ignored the question. "What do you want, Belle? You run out of that shit you shovel in your column?"

"Nah, honey, there's plenty of manure around here. Thought you might want to know you missed a staff meeting this morning. You look awful. Late night with what's her name?"

"Actually, too much sleep. I didn't hear the alarm this morning. Want to tell me what I missed?"

"Nothing! You missed exactly nothing. Nothing worth talking about. Nothing worth printing. God, for a college town, you'd think something would happen around here. Dullsville! Well, I'm off to town with my pooper-scooper. Got to know who's who on the list for the Harvest Moon Ball. By the way, Ben wants to see you. Better wake up, sonny boy, the boss ain't in a good mood."

Jeff styled himself as the science reporter for the Knoxville Chronicle. The truth was, he handled any assignment handed him. He kept writing a technical column; sometimes it even got printed when they needed to fill in space. I'll get the Pulitzer for this story, he thought. Karen had shown him enough. He knew they were working on propulsion systems in Oak Ridge and the UT Space Center at Arnold Air Force Base. The Air Force base included a big wind tunnel that tested aircraft parts and other highly guarded secret paraphernalia for the government. It also provided other avenues for research along the same lines as Oak Ridge. The research facility was managed for maximum security within the confines of the military base. Briefly, he had been allowed access, but his informant at Arnold had been transferred, so he was concentrating on Oak Ridge right now, and maybe, just maybe, it would pay off.

He had met Karen Fielding at synagogue. Not that he cared much about religion, it was a good place to meet some of the higher echelon who ran the government funded National Laboratory in Oak Ridge. It was general knowledge that the Lab was looking for an alternative fuel. Even the American Museum of Science and Energy had information on that level. The technology Karen had allowed him to see was way past that. Mind boggling, was what it was.

He had to know more, and he would if he could hold up. She did that to him, piecing out the information in return for sex. He had to play the whole part, too. Romance, dinner, gifts, but he'd go the distance for this one. So far she hadn't asked for commitment, but was becoming more and more demanding. He had been with her two nights in a row and the effort showed in his red-rimmed eyes.

She clamed up, turned stone deaf when he quizzed her about the little moon buggy. The only tid-bit he could pry out of her was a full size model and test track were being built in the old K-25 area in Oak Ridge. He would cool it for a while. She would loosen up if she thought he would drop her. And I could use the rest, he groaned.

Jeff picked up his coffee mug and went down the hall to the editor's office. He switched on a voice activated tape recorder and stuck it in his shirt pocket before he went through the door. His boss, Ben Parry, looked up from some official looking documents and motioned him to sit down.

The phone rang, and Ben picked up the receiver, nodding his head toward the door. He turned away, hand cupped over the end of the phone. Jeff got up and walked back out into the hall. He lounged against the wall, sipping his coffee and let his thoughts roam over the last few weeks. It was not just Karen. He had made a bargain with his brother. In return for keeping an eye on Karen and her research, his U.S. Senator brother would help him get his life back on track and would pay him a considerable sum of money. Bargain, yeah, big brother taking care of him again, but Jeff had something better in mind for himself. Big brother could keep thinking the agreement would keep Jeff away from Washington. That suited him fine. He didn't want anything more to do with the government. Besides, it wasn't like he was stealing military secrets this time. It was only the same information he would publish when he got the chance. And if his plans all jelled, big brother could go to hell.

Ben came to the door and waved him back in. "What freight train hit you? You look like shit."

"Thanks for the compliment. I'm all right, just tired. Haven't been able to sleep much lately. What can I do for you, boss?"

"Get yourself some melatonin, helps you sleep. Now, if you can stay awake long enough to drive to Carthage, the Vice President is going to meet with some tobacco farmers this afternoon. An off the record, last minute set up, probably just for some publicity, but you might find a different angle to write it up." He handed Jeff the fax off his desk. "Both UT and Vanderbilt are experimenting with tobacco for pharmaceutical use. A lot of other companies, too. See what you can come up with." The editor turned back to his telephone, then paused. "Oh, Jeff, don't miss another meeting if you want to stay on this staff." He picked up the receiver.

Jeff shambled back down the hall to his desk. He checked his watch 11:30am here on Eastern Time. The Vice President's hometown was on Central Time, 10:30am now. Plenty of time to get there, maybe a two hour drive. He glanced at the fax sheet with the meeting information. Yeah, he had been there before, he could find the middle school okay. A waste of time, anyway. It would be a political rally, no real information. Just what I need, he shrugged, an afternoon in the country, and I can tell Karen I'm out of town on assignment. If he stretched it out he could put dinner on the expense account.

He pulled a folder from of a drawer. He had already collected some data on the medical angle. He could make up something while he drove. He went to the restroom to wash his face, and smiled into the mirror as he patted dry with a paper towel. He didn't look too bad. When he remembered the tape recorder in his pocket, he switched it off.

****

Ahmed tapped his fingers on the steering wheel and glanced at his watch for the fifth time. The State Troopers were enjoying a leisurely lunch. An hour had passed and the cruiser was still parked in front of the restaurant. The timing was essential. He must arrive at the target destination after the security sweep of the area, but before the arrival of his mark. Finally the State Police returned to work. He watched until the cruiser pulled onto the interstate.

At the Park and Ride, he turned in beside the old pickup truck he singled out yesterday. Quickly glancing around, he reached for the door handle of the truck. It opened easily. No steering wheel lock on this old model. Forty-five seconds later he had the motor started. He transferred his belongings and the special equipment to the front seat of the truck. Again checking the parking lot, he used the dish towel he brought to go over the Bonneville and made sure the inside of the vehicle was clear of any trace of him.

He climbed in the driver's seat of the pickup and revved up the big engine, surprised to find so powerful a response in a truck with bondo sides and a missing tailgate. With squealing tires, he pulled out of the lot and onto the interstate. A glance at the fuel gage showed three-quarters full. Another good sign. Maybe his luck was changing.

****

Ellen dialed Liz's number and she picked up on the first ring. Yes, the VP would see them, right after the town hall meeting, if that was okay. If they could be there for the meeting, it would save him some time. Bobbie was here, okay if she goes? They made arrangements for Liz to pick them up at the office.

****

David finished up around noon at the VA Hospital. He drove a new SUV, with an automatic shift. No problem, he didn't need any hand controls since it was only one leg that was missing. He counted his blessings as the high powered vehicle sped north. It would have been closer going the back roads, but he was thinking about stopping for the town hall meeting with the Vice President. A lot of tobacco was raised around this part of the state. He looked at his watch, he could just make the meeting.

****

Ahmed pulled off the interstate, crossed the bridge over the river and drove through the business district to the middle school. No students here today, the time designated for teacher training, but several people were out front of the building where the meeting would be held. A Tennessee State Police car sat blocking the far end of the circular driveway. The uniformed trooper stood by the car, talking to the gathering crowd. Two men, in almost matching gray business suits, stood by the double entrance doors. Ahmed knew the men would be the advance Secret Service detail. There was no sign of other security agents, but he knew they were there. Apparently security arrangements had changed little in the years Ahmed was inactive. If the truck was seen passing the school it would not be a problem. There must be a dozen pickups parked up and down the street. Driving slowly, he saw through the rear view mirror a city police car pull across the middle of the road behind the State vehicle. The policeman started directing traffic down a side road, away from the school. Ahmed smiled, maybe he still had the old touch. His timing was perfect.

Past the school, where the houses thinned, Ahmed turned the old truck on the dirt road he had marked for use. The road ran behind an older residential neighborhood, then angled back toward town. He passed a rundown dwelling, with the remains of a rusted automobile in the yard and neglected flowers planted inside discarded tires. The house looked deserted now, but a cheap plastic tricycle and toys littered the yard. A couple of empty weed grown lots, then he found the small forested area marked for him on the aerial photograph.

He parked the truck under the trees, as far in the brush as possible. No one was around. Wearing latex gloves, he quickly pulled the coveralls over his clothes and put the rubber boots over his shoes. He loaded the automatic and deposited it in one of the large pockets. The magazines for the rifle went in another pocket. He covered everything left in the truck with the army blanket. Wearing a cap and the yellow sunglasses, he checked his location again and moved deeper into the heavy underbrush of the woods.

The forested area ran for a little over a hundred yards back toward the main part of town, then turned to neglected pasture. Sapling trees and tall weeds were underfoot. An empty, half demolished clapboard house claimed a spot under a huge spreading oak. A forlorn 'For Sale' sign sagged from a rotted stake at the front of the house. Ahmed found the place he had noted before. Between the old house and a rusty storage shed, low bushes of wild blackberries grew thick and heavy along the tatter of an old wire fence. Parallel to the bushes, a partially graveled overgrown track ran along the other side of the fence. Young cedars and hickory were beginning to show at fence level, building an effective screen if a man stayed low. The angle wasn't good, but he could see the curve of the driveway in front of the school building.

Ahmed tunneled beneath the blackberries, ignoring the thorns that clung to the coveralls. A little more elevation would be better, but a shot was possible from here. He could see the street at a distance of three hundred, maybe three-twenty yards. The air was calm, the sullen sky still promising rain. An empty field, with deep wiry grass was behind a rusted garbage dumpster back of the brick building, the track and playing fields to the other side of the school. A single door opened to concrete steps, the window covered with heavy wire. A van with dark tinted windows was parked behind the school. Staying far enough back in the bushes to keep light from reflecting on the gun barrel, he trained the gun's sight on the building. As he expected, a figure was stretched flat on the level roof, facing to the front. He could see a dull flash of metal as a rifle was moved into position. Using the scope, he spotted two more concealed agents, one by the dumpster and the other at the far end of the building. There would be another on the roof, more in front and across the street. Moving the gun, he checked the area to the west of the building. He adjusted the scope until the cross hairs were centered on a street stop sign, barely discernible past the corner of the school.

He looked at his watch, again. The field with no obstacles would mean he had to move very fast. With no cover, it would keep the agents who guarded the Vice President from crossing immediately, but it also gave them a good view of his location. He would be required to take down one, probably two, when the rifles were turned in his direction. For a moment he closed his eyes, knowing his heart was not in this. Then the instinct for survival took over. Ahmed took a deep breath and willed himself to relax. He was a trained marksman. He would not miss.

The cavalcade came first. Police cars, dignitaries and secret service, then the Vice President. A group of people pushed forward as the black limousine pulled in the drive. Ahmed adjusted his sights and waited. The Vice President stepped out of the car, looking relaxed and unhurried.

Dressed in casual clothes with an open neck shirt, he began to shake hands with the people who welcomed him, pausing for the photographers to get their pictures. The police began to move the spectators back and the shot would be clear. No! The Vice President looked over the heads of the crowd and smiled, waving to someone closer to the building. With a word to his guard, he walked forward, away from the limousine. With one man beside him, and another at his back, he headed for a group of people standing by the corner of the building. Obviously friends, the Vice President kissed the cheek of a silver haired woman, then took the hand of the lovely girl beside her. He turned toward the door, taking the girl with him. Ahmed tensed, sweat drenching his armpits, as the group turned to the building.

It was now or never. Ahmed, on his stomach, gun steadied on his arm, concentrated, and squeezed the trigger. The bullet went high, slightly to the right and struck the secret service agent behind the Vice President. The force of the bullet seemed to jerk the agent's head apart, knocking the lifeless man forward into the Vice President and his companion, knocking them to the ground. The girl threw herself over the Vice President, keeping him down. Immediately another agent knelt, using his body to shield them. Ahmed cursed and adjusted for the defective scope. He squeezed off three more quick shots. The first struck the kneeling agent, sending him into the tangle of arms and legs on the ground. The next bullet found a mark and a woman screamed. The third felled an agent as he rounded the corner. Someone dragged the Vice President out of sight behind the corner of the building, the girl still with him.

People ran in all directions, with the police yelling for them to get down. The limo driver was desperately trying to get the armored vehicle to the Vice President. People scattered as it crossed the sidewalk and finally blocked Ahmed's view of the scene. He saw the other shooters turn their scopes in his direction. Reloading he fired again and the man by the dumpster went down. In only seconds, the roof rifleman would find him. A few bullets zinged across the field as the town policemen shot wildly at Ahmed's location. Sirens were blaring and people screaming in confusion. He wiggled out of the bush, firing rapidly again, chipping brick at the edge of the rooftop, forcing the rifleman back. He fired a volley at the building with the hand gun, knowing it was out of range, but it kept the police from coming around the corner. He faded back behind the old shed, as bullets from the other rooftop rifleman plinked through the metal. Taking a deep breath, he sprinted across to the abandoned house, then screened by the house, skirted the pasture until he was in the trees.

The black van careened through the empty field, one agent riding the running board; bullets shredding the blackberry vines. Police sirens were coming around the building through the empty lot along the gravel ruts, as

State Troopers rushed to the back. Ahmed's training took over, and he calmed his rapid breath. He moved quietly from tree to tree until he was sure he could not be seen. He was through the woods, and made it to the truck before any of the agents or police ventured out of their vehicles and across the fence.

He quickly shucked the camouflage coveralls and hat, stuffing them behind the seat with the rifle and yellow glasses, covering them with the blanket. He leaned under the dash and the big engine roared to life. Backing out of the shelter of the trees, he realized it had begun to rain. If he hurried, the tire tracks wouldn't be deep enough to last long on the muddy road.

He turned on a side road past the residential area, and came out half a mile down from the site of the shooting. An ambulance was screaming down the road with cars scrambling to get out of the way. He turned up the street behind the ambulance. A young patrol officer stopped him as he reached the school.

"What happened, Officer?" Ahmed knew this was necessary to lead the police to the trail he had taken pains to establish. If he were detained now, it would be all over. Maybe that would be for the best. He was tired of the life he was trapped in. Still, it was not in his makeup to give in so easily.

The young man was visibly shaken. The light rain dripping from the bill of his hat ran down into his face. He kept brushing at it with his hand. "Somebody shot the Vice President. Killed other people, too. You can't go through here. Turn down that street and go around. Uh, where you going? I need to write down your license plate too."

"Can't say as I know it. This is my brother-in-laws truck. I just borrowed it to move some stuff. Wilson County is all I know. You can get it when I turn the corner. I was headed home."

The rain was increasing and the young officer waved him away as he swiped a hand over his face again.

The scene at the middle school was utter chaos. The senior secret service agent pushed the Vice President inside the limousine and gave the order for the driver to leave. Again, people were pushed out of the way of the retreating automobile. Radios blared, sirens wailed and the police milled around, dazed to think this could happen in their town. People huddled behind whatever they could find. Maggie and Liz were on their knees beside Ellen Taggert. Maggie pulled off her sweater and tied the arms around the upper part of the thigh, while Liz screamed for a medic. A paramedic started over to Ellen, as David swung up on his crutches.

In an instant David was down beside Ellen. She was trying to get up. He held her shoulders. "Be quiet Ellen, you're hurt. Wait, here comes help." He looked at Liz and Maggie. Blood was everywhere.

"Help me." Maggie took his hand and placed it on the wadded up sweater around Ellen's thigh, "Push hard, here."

Ellen grabbed his arm in a crushing grip. "Where is Bobbie? David, go find Bobbie." Her voice was shrill. "Oh, Dear God, she's dead. I saw her fall. They shot her, too."

The medics were pushing him away. He found his crutches and struggled to stand. One of the men gave him a hand up, then turned to the patient. "Looks like it went all the way through her leg. Lost some blood. She'll be all right."

David made his way to the building. Bobbie was not in sight, no body, no blood, except the blanket covered agent. Panic was building in his bloodstream. Then he saw her in the window, frantically gesturing to him. She wanted him to come inside. The relief made him weak. He banged on the door with his crutch.

While he waited for the door to be unlocked, he heard an elderly, denim clad bystander voice his opinion of the shooting. "Boy needs to remember where he comes from." The man spit a stream of tobacco juice into the gutter. "This here's tabaccy country."

CHAPTER FOUR

It started to rain. A late summer drizzle that brought steam from the asphalt and sidewalks. Outside, the building was a scene of mass confusion; inside the senior Secret Service agent was efficiently insuring the safety of the Vice President. Tantamount to the safety of the President, it was his main priority; finding the shooter came second. That, for the present, could be left to the State Troopers. His charge was safely out of range and on the move to a pre-arranged destination by backup means. David was allowed in the building after verifying his identity to a State Trooper who cracked the door with drawn gun. He stood still, submitting to a search. A Trooper took his crutches, until David pointed out he couldn't walk without them.

Members of the Vice President's entourage milled about the hall. Voices were raised in disbelief. Accusations and excuses were made. How could this happen in his hometown, for God's sake?. Someone was heard to say they didn't think this kind of thing would ever happen here in the middle of Tennessee. The answer was given in all sincerity. "They didn't think it could happen in Oklahoma, either."

The Washington agent, on his cell phone, nodded as David was ushered into the room. Bobbie threw herself at David, knocking him back against the wall. He dropped his crutches and hugged her close to him. She was dry eyed, but trembling.

"Hey, lil'bit, just what do you think you are doing in here? Couldn't you get into enough trouble by yourself, huh? Had to go get shot at?" He had his mouth close to her ear, soft voiced, soothing her with his hands.

"Don't tease me, David. I was so scared."

"It's all right to be scared, honey, that's the reaction setting in. You were terrific. The cops said you saved his life."

"Just who might you be?" The agent, snapping the cell phone closed, was standing in front of them.

David kept his arm around Bobbie. "David Middleton, Attorney, sir. This young lady is my fiancée, Roberta Foster. She is a Deputy Sheriff in our county. I was driving up when I heard the shots."

"What the..." The agent turned to the glass front window. "Somebody get that television camera away from there. Jesus, where'd all the media come from? Somebody get out there and move those people away. Do I have to do it all myself?" He turned his back on David, put a finger to his ear in answer to a radio page. After listening for a moment, the agent went over to a desk and sat down, head in his hands. "Jesus," he said again, "Joe was a good man."

David bit his lip and shook his head. "The first man hit didn't make it," he told Bobbie. "I saw another agent who got the wind knocked out of him. Had a vest on."

The Secret Service agent interrupted. "Another of my men was hit, but alive. We are still accessing the situation. They tell me a woman caught a bullet."

"My paralegal," David answered, "Ellen Taggert. Bullet went through her thigh. The paramedic's said she'll be all right."

Bobbie tensed at his side. "Aunt Ellen is hurt? I heard someone scream, I didn't know it was her. David, let me go. I've got to get out there!"

"I see the ambulance leaving now. It's raining, too." The agent scrubbed his face and sat up. "You can go in a minute. I need you to tell me what happened. There's going to be FBI, NSA, TBI, and maybe even CIA here in a few hours. By the way, my name's Jim Orson. I'm the Senior Agent on what was supposed to be light duty. Retirement coming up in two months. Hell, what's that old saw about a politician and his home town? Only place he's not welcome?"

Bobbie handed David his crutches and they crossed the room to sit in chairs beside the desk. "I can't tell you much." Bobbie was nervously kneading David's hand. "We came to see the Vice President about an environmental issue. My aunt, the lady who was wounded, is a friend of his family and I know him, too. We had an appointment after the meeting. Maggie Lewis and Liz Tidwell were with us. When the Vice President got out of the car, he recognized Aunt Ellen, and stopped to say hello to us. I heard what sounded like a firecracker, then the other agent staggered. He fell into us. The Vice President grabbed my arm and we both went down. He tried to get up. I didn't think, I just pulled him down again, and held on. Then you came out the door and dragged us around the corner. I'm… sorry about the other man."

Bobbie's voice was shaky, and David thought his fingers might be broken from her grip. He caught her hand and held it still.

"I was inside, at the door. We wanted to bring the limo closer, but this is his hometown crowd. He wanted to get pictures with the people when he arrived, so we stopped out in the drive. Couldn't chance taking him back into the line of fire to get to the car. You probably did save his life. You and the lady who got in the way of a bullet. Glad she'll be all right." Jim Orson gave Bobbie a reluctant smile. "The Vice President is okay, too. Shook up, but okay. I don't think it has set in yet, the bullet was meant for him. We sent the limo off with a decoy inside. If there was more than one shooter, it should throw them off. Now, what about you?" He looked at David.

"I can't add much. I decided to stop in here on my way home from the VA Hospital. I represent some farmers in the area. I was late, and drove up to the road block as the first shot hit your counterpart and I saw Bobbie and the Vice President go down. Then I heard the other shots and punched the truck around the corner. I left my truck in the street and came back as fast as I could. By the time I talked my way past the police and pushed through the crowd, the paramedics were getting here. I saw Ellen on the ground. She told me to find Bobbie." He turned to her, "She thought you were shot, too. I almost went crazy when I didn't see you."

"You two can compare notes, later. What else can you tell me?" The agent claimed their attention.

David gestured to the back of the building with his hands. "I can tell you there was only one shooter, located behind here and to the left. The first bullets came from a hunting rifle. A semi-automatic thirty ought six. I heard the reports."

The Washington man narrowed his eyes. "You could tell that by the sound? Army Specialist?" Sharp shooter, maybe? That how you lost your leg.?"

"Yeah, I left it in Kuwait," David shrugged. "I've hunted these hills and hollers since I was ten. I know a deer gun when I hear it. The shooter was a trained marksman. The distance is too far for an ordinary hunter."

The door opened to admit another agent, moisture dripping from his poncho. Jim Orson went to confer with him, and cursed again. He turned back to David and Bobbie. "They didn't find anything except shell casings. You were right about location and the gun. The shooter was more than a marksman. He had backwoods training. No sign of tracks that the rain hasn't wiped out. I'll need a statement from you both, then you can go, but stay at home. I'm sure a lot of people will want to talk to you."

****

Jeff Fischer had switched on his recorder even before the first shot was fired. A gray suited Secret Service Agent came to open the limo door, then the Vice President exited the car and stopped to shake hands with his welcoming committee. Jeff watched as the VP turned to a strikingly beautiful older woman in the crowd. It was obvious that she was a friend, then the VP extended his hand to the lovely girl beside her. He took her arm and together they turned toward the building. When the first shot took down the bodyguard, they both went down on the sidewalk.

Jeff stood for a moment, stunned like everyone else, then his mind kicked in and he threw himself down as more shots split the air. The limo barely missed him as it lurched across the flower bed, trying to maneuver around the crowd and reach the Vice President. He crouched helplessly on the pavement as town police pushed past him to the corner of the building.

Gunfire erupted from the back as the police fired into the bushes. He instinctively covered his head with his arms, staying on the sidewalk. When he could, he stood up, only to be pushed away by the crowd trying to see who was hit. The silver haired woman who had been behind the Vice President lay on the ground. By this time the limo was backing to the street, again across flower beds. It screeched down the road with the State Trooper motorcycle escort. He reached for his cell phone and the 911 button. Busy signal, others had dialed first.

Now he was talking into his phone, trying to describe to his editor what had just occurred in this little out of the way town. He was crowded up under the dripping eve of the building, as the overcast sky emitted a soft, misty rain. An ambulance roared up and he could barely hear over the din of siren and screeching tires. He held the recorder out to catch what the Channel Four television reporter from Nashville was saying as her cameraman panned the crowd. "I'll call you again when I find out if the VP was hurt." Jeff clicked off his phone, but left the recorder running.

Things were moving fast; the State Troopers taking over, the town cops sent to direct traffic and disperse the crowd. Jeff took a deep breath. People jostled him as he pushed toward the woman on the ground. Two more women were kneeling beside her. A man on crutches shouldered his way to the women, then Jeff saw one of the women stand and stare after an old blue pickup truck. He tracked it with his eyes, as police waved it around the corner. The woman said, "I know that man! It's him. From the campground."

Then the paramedics were there and Jeff was pushed aside again. The injured woman was quickly loaded on a stretcher. One of the women got in the ambulance with her, telling the other woman they were going to the hospital in Lebanon and pitching her a ring of car keys.

Jeff introduced himself. He wanted to know more about the woman who was shot and the girl who was with the VP. "Jeff Fischer, here. I'm a reporter for the Knoxville Chronicle. I thought this would be an easy assignment, just politics. If this is politics, it sure turned nasty. Will your friend be okay?"

"Maggie Lewis is my name. Yes, she will recover. They said the bullet went all the way through her leg. Excuse me, I've got to find David and Bobbie."

"That the girl with the Vice President?" Jeff moved along with the older woman, ignoring the rain. "I'll help you look. If I can get the first interview, that's big news."

Maggie was good at sizing up people. Jeff was a tall, lanky man, somewhere between thirty-five and forty, she guessed. He had that down and out look, rumpled clothes, run down heels, and too many cigarettes smoked short had stained his fingers. The light rain slicking back his thin hair didn't help, either. Aside from the hang-dog look, she suspected he was a man who had seen better times. "Come on, I think Bobbie is inside the school."

They rounded the corner of the building to where they could see in the front window. A State Trooper came out in a slicker and pushed the TV crew back from the building, telling them the Vice President was not hurt. A statement would be made later. David and Bobbie could be seen through the glass.

"That her name, Bobbie? Who is the guy on crutches?" Jeff stepped under the roof line as the Trooper went back to the door.

"Her name's Roberta Foster. She's a Sheriff's Deputy in our county. The man is David Middleton. He's a lawyer. Her aunt, the lady who was shot, works for him. She told him to find Bobbie. We thought she might be hurt, too."

The Trooper motioned for them to move on, back from the building. Maggie held up the car keys. "The girl inside, she's with me," she told the man. The man nodded, and she and Jeff only moved a few feet to clear the door.

The crowd was beginning to thin, the rain dispersing them better than the police. Witnesses were anxious to get home or on the telephone to tell friend and family what they had seen. By the time David and Bobbie were released, several phone calls had been made to The Enquirer. One claiming to see a black man firing the gun, another swearing it was a setup by the tobacco industry; one anti-abortionist claimed responsibility. The other callers promised to tell all when money was received.

In Washington, it wasn't much better. Security was doubled around the Chief Executive, who, already unhappy about current events, was not in a mood to cooperate. The White House was closed to visitors with no explanation; a tour bus full of senior citizens thrown out before they got their money's worth. A Marine helicopter stood ready and the war room opened. Within minutes, news agencies around the world were monitoring satellite broadcasts of the transmission tapes from Channel Four. Correspondents assigned to the White House and Capitol Hill were demanding information. At the Pentagon, orders were given to move up to yellow alert, and hold for red. The FBI and CIA each, had a plane in the air, only minutes behind the NSA.

A spokesman for the Vice President came out to the news reporters present and made a short announcement. The Vice President was unhurt and would make a brief statement to the public via television at 7:00pm Central time. No, no one knew of any reason for the attack. He couldn't say more now. A full investigation would be made and details disclosed then. A short question and answer session followed.

Jeff Fischer knew an opportunity when he saw it. The spokesman was giving the reporters the usual bullshit, but he was witness and here with someone who could give him more firsthand information.

Bobbie and David were released after being warned not to make any public statements. They joined Maggie at the door to the building. "Liz went with Ellen in the ambulance," Maggie told them. "They took her to Lebanon. I've got the car. Don't know what all the bullet did, but they said the wound was clean. Bobbie, you need to let her know you are all right."

David looked at the man with Maggie. Jeff extended his hand. "Jeff Fischer. I'm a reporter. Do you mind if I ride along with you?"

David gripped the hand. The guy looked seedy, but the handshake was firm, and he topped David's six foot two, by an inch or so. "David Middleton," he responded. "You can go with Maggie if that's okay with her. Bobbie is coming with me."

Maggie shrugged, "I'd better call John, first. You two go on. I'll be there right after you."

Bobbie had said nothing at all, after they left the school building. In the truck with David, she continued to be silent. Noticing she seemed flushed, he reached a hand over to touch her cheek.

She brushed his hand away, and continued to stare straight ahead through the windshield wipers. "David, I seem to have missed something."

He glanced her way, but she didn't look at him. "Missed what? I don't know… Can you explain?"

"I was hoping you would. You told Jim Orson I am your fiancée. Funny, I don't seem to remember our engagement."

David had a rather ordinary face until he smiled, then even Hollywood was envious. "Oh, so you don't remember the little pest in the ninth grade, who told the captain of the high school football team she was going to marry him?"

"Good Lord, David, that was years ago. You and my brothers teased me so unmercifully, I just wanted to get even. I'm surprised you even remember."

"I was kind of hoping you still feel the same way. I won't be playing football again, so if you think you can put up with a fellow who gets around on sticks, I'd like to take you up on that proposal."

Bobbie laughed softly, still not looking at him. "David, are you asking me to marry you?"

"Yes," he said, keeping his eyes on the road, afraid to look at her again. He had waited three years, giving her time to realize what a real handicap the loss of a leg was to him. Giving her time to know that he was not the same person who joined the National Guard and marched off to war. Giving her time to find someone else. Someone whole. Not anymore. Now, there would be no waiting. God help him if anything had happened to her.

Bobbie had turned to him. "David, I will marry you if you promise never to let your loss come between us. You are the least handicapped person I know. I love you David; I love the man you are, good, kind, honest..."

His hand found hers across the console. "Lil' bit, you forgot intelligent, handsome, sainted..."

She squeezed his fingers. "While we're wheeling and dealing, how about forgetting that ridiculous nickname you and my brothers put on me. After all, I grew up to be five foot eight. Do we have an understanding?"

"Yes'mam, we do. Soon too. Quick as we get Ellen out of the hospital. Okay?"

"You're on, Mister."

****

Ahmed turned toward Lebanon on U.S. Highway 70N. It would be slower, but he needed time to think. At any rate, his luck was holding, he was away from there before road blocks could be set up. The rain continued, more nuisance now than help. The windshield wiper blades needed replacing and screeched every time they crossed the glass. Ahmed could have screamed with them.

He should have taken time to test fire the gun. He would have known the scope was out of calibration. People went down, men who were only doing their job and an innocent bystander. He had never killed needlessly. He drummed his hand on the steering wheel in frustration. *I meant to miss the mark! That was my plan and others paid for it!* That he had gone through with it would have to be enough to satisfy Ibrahim, whose fanaticism would expect total self-sacrifice in the line of duty. The only thing he could do now was get back to the Park and Ride, retrieve the green sedan, and somehow get back to his real identity in hopes he could evade the law. He pulled out the Tennessee map and cursed again at the lack of detail.

Finally finding his way to the interstate by following signs, he found he had gone one exit too far. Nothing to do except turn east again. He tried to judge the traffic from the overhead bridge. It seemed to be moving smoothly. No police roadblock here. He pulled into the Park and Ride and quickly turned into a front row parking place. He bit his tongue to keep from screaming aloud. A police cruiser kept watch as a wrecker truck towed the green car from its parking place. Ducking down to keep from being seen, he straightened to see the truck turn toward Nashville. The police car followed without checking the other vehicles.

This trip had been cursed ever since he arrived in this miserable, God forsaken place. First the mix-up at the airport and finding Ibrahim alive, then the black girl. And now today and what it could mean to the life he had created for himself. He could feel the gun in the seat at his side. Maybe that was the answer. For a moment he let the thought of the boy who would be the only son he would ever have creep into his mind. After all, Ahmed Faziz was a man of some importance in his own life. He needed to settle down, shave the beard and get into the business suit and oxfords. It was worth a try.

Not in this truck, though. He had made sure people in the area would remember a man with a beard. He would leave the truck here with the guns and overalls inside. That meant he had to have transportation. Whether it was fate or luck, he could not tell as a mini-bus marked Opryland Hotel, turned in and women in maids' uniforms exited its doors. Ahmed could hear Spanish spoken and he approached one of the women.

"*Buenos Dias, Señorita,*" he continued to speak Spanish, complete with a north Mexico accent. "My truck is broken down, could you give me a lift into town?"

No, her car was already full, but the bus was going on to Lebanon. Maybe he could get a ride.

Sure, the bus driver, also Hispanic, was glad to help. Ahmed retrieved his luggage from the truck, careful to keep the guns covered with the blanket. The bus jolted back onto the interstate with the remaining women keeping up a constant chatter. Ahmed joined in, claiming a persona he had used in the past. Maybe this would turn out for the best.

****

Ellen was still in surgery when David and Bobbie arrived at the hospital. They joined Liz in the waiting room. Liz was silent for maybe the first time in her life. "I'm so sorry. If I hadn't insisted on coming, Ellen wouldn't be hurt."

"Not your fault, Liz. The Vice President owes you too. If Ellen hadn't been there, he might be the one in surgery now." David could always be the voice of reason. He and Bobbie took the chairs next to her.

Bobbie slumped in her chair and tried to smooth her disheveled hair. "David said the bullet went through, so it didn't hit the bone and Aunt Ellen will be okay. That's all that matters now. Don't beat yourself up over it."

"I still feel bad it happened. Every time I try to be a do-gooder, I cause trouble. But you," Liz gave Bobbie a big grin, "you are the heroine of the day. Wait until all the talk shows make you offers."

"They will have to check with my fiancée to see if I am available." Bobbie turned to look at David.

Liz, who never missed much, raised an eyebrow. "Well, glory be. I wonder who will win the pool. Everyone in town has been betting on when he would pop the question."

"You've got to be kidding," Bobbie was actually blushing. "We want to let Aunt Ellen know first. Don't give us away, please."

"Who, me?" Liz had a finger in front of her lips.

Maggie and Jeff Fischer arrived just as the Doctor came through the swinging doors. "Mrs. Taggert is fine. A bullet that size leaves quite a hole. The bone was barely chipped, but everything is stitched up nicely. We want to keep her a few days to be sure no infection shows up. She will be in a room in a few minutes, but still groggy. Keep it short, will you?"

The quiet of the hospital, with the silent tread of the nurses moving about their duties, was finally allowing the enormity of this afternoon's history making incident sink in on those who had been witness. Bobbie and David went to Ellen's room first. Assuring a sleepy Ellen that Bobbie was all right, they broke their news to her.

"We need you to get back on your feet," David whispered to her. "You know I can't run the office without you. Besides, we need you to stand up with us when Bobbie and I are married."

"Oh?"

"Aunt Ellen, it's true. I finally out waited him. We don't want to wait any longer, so as soon as you can be there..."

"That's nice, dear," was the only reply. The engaged couple slipped from the room.

News crews had found the hospital and Liz and Jeff were keeping them at bay. Maggie was sitting to herself, looking a little pale. Bobbie sat beside her when David went to confer with the medical staff.

"That was something, huh, Maggie. Enough to give us all something to think about. I'm in law enforcement, but that was the first time I've been under fire for real. Can't say as I like it."

Maggie's voice was soft as she turned to Bobbie. "I called John. Remember the other day in the campground? The dress and the strange man in the green car? Well, guess what? The Corp of Engineers has been lowering the lake water level to winter pool. A body turned up. A body for that dress!"

"Wait a minute. You mean...?"

"Yes, John said to tell you it was tangled up in some brush under that rotted bridge on Kinkaid's farm. A little black girl, buck naked. Stabbed to death. She would fit that dress. Bobbie, I saw that same man today at the school. I know it was him!"

"Are..., are you positive?" The coincidence seemed unlikely.

"There is something else." Maggie continued. "I swear I know that man. It couldn't be, though. John says I'm imagining things. It was a long time ago."

Bobbie went to get David. He left the news conference and Maggie told him of the discovery. He handed her his cell phone. "Call in and tell the sheriff. Let him call the highway patrol. With everything going on here, it will be hard to get anyone to pay attention. It's getting late. We will have to sneak out, lil', uh Bobbie. You are a celebrity, now."

David had arranged for hospital personnel to deal with the media. They issued a statement on the condition of the injured woman, taking full advantage to the publicity. He presented himself to the reporters and cameras as the attorney for Miss Foster. Other than giving them her name, he offered no information and declined an interview with her. Somehow it had surfaced that she was a sheriff's deputy and that would be headlines enough for now.

Jeff Fischer took over, giving a first hand account of his experiences. It was taken for granted that he was part of the group of friends at the hospital and he did nothing to correct that impression. He told David to get Bobbie away and he would ask Maggie to drop him by to retrieve his company car.

David agreed and the two exited by the doctor's door. David was not easily impressed by strangers, but Jeff seemed to know his stuff, and the help was appreciated.

****

6:30pm, Eastern Daylight Savings Time, a disgruntled woman with an Israeli passport, carried her briefcase past the guard desk at the National Laboratory in Oak Ridge.

"Going home early for a change, Dr. Fielding? I need to check your case, you know."

"Here it is, Charlie." She placed the satchel on the desk and unzipped the top. "You're just nosy, my man. You know I take work home all the time."

The guard stirred the contents of papers, thermos bottle and candy wrappers with his hand. "Want me to throw these away?" He held up a Mars bar wrapper.

"No, I need to keep a tally on my calories. I'll throw them out after I write it down. Keeping a Weight Watchers diary, you know."

"Aw, you look more like you need fattening up to me." The guard handed back the bag.

"That's sweet of you, Charlie. Good night, see you in the morning."

CHAPTER FIVE

The teenager watched as the blue truck pulled into a parking place. When the driver took his bags and boarded the bus, he wondered why. Curiosity more than anything made him cross the highway and try the door on the truck. It was open, he looked around then slid behind the wheel. No keys, no problem. He had learned to boost a car at the last meeting. A corner of an old wool army blanket protruded from behind the seat. He reached over to the passenger side, released the hinge and the back of the seat leaned forward. The blanket concealed an unloaded 30.06. Hunter, he guessed, then the gleam of metal beneath camouflage coveralls and rubber boots caught his eye. An automatic handgun, loaded, nestled there as well. Grinning, the boy reached under the dash for the wires. They were already loose, but he didn't stop to wonder why.

* * * * *

When the mini-bus discharged its passengers, Ahmed asked to be let out at the first motel by the interstate. Leaving the bus, with *mucho gracias* to the driver, he watched until the bus was out of sight, then carried his luggage across the bridge to the opposite side of the interstate highway. He walked into the lobby of a small motel and used his real identity and credit card to rent a room, explaining to the clerk his rental car broke down on the interstate. No, no, he had called the company and they would take care of it. He had friends in the area, they would pick him up tomorrow. Thanks anyway.

In the room, he neatly hung his clothes in the closet, put away his shoes, everything lined up even. These small tasks helped calm his nerves. He took his shaving kit to the bathroom and used scissors on his beard, leaving a mustache. A razor scrapped his skin bare, but he managed with only a few nicks. He carefully made sure all the hair went down the toilet. The water in the shower was steaming hot and he stayed under the spray until the aches left his muscles. Naked, he turned down the bed, fluffed the pillow, and slept.

* * * * *

When David drove up in front of Bobbie's apartment building, the Sheriff was waiting. "About time you got here," he growled. "What do you think you were doing, girl, pulling a stunt like that? It's all over the TV and radio." A big grin softened the gruff words. "You sure made us proud today, lil'bit."

"Thank you, Uncle Steve, but I'm no hero. I didn't even know what happened until it was over," Bobbie answered from the passenger seat in David's truck. "I was scared, Uncle Steve, I was so scared. When the man fell into us with his head almost gone... I just knew we would be hit, but it was Aunt Ellen..." The tremor in her voice revealed nerves still strung tight.

"You did good, Deputy." Steve reached through the window to pat Bobbie's shoulder. "I checked on Ellen over the police radio. Paramedics said it was clean. I'll go over there tomorrow, myself." Steve Milloy and Ellen Taggert were brother and sister. This was a small town; almost everyone was related to someone. "David, you better get your claim on this little girl before she gets offers from the big cities."

David reached behind the seat for his crutches. "We have done everything but set the date." he grinned at the Sheriff. He liked Bobbie's relatives and looked forward to being part of the large family. He opened his door, as Bobbie stepped out of the truck and came around to him. "Right now we have a problem. I think we were followed. Bobbie needs some rest, could you set a guard for her? The media has her address by now. It will be a zoo around here."

"Why don't you stay with her? What with finding that body out at Center Hill, I'm short handed. We are going to join the Rangers and Tennessee Wildlife as soon as it's light enough to search the creek and the cove where it runs into the lake."

David gave Bobbie a questioning look. She blushed becomingly, then said, "We have waited this long, Uncle Steve, we thought we might as well wait until we say I do. David, go on home. I know you're tired, too."

"No, honey, I'll stay, but it might be better if you go over to Paula's. Think you can do that?"

Bobbie looked at Steve. "I need to get to work in the morning. Paula's farm is over in the next county."

The Sheriff clapped David on the back. "Good idea, son. Take a few days off, Bobbie. My staff will enjoy telling tall tales to the news media. You'll be the biggest hero since Davy Crockett. I'll call you if anything turns up in the search. I can see headlights over on the main road. Grab your stuff, and get going. I'll call Paula and tell her you are on your way. David, take the patrol car, I'll take your truck home with me. That should throw them off."

* * * * *

David parked the patrol car in the allotted space behind the Sheriff's office in Smithville. It was only a couple of blocks to his building. Bobbie was safely at her sister's. He would call her in the morning. Now he was looking forward to some supper and his bed. Having only one leg put a lot of strain on it; he really was tired. He went to the front door of his office, fumbling with the key in the dim light from a corner street lamp. A white car pulled to the curb.

The window rolled down, and Jeff Fischer called to him. "Hello there, could I ask a favor?"

David grimaced and stayed at the door while the man got out of the car. "Depends," he said curtly. He was tired and didn't want to be bothered by another news reporter, even one he knew.

Jeff approached with a timid smile that made him look like a homeless puppy. "Maggie Lewis said you might put me up for a night. The motel is full, fishing tournament in town they said."

"It's not late. Why don't you drive home?"

Jeff stuck his hands in his pant's pockets and rocked back on his heels. "Yeah, okay. Don't want to bother you. Thought I might pick up more of the story tomorrow. I sure could use the help."

David motioned toward the door. "Just so you don't snore." He flicked the switch inside the door and an overhead fixture in the hall came on. "Go park the car in the alley behind the building, I'll open the back door. We don't need more of the media to know we are here."

The streetlight through the windows outlined furniture in the upstairs front room. David crossed to pull down heavy shades. He switched on a table lamp and laid out the ground rules. "Bedroom in the back is mine, you get the sofa. I haven't finished the walls in the other bedroom. Bath is between the two. I'd prefer you not to smoke, either. Are you hungry?"

"Look, I'm sorry about this. Don't put yourself out for me. It... I mean, I could really use a break."

"It's okay. I haven't had it so easy myself. What division were you in?"

"The 101st. I'm not a paratrooper. I crewed choppers. Saudi Arabia wasn't so bad. How about you?"

"I went with the National Guard when they were called up. Kuwait. Hey, sit down," David sank in a chair. "My legs get a little tired this time of night." He shook his crutches.

Jeff sat on the sofa. "You want me to go out and get something?"

"No, I've got a freezer full of food. You like Lasagna? There is beer in the refrigerator and Black Jack in the cabinet."

Jeff got two cans of beer and handed one to David. "Tell me why you decided to be a lawyer."

* * * * *

Karen Fielding was furious. The message on her answering machine said he was out of town on assignment, didn't know when he would be back. He would call. She needed him to be here tonight. She was counting on it. This would be the last time. The great lover, acting like he was doing her a favor. He was a good fuck, she admitted. She would miss him. She wanted to see his face when she told him he was only her alibi.

She paced in front of the telephone, chewing on a fingernail. Couldn't be helped, she would have to think of something. She went to the small kitchen of her apartment and emptied the contents of her briefcase on the counter. Cold tea from the thermos went down the sink drain. She rinsed the jug and left it to dry. She sorted the sheets of paper, most of it was old work she had completed, none of it classified. The candy wrappers were laid aside. Carefully, she unfolded the wrappers, smoothing them flat with her fingers. Turning them over, she placed her palm over the thin material. When she took her hand away, the heat had brought out numbers written on the inside. She smiled and checked each of the three. All were readable. The oldest trick in the book. Invisible ink.

The ink was fading again when she placed the wrappers in a plain white number ten size envelope. She wet her finger with water from the tap to seal the top. There was no address. Time to make a phone call, she couldn't put it off any longer.

In the bedroom, she opened the drawer in the bedside table and picked up a cell phone. The number she dialed was answered immediately. "The canary is out of the cage," she whispered.

"Speak up," a man replied. A background noise of hard rock music came through the receiver.

She cleared her throat. "The canary is out. The cage is empty."

"Good. You know the procedure."

The phone clicked dead.

Karen sat on the bed and cried. She should be happy. It was almost over and the bastards would pay. The tears she shed were not in remorse for the treason she committed. They were for Ibrahim, for the man she loved, the man she was to marry, until the Israelis executed him simply because he was a Palestinian.

She rose from the bed and changed into a sexy, short black dress. Carefully, she applied eye makeup, rouge and lipstick. She twisted her shoulder length hair up with a butterfly clip, leaving tendrils along her cheeks. A pair of six inch heeled sandals and she hardly looked like the eminent Dr. Fielding, the Israeli contribution to the international team of scientist working with the U. S. Government at Oak Ridge. She thought once again of Jeff Fischer. Damn him for not being here. At least he had kept her from being lonely.

It wasn't until she walked into a bar on Gay Street that she saw a television. Not quite 8:00pm, the news should not be on. Then she saw it was a special segment. The U. S. Vice President was assuring the citizens that he was alive and well.

A major network news anchor came on to explain what the Vice President said. Again, it was irradiated that no one knew of any reason for the attack. Several groups had claimed responsibility, none believable. It was thought the work of a lone gunman. One secret service guard killed and a local woman wounded. The President declined comment. On and on, as though the American public was too stupid to understand what the Vice President had just told them.

Karen pressed through the crowd around the bar, went to the back of the room and found a table. She ordered vodka over ice, and shifted nervously in her chair until the drink was delivered. She asked to run a tab, then sat back, sipped and waited.

Fifteen minutes later Karen was on her second vodka when she was joined by another woman. "Hi, girlfriend. Sit down and have a drink."

The woman sat, to the stares of every man in the room. The short skirt pulled up, leaving long, gorgeous legs in plain view. The luscious curves of her full breasts rose and fell with every breath. She brushed back long blonde hair, an unconscious gesture. "Karen, you are smashed. Why do you drink vodka when you know what it does to you?"

"Don't start, Nadja. Not tonight."

"Where's lover boy?"

Karen shrugged and chewed ice from her drink. "Out of town. Working, he said. On the answering machine."

"Did you hear about the Vice President? Somebody tried to off him."

"Not until I got here. What was that all about? The TV was making a big deal of it."

The blonde woman held out her hand. "You got the envelope?"

Karen took the number ten out of her purse and handed it over. "This is it, then? You won't need me again?"

"Go home, Karen. It's not up to me." The long legs uncrossed, she stood without bothering to pull down the tight skirt. "So long, girlfriend."

As the blonde crossed the room with a leisurely step, every man in the place felt like he should stand and applaud. The woman was the epitome of male desire. Until you looked in her eyes. They were dark, shiny, cold and unblinking, like a snake..

Karen ordered another drink. She watched couples dancing. She watched them talking and laughing at the tables. She sat alone and drank more vodka. The waitress came over to ask if she was okay. This time Karen paid her bill, plus a ten dollar tip. She gathered her purse and tried to imitate Nadja's walk across the room.

Almost to the door, she stumbled, twisting her ankle on the high heel of the sandal. A hand grabbed her arm, steadied her.

"Here, let me help you."

"Sorry, I didn't mean to be so clumsy." She realized her voice was slightly slurred. "I'm all right, really." The man let go of her arm. She swayed back against him, "Maybe I'd better sit down."

He pulled a chair from a nearby table and helped her down. "I saw you come in. Hasn't been long ago. You don't drink much, do you?"

Karen focused her eyes. He was a big man, and good looking. She didn't mean for the giggle to come out. "Jilted," she hiccuped. "Working out of town, yeah. Like I believe that story. He didn't show up."

"Let me see you home. I'm ready to leave."

"Why not? Sir Lochinvar to the rescue. My shining knight." She almost fell from the chair when she tried to bow.

"Come on Princess. Where do you live?"

Sometime later, Karen woke in a panic. The room was dark, the only light coming from down a hall. Then she realized she was on her own sofa. When she sat up, she felt the blood rush from her head, leaving her dizzy. Stupid, she thought, I'm really stupid. I never drink that much, only tonight was special. Ibrahim would have understood.

The man who brought me home? She didn't exactly remember his face. Holding on to the furniture, she took a few unsteady steps toward the light. At a doorway, she blinked in the brightness of the overhead ceiling fixture. The room was empty.

She went into the bathroom, leaving her clothes dropped along her route. She turned on the shower, waited until the water warmed, and stepped in the glass enclosure.

She never heard the pop of the silenced gun. She slid to the floor, legs folded under her. Before the blackness closed in, her eyes were seeing Ibrahim's face.

****

The telephone woke David from a sound sleep. The Sheriff's voice came through the haze of a sleeping pill. "We need you, counselor. Kid here won't talk without a lawyer." The lighted clock showed two fifteen am.

"Give me twenty minutes," David grudgingly sat up. "What's this about, Steve?"

"Skinhead kid, sixteen, maybe seventeen. Tattooed swastika on his arm. Got stopped on 70 for speeding. Mouthed off at the deputy, so they searched. Guess what? The truck matches the description that's posted. AND guns concealed. Same type of guns used on the Vice President."

David whistled. "I'll be there quick as I can."

Still groggy, David switched on his bedside light and reached for the clothes he had left on the chair. He didn't need the prescription sleeping pills often. Only when the phantom pain came. Even though his leg was gone, the nerves in the spinal cord re-created it, remembering with excruciating pain the destroyed bone and flesh of the wounded appendage.

He struggled into his shirt and pants as his head cleared, tucking the empty pants leg up under his belt. Finding his crutches beside the bed, he went into the bath and splashed cold water on his face. A couple of aspirin helped, and he hoped the sheriff had some fresh coffee.

Before leaving the apartment, he checked the living room. The covers on the couch were thrown back, the cushions empty. Maybe the telephone woke him. Probably outside for a smoke or maybe he decided to go on home after all. David didn't have time to worry about his guest.

He left by the front door, leaving the light on in the downstairs hall, in case Jeff came back. On the other side of the courthouse square the Sheriff's Office and County Jail blazed with lights. David swung quickly on his crutches toward the building. He wanted to get to the kid before more law enforcement arrived. The truck and the guns would bring in the Highway Patrol as well as the TBI, maybe the FBI. If the guns proved to be the weapons used in the shooting, no telling who else would converge on this small town.

The front doors were open, with a deputy behind the reception desk. "They're waiting for you, David. Steve's office." The deputy nodded toward the hall.

"Thanks." David turned down the hall. At the door of the office he looked through the high glass window. The kid was seated in a straight chair beside the desk. The Sheriff paced in front of the desk, and a senior deputy stood to the side, arms folded across his chest. David watched the boy. Under the facade of bravado, he could see the kid was scared.

He knocked and Steve held the door open as he entered the small room. "This is David Middleton. He's a lawyer."

The kid bolted up from the chair, his young face contorted by an ugly sneer. "I ain't gonna talk to nobody!"

David looked at the Sheriff, "If we could have some privacy?" Steve nodded to his deputy, then both men left the office.

David went behind the desk, unhooked the crutches from his wrists and sat in the swivel chair. "Look, I don't want to be here anymore than you do, so let's make this fast. Okay?"

The boy sat back down with a plop. He bent forward, elbows on his knees, head in his hands. The growing hair on his shaved head gave it a black shadow. His voice came muffled by the hands. "I told that SOB of a sheriff I don't know who the guns belong to. I don't know what the hell he means about the Vice President. I been in school all day."

"That right?" David waited while the boy straightened in the chair. "What about the truck?"

"Ahh…, belongs to my cousin. He lives over in Sparta."

"Guess he owns the guns, then."

"Ahh…, no, never saw them before." The boy stood up and bent to look David in the face. "Who the hell are you, anyway? I want a real lawyer, not some cripple!"

"Cut the crap, kid. I am a real lawyer. It takes brains, not two legs. You know someone else? Make up your mind, you want my help or not?"

Deflated again, the boy sat. "Yeah, I mean maybe. I need to call Buddy. It's over in Sparta, will they let me call there?"

"Sure." David picked up the phone, "Deputy, we have a phone call to make. Put us through." He handed the phone to the boy.

"Uh uh," the kid shook his head. "I want a pay phone."

"Suit yourself," David swung up on his crutches. He reached in his pocket and tossed the kid a couple of quarters. Out in the hall, he told the deputy to take the kid to the phone in the back.

"I don't know if he will talk to me. He's scared." David walked with the Sheriff to the end of the hall where a coffee pot gurgled, making a fresh batch.

Steve poured the black brew in two mugs. "Why doesn't that surprise me?" He shook his head. "These kids join the militant groups before they know what they are getting into. The men who run them fill their heads with all sort of nonsense. Most of the time the organization is a sham, just an upper for somebody's ego. Captain Strickland from the Highway Patrol is on his way over. TBI is sending their domestic terrorist expert. Somebody named Smith. I don't know him."

"Have they notified the Feds yet?"

"Probably, I haven't heard.

The deputy came down the hall, the boy in handcuffs before him. He removed the handcuffs, shoved the kid into another room, then handed the Sheriff a slip of paper. "Here's the number he called."

"Shit," Steve said, "don't ever do that in front of a lawyer." He folded the paper and put it in his shirt pocket. "See if you can get him to make a statement." He nodded curtly to David and went back to his office.

David entered the room, set up for interrogations with plain walls, a table and two straight chairs "What's your name?" He set the mug of coffee on the table and pulled out a chair, leaving the boy standing.

"Orville Wright." The boy lowered himself in the chair across the table.

"Yeah, and I'm Wilbur."

The kid gave a resigned shrug, like he had heard it before. "That's my real name."

David looked at the boy. He had blue eyes, very intense blue, and he was looking straight at David. Whoever was on the other end of the telephone call had apparently told him to cooperate.

"Okay, Orville, you want some coffee? Is that what they call you? Orville?"

David reached over with one crutch and tapped on the door. It was opened by the deputy. "Some coffee for my client, please." The man nodded and closed the door.

"Are you my lawyer, now? Buddy said it was all right. Said he'd be here to bail me out. When can I leave?"

"I don't know, Orville, you are in more trouble than you know. Who is Buddy? That who you called? How old are you anyway?"

The boy shrank down again. "Buddy's my cousin. That's why I called him instead of Ma. He lives closer, too. Sparta."

David sized up the youth. Tall, but about as big around as a jack pine. No sign of a morning beard. Gangly, with oversized hands and feet, like a growing hound pup. He repeated, "How old are you?"

The boy ducked his head, "Fifteen."

Just my luck, David did a mental about face, a real juvenile. What rotten luck. The news media will have a field day with this one after all the high school shootings. It was an effort to keep his face bland.

Orville sat up straight again when the deputy put a mug of coffee in front of him. "Anything I can do for you, David?" the deputy asked before closing the door.

"Please bring me a list of the alleged charges against my client. And tell the Sheriff to honor my clients rights as a juvenile." Steve would know what he meant. The Sheriff was obligated to notify a guardian, before any legal proceedings took place.

David turned back to Orville. "When the deputies arrested you, did they read you your rights?"

The kid nodded, "Yeah. I watch those cop shows on TV. He had it down on a card, but I knew what it said."

"You understand what it means?"

"How many times I got to say it?" Orville was beginning to be angry. David wondered if he really understood the trouble he was in.

51

"What did you say to the deputies that made them search the truck?"

Orville fidgeted in his seat. "I thought you was supposed to be on my side. How come all the questions? I told them I didn't know nuthin' about the guns."

"Just answer the question, or I'll get it from the deputies. If I'm going to help you I need to know everything you can think of to tell me." David was tired and in no mood to put up with a snot nose kid, who just might go to jail for the rest of his life.

"The deputy, the one who had the Miranda on a card, was one big, black motherfucker. I told him no nigger was going to tell me what to do."

David had a hard time suppressing a smile. Jim Ed ran the gym in the mornings, then drove a patrol car for the County on the late shift. Meeting up with Jim Ed in the dark, uniformed as a cop, was enough to scare the hell out of most adults. The kid had guts, if not sense.

"Do you live at home with your mother?" David hoped the answer was no.

The boy didn't reply, just nodded his head yes. "When can I go? Buddy should be here now."

A knock on the door and the deputy brought in a computer print out. He handed it to David and left the room without looking at the boy.

David read the information on the sheet. His gut feeling about this whole thing sank even lower. The truck had been reported stolen from a Park and Ride close to Nashville. That was enough to hold the boy. David shook his head, trying to recall his memory of the afternoon. Maggie Lewis had said a bearded man was driving it in Carthage. Was there a connection between the truck, the man, the boy, and the shooting?.

David took a hand held tape recorder from his pocket. "Orville, I want you to tell me everything you did yesterday, from the time you woke up, until now."

* * * * *

At exactly 4:00 AM EDT, an explosion strong enough to register on the Richter Scale rocked Oak Ridge. The blast leveled the central building of the National Laboratory. Simultaneously, an explosion destroyed a minor production facility in the K-25 section.

Startled residents of the nearby town ran outside, fearing an earthquake. Panic stricken deer in the surrounding mountains ran blindly off bluffs in the pre-dawn dark. Birds were knocked from their perches in the trees. Eight people died on site, three lab technicians working on night projects, and five security guards. Seven people, four from the janitor staff and three more security guards went to the hospital, five with critical injuries. Three injuries were reported from K-25, all security guards, all minor.

Fire fighters and medical personnel were called in from the city of Knoxville. Police from neighboring towns helped secure the area. The city of Oak Ridge was as effectively shut down as it had been fifty years ago, when walls, fences and manned gates isolated the town to protect the production of the first atomic bomb.

CHAPTER SIX

The attempted assassination of the Vice President of the United States was international news. Broadcasts around the world speculated on the event. Heads of nations called subordinates on the carpet, then issued statements denying responsibility. The President of Russia called the President of the United States personally, as did the Premier of China, England's Prime Minister, Germany's Chancellor, the President of France, along with many other VIPs who could not get through. On Capitol Hill it was intimated that the whole thing was staged to get sympathy and votes for the VP in the upcoming election. On the other hand, Democrats blamed the Republicans and a no holds barred fist fight broke out in the House of Representatives. Lobbyist for the tobacco industry made themselves scarce, as did the gun lobbyist. Environmentalist blamed the capitalist, and the general public held the news media responsible.

On the opposite side, several international terrorist organizations took the credit, saying it was only a warning. Next time it could be the President. White Supremacist groups issued a statement saying they would not have missed the first time, and The Tennessee Liberty Army marched before the White House carrying placards worded *DOWN WITH TAXES! NO TAX ON WHISKY! TAKE TAX OFF TOBACCO AND GASOLINE! INDEPENDENCE FOR TENNESSEE!*

The Vice President was still in seclusion and the early morning news shows carried no mention of the explosion in Oak Ridge.

* * * * *

Bright sunshine coming in the window woke Bobbie. She stretched, still feeling drowsy, trying to hold on to sleep for a few more minutes. Every muscle in her body felt stiff and sore. The white, freshly starched curtains over the open window clued her that she wasn't in her apartment. She stretched again, sleep had been a long time coming last night. The sound of gunfire kept echoing in her head. No stranger to guns on the firing range, she shivered now, knowing this time it was for real. Then thoughts of David moved into her head. Tragedy and joy, all at the same time. She was happy David finally opened up to her, but then remembered that a man had died just inches from her.

Well, if it took danger to cut through the wall David had built around himself, yesterday had done it. Last night, before he left her at her sister's house, he told her he loved her. He had known that he loved her for a long time; loved her enough to let her find someone who was not maimed, someone with two legs. She knew he was giving her one more chance to say no, before the rest of the town knew of the engagement. Neither of them mentioned the afternoon's events, but the threat of losing each other was very present.

Bobbie took the initiative, even tired as she was. Told him to turn around and go back to her apartment. If he was backing out, at least she would have one night to remember. Or he could stop the car right now.

Maybe that's what we should do, he had told her, with one of his rare smiles; not wait for a wedding, but if you got in the back seat of a patrol car you couldn't get out. The doors had to be opened from the outside. They both had laughed at the thought of making love in the Sheriff's car.

David sobered then. He knew he could perform sexually. He confessed to a brief affair with a friendly nurse at the VA Hospital. He had been as chaste as a celibate priest since he came back to Smithville, but now, just looking at Bobbie made him hard as one of the granite tombstones in the cemetery plot they passed. It was a good thing she could stay with Paula tonight. She really wouldn't be safe with him, wedding or no wedding. Bobbie teased him with a seductive grin and pouted that he had turned down her offer, as he parked the police car in Paula's driveway.

When he turned off the engine, she made a confession, too. She was not a virgin. He protested, not wanting to hear, but she continued. It had happened when she was in college, when she thought David would never come back to her.

David sat still for a moment, then without a word he gently placed a finger across her lips before she could say any more. He tilted her face to him and kissed her, hard and long enough to leave them both breathless. It was all she needed to know. Paula and three of her kids spilled out the door and caught them making out in the Sheriff's car.

Bobbie helped Paula put the younger children to bed, then told Paula everything that happened in Carthage. Paula had seen the six o'clock news and tried to call Bobbie at the hospital. She was thrilled that Bobbie and David finally decided to marry. Like almost everyone, she had believed it was only a matter of time. "Everybody in town knows you've been mooning around after him, but who would have thought it would take national news to get the two of you together. Anyway, I'm happy for you, sis."

Bobbie could always talk to Paula. Paula never judged or criticized. She told Paula what had transpired between her and David in the car.

"Don't sweat it, kiddo. He's one lucky fella to get you. He had reasons for what he did and abstaining now, but you, you could have anyone in Tennessee, or anywhere else for that matter. Ever look in a mirror? You look like Aunt Ellen. You're one gorgeous woman!" Paula gave a serious smile to her sister. After a sisterly hug, they made their way up the stairs to bed.

Wide awake with the morning sun, Bobbie climbed out of bed and picked up a hairbrush from the dresser. Her tangled brown hair and oversized tee shirt sure didn't go along with gorgeous. Giving up on her hair, she pulled on her jeans and went barefoot down the stairs.

Paula was all ready working at a farm wife's chores. Canning jars lined the kitchen table waiting to be filled from kettles of cut corn. Bobbie went to the stove and poured herself a cup of coffee, added milk and sugar and sat at the table with a yawn.

Paula went out on the kitchen porch and came back with a bushel basket full of green beans. "You okay this morning kiddo? I mean with all the excitement yesterday?"

"I'm just tired. Didn't really sleep much." Bobbie pulled the basket over and began to snap the beans. Suddenly she stood up. "Umm," she finished the coffee, "I told David I would call him in the morning." Her sister snickered when she went to use the phone in the living room.

The telephone rang several times, until a strange voice answered with only a hello. "Who is this?" Bobbie blurted out, then realized she sounded rude.

The man on the other end didn't take offense. "Jeff Fischer. May I ask who is calling?" he asked politely. Then she remembered he was the reporter who had been with them yesterday.

"Ah... I need to speak to David. Tell him Bobbie is calling."

"David is still sleeping. He had to go out sometime in the night. Didn't get back in until morning. He put me up last night, the motel was full. Thought I would return the favor and stay to answer the phone for him. Hey, you're the girl who saved the Vice President. Can I set up an interview? I was there, too, remember.?"

"Please don't wake up David. Tell him I'll call later. I don't know about an interview until I talk to David. Thanks for helping out yesterday." She remembered him from the hospital, too. She hung up the phone, feeling disappointed.

Back in the kitchen, Paula had turned on a small television to entertain her youngest while she finished the canning. Bobbie held out her arms to the baby in the playpen. He pulled up on the mesh side of the crib and held up his arms. She picked him up and turned to show him the TV when a news break came on. "Paula, come see this."

Paula put down her spoon and came to that side of the kitchen. Oak Ridge, the National Laboratory destroyed by explosion and fire. Under control now; the National Guard called in to cordon off the area. The cause was not known at present. People were being evacuated from the immediate vicinity of the explosion. The reporter emphasized that no one should try to go in the area. Programming would be interrupted as news broke. The report was low key, directed more to the safety of the residents in the surrounding area. The screen flickered and a commercial came on.

"What is happening to Tennessee?" Paula took the baby from Bobbie and put him back in his pen. She shook her head with dismay.

Bobbie didn't have an answer, only an uneasy feeling. She gestured at the canning jars. "Can you leave this long enough to take me in to my apartment?"

"Yes, but is that wise? Steve said you need to stay a couple of days."

"I want to get my car and uniform. The office will need help with what's going on. I'm a big girl, I can handle the pressure. Besides, I want to see David."

"Okay, I'll get my purse. Here, hold Skeeter. He'll have to come with us." Paula switched off the stove, covered the corn and beans, and went up the stairs. She stopped on the first riser and waggled a finger at Bobbie. "You owe me a bushel of snapped beans."

Paula dropped Bobbie at her building, hurrying to get back and finish the canning, so she could see Aunt Ellen in the afternoon. Bobbie felt guilty asking so much of her sister, but only said she would call later. Tell Aunt Ellen, she would be there this evening.

In her apartment, she quickly showered, subdued her curly hair by twisting it up and pinning it to the back of her head. She put on a fresh uniform and surveyed herself in a full length mirror. She enjoyed the prestige of the Deputy's uniform.

She had gone to college, wanting the pre-requisites for a major in elementary education. In her second year she left without a degree and returned to the family farm to care for her mother. All the older siblings were married, with families to support. Only she and one brother were left to care for Ma.

Seeing someone you love die was not something everyone could handle. Aunt Ellen had been through it with her husband, and was Bobbie's main help and support during the year it took the disease to kill her mother.

Ma, all eight kids called her, a beautiful woman like her sister, had stayed alert and cheerful to the last. Her body had shrunk and withered as the cancer spread, but her spirit could not be conquered. Her last words to Bobbie were, "Don't grieve for me, child, Pa is there. We will be together again. All of us will be together one day. Never be afraid to love. It is what makes life worth living."

It was that memory, and the way her mother had loved the stern, quiet man who was her father, that kept her love for David alive. David, who excelled in sports; David, who had gone to the University of Tennessee on a football scholarship; David, who loved to dance, would never do those things again. He had come back from the war a far different person from the laughing, teasing youth who wanted to be a policeman like his father. When he joined the National Guard, it had been with a sense of duty, never knowing what it would cost him. When called up, he and his unit left on the high note of adventure, then he came back with no prospects for anything.

Bobbie held onto her love for him when he went through his self pity phase. She held onto her love when he rejected her, told her to stop bothering him. She held onto her love when he went away again, this time to law school, and when he had come home again to set up his law practice. There were times that she had wondered if he was worth it; times when she was attracted to other men; times when she felt sorry for herself, too, but it was her mother's words that carried the day. Don't be afraid to love, even someone who thinks himself unlovable. Now Bobbie knew he was worth her waiting. David did love her. He had proved to her and the entire town that he was a whole person, despite the handicap of losing a leg.

Uncle Steve had given her a desk job after her mother died. She liked the work and wanted to be a full fledged deputy, took the test and won an appointment to the police academy where she graduated top of her class. She was the one who had gone into law enforcement, and David had gone into the law itself. They would be good for each other.

Bobbie didn't spend a lot of time thinking about all that had transpired in the last few years, it just passed through her mind. She got her car from the parking place out front of the building. She noticed a white car with a Channel 2 sign parked at the corner of the entrance. Swinging the car around to the rear, she drove out a side exit. She would go to David's office first, then to work.

* * * * *

In Nashville a minor corporate official walked in the shack by the gate of the Davidson County Sheriff's impound yard. "Paper here says you have a car for me." He held out a half page of print to the man lounged behind the desk.

"Yeah," the man took the document, "yeah, it tallies. Green 1999 Pontiac Bonneville. How did you lose that car and not know it?"

"How the hell should I know? The high and mighty types get to take their cars home with them. They just told me to pick it up."

"Number sixteen, third row back. That's fifty-five dollars. Thirty for towing, twenty-five for storage." He held out a dirty hand.

The official dug in his pocket and pulled out three twenties. He slapped them down on the desk and snatched up the car keys. Mumbling obscenities, he went to find the car.

On the top floor of a downtown office building, another man, with the style and appearance of a well-dressed gentleman, stood looking out over the Nashville skyline. He could see the river and the new NFL stadium rising on the opposite bank. His hands were folded behind his back, emphasizing his relaxed posture. The woman standing just behind him was almost as tall, easily able to see over his shoulder. She unconsciously brushed back long blonde hair.

"So the idiot stole a license plate."

"Yes," she smoothed her hair again, putting it behind her ear. "That is how the police recovered the car. The license plate was reported missing."

Behind them, sitting in the shadows, was a stocky man with a shock of brown hair and a bushy beard. "I made sure the drive out tag had plenty of time on it when he picked up the car from the lot. The police never notice those dates, anyway. The car has been retrieved?"

"Yes, we have the car." The man at the window answered in a well modulated voice without turning.

The blonde shrugged her almost bare shoulders. "Somehow Ahmed felt the car was compromised, so he took the truck. He has been accepting assignments for almost twenty-five years. We should have anticipated that he would adjust his plans. He is clever, experienced, and dangerous. He knows what he is doing. It is also possible he will complete the contract."

The man turned and Nadja stepped swiftly back. Rage mottled his normally florid face. "Are you an idiot, too? There will not be another attempt. I told you, the plans have changed." Nadja backed up another step. "Where is Ibrahim Hassim? He was hired to arrange the contract and tie up the loose ends! You, and you," he pointed to the bearded man, "get out! Find Faziz, and don't come back until you have him."

When the pair left the office, the man sat down to a computer. It was all coming together, the idiots he hired were doing exactly what he wanted. The main objective was accomplished. The magno-electronic project at Oak Ridge was finished. Congress would never fund the research necessary to rebuild the project. Now, private industry would build the car, and with luck, his company would market it first. It didn't matter if the Vice President was still alive. His interference with the government project would mean nothing now. If he should become President, additional steps could be taken then.

* * * * *

Ahmed picked up the cellular phone from his suitcase and dialed a pre-arranged number. The call was answered immediately. The din of loud music blasted his eardrum, but a man's voice came through clear. "Yeah?"

Ahmed cleared his throat, "This is the Doctor."

Silence on the other end as the music was turned off. "Where are you?"

"A motel next to I-40, thirty miles east of Nashville."

"Wait there, we'll bring you in.. Give me the name and directions, someone will pick you up. I repeat, stay there!" Urgency was in the voice.

"I'll wait." Ahmed gave the information to the man. "How long?"

"As long as it takes!" The phone went dead.

Ahmed knew without being told, he was in trouble. If his mission had been successful as in the past, he would have been told to proceed as planned. He threw back the covers and showered quickly, dressing in his new suit with the English wing tip oxfords. His face looked fine without the beard, except for being pale. He had used this deception before and was prepared. He found a small bottle of women's makeup in his shaving kit. After he shaved, he applied the foundation to the light part of his face. Satisfied with the results, he went to pack his luggage. Ready to go, he started to the lobby of the motel where breakfast was available.

Two girls were already soaking up the bright morning sunshine by the small pool. They were stretched out on lounges wearing tiny thong bikinis. Ahmed could see from where he stood they were very young. Skinny kids with hardly any breasts, as young as the black girl. He felt the deep sadness in his heart. Why hadn't he tried harder to help her? He cursed himself again. It made little difference, she would have died anyway. He should have called the authorities. After all, he was in the United States on a legitimate visa. But then, how could he explain why he was in the old motel with a prostitute dying of knife wounds?

Ahmed had to lower his eyes. One of the girls was not asleep. She sat up and yelled, "What you staring at, Jack?"

Ahmed remembered where he was. He ducked his head and quickly entered the lobby. Over a cup of tepid coffee, he began to assess his situation. The trouble could be mild or it could be bad. If he could get to Ibrahim's employers he might have a chance. They would have no idea he had deliberately failed to accomplish the mission, but evidence would show it was not entirely his fault. Ibrahim had given him unreliable information and equipment unsuitable for the distance. What did they expect? He was not superman. The defective scope had killed the secret service agent. He was aiming at the vest he knew the men wore. He would never shoot to kill men who were only doing their duty. Damn the woman who got in the way of the second bullet. Never had his work been so sloppy. Too late now to worry, except for himself. He had been told to wait. Suddenly he knew he could not wait. It would be dangerous. He would rely only on himself.

He went to the desk and checked out. The clerk was most solicitous. Was everything all right with the room, Dr. Faziz? Be sure and have some breakfast. Come back if you are in this area again. Ahmed brought his charm to the front, assuring the man he had been most comfortable.

In the room, he gathered his belongings and checked the automobiles in the parking lot. Not much available now, most overnight guests had left, but there was a large shopping mall across the street.

He was pulling his wheeled suitcase through the parking area, when a dark blue sedan turned in the drive. It stopped beside him and a window lowered. "Going somewhere, Dr. Faziz?" The voice was smooth, melodious, with a hint of sarcasm.

His heart beat a tattoo. "Hello, Nadja."

* * * * *

David woke up to the sound of the television. He pulled on a terry robe, picked up one crutch from the side of the bed and hopped into the living room of his apartment. Bobbie and Jeff Fischer had their backs to him watching the TV. Bobbie was in uniform, and Jeff looked as rumpled as yesterday. What time was it, anyway? The clock in the kitchen alcove blinked from 10:30 to 10:31 AM. David stifled a yawn.

The next instance Bobbie had her arms around him, holding her face up for a kiss. He gave her a little peck. "Wait a minute, honey, I'd like to keep a few secrets until our wedding night. Why aren't you at Paula's?"

She laughed, a happy, contented sound, "You need a shave, big man." She reached up to rub his dark stubble of beard and kissed his cheek. "I wanted to see you."

Jeff poured fresh coffee in a mug for him. "Thanks for everything last night, David. I'm leaving now, something has happened in Oak Ridge. That's my beat. Bobbie said she will be glad to give me an interview when you can be present. I'll call quick as I can; that's important to me." He winked at Bobbie, "I'll see if I can throw off the news hounds for you."

The two men shook hands, as Jeff congratulated David and Bobbie on their engagement. He left a card with his telephone numbers.

"So what kept you up all night?" Bobbie poured more coffee in David's cup and seated herself opposite him at the small kitchen table.

"The pickup truck Maggie reported turned up here in town."

"The man with a beard?"

"No, the driver was a fifteen year old kid, but that's not all. A 30.06 and automatic, along with camouflage coveralls was behind the seat. Steve called me when he realized what he might have."

"Jeeze," Bobbie shook her head. "The same type of weapon used in the shooting, and we can place the truck in Cartage at the right time. But Maggie recognized the man from the campground driving the truck." Bobbie picked up the cups and put them in the sink. "I'd better get over to the office. Something over in Oak Ridge, too. The station broke into the programming, but only said an accident at the National Laboratory. The area is sealed off, no one in or out. Jeff called his editor and was told to get back quick. What do you suppose that's all about?"

David shook his head in the negative. "The kid picked up here is from Nashville. I've got more to do than worry about government secrets in Oak Ridge. What did Jeff mean about the news hounds?"

Bobbie looked a bit guilty. "I couldn't stay at Paula's with all this going on. Somebody followed me from my apartment. They're out front now."

David gave her a wry smile. "I guess you will have to make a statement before the day is over. When you feel up to it, we'll go down. Say, lil'bit, oh, sorry Bobbie," David's grin wasn't a bit sorry. "That's going to be a hard habit to break. Steve said for you to take some time off. It would be a big help to me if you could stay and answer the phone today. I've got two cases for the County coming up and now the kid who drove the truck. I'll check Ellen's computer downstairs, but Judge Jenkins is on the bench today, you know how he is. Besides, I don't think the reporters will bother you so much here. I'll pull the drapes downstairs when I go out and tell them I won't be back today."

Bobbie frowned, "Well, I guess I could call in and tell the office I'm here in case they need me, but I'm not Aunt Ellen, you know. No super efficiency here, I just muddle along at my own speed."

David stood up and steadied himself on the edge of the table. He reached over and grabbed Bobbie's arm, pulling her to him. "Hey, lil'bit, you don't want the job?" He put his face down and nuzzled her cheek, teasing her with his unshaved chin. He wanted nothing more than to pull the pins from her hair, to unbutton her shirt, to...; he made do with a kiss.

She leaned into him, feeling the solid bulk of him. "Humm. Well, if this goes with the job..."

David shaved and dressed quickly in casual slacks and white shirt. He rolled up a tie and stuffed it in the pocket of his sport coat, just in case he would be needed at the courthouse. He looked himself in the eye at the bathroom mirror and said, "Liar."

What he wanted to wear was a uniform like Bobbie. All he had ever wanted was to be a State Trooper like his father. Now that dream was shattered. The need for Bobbie to stay in his office was an excuse. He knew his schedule as well as Ellen Taggert. He should be the one in the uniform, the one who might be in danger, not the woman he loved.

David was surprised at the intensity of his feelings. He usually buried his emotions, putting the past where it belonged. In a moment of weakness he had let Bobbie know how he felt about her, asked her to marry him. He had no right to ask her to marry a crippled man, no right to ask anything, but he would ask her to give up the job. Never would he convince himself to let her be in danger. He thought of yesterday's shooting and the helpless feeling that hit him when he couldn't find her. He shuddered and looked the mirror in the eye again. "Just what were you thinking? You're a damned cripple," he told the reflection in the mirror, "how do you think you could protect her?" He continued to watch, as what he saw as a sorry excuse for half a man stared back from the mirror.

Downstairs, Bobbie brought up his appointments on Ellen's computer. It was not a busy day, so except for the new case with the boy, why did he need her to stay? She shrugged and scrolled through the next few days. Most of the work was for the county in his capacity as public defender, nothing big coming up. Bobbie had not realized things were so slow for David. Aunt Ellen's duties included a lot more than what Bobbie could do, secretarial, bookkeeping, and legal research. All of the files were current, nothing left over to complete. It would be some time before David would really need office help. Aunt Ellen should be back by then.

Bobbie moved some papers around on the desk. She would stay today, but tomorrow she was going back to the Sheriff's Department and her duties as a Deputy.

CHAPTER SEVEN

Dr. Ahmed Faziz stowed his luggage in the trunk of the blue sedan. He took the front seat beside the driver. The woman pushed up dark sunglasses and gave him an admiring look. Her smile was lazy, seductive. "Ah, you look much better. I never liked your beard." She put the car in gear and turned toward the interstate.

"What are you doing here, sevgili? (sweetheart). When was it I saw you last? Three years ago in Istanbul?"

The woman unconsciously brushed back her long blonde hair. "Umm. Istanbul, yes, it has been that long. I was here in the area. When I checked in, I was told to pick you up." She kept her eyes on the heavy traffic as she took the east ramp.

Ahmed had a sinking feeling in the pit of his stomach. "You were here? Looking for me?"

The blonde shifted her shoulders and the vee neck blouse showed the round fullness of her ample breasts. "Relax, old friend, there has been a change of plans."

Ahmed turned his head to look out the window. "We are going east. I need to go to Nashville. I am scheduled to speak at a seminar Friday at Vanderbilt University. I am expected. The University sponsored my visa into the United States for that purpose."

"I told you, plans have changed. It was taken care of. They regretfully canceled your participation when you fell too ill to appear." Nadja drove skillfully, just beyond the speed limit.

"I was prepared. I could handle it, then be in the clear to use the airline return ticket on Monday."

"Ahmed," the woman's laugh was musical, like soft bells, "you are getting old and set in your ways. A stroke of bad luck. The truck you used was stopped for speeding. The guns were found."

Ahmed shrugged, "It was clean, I left no prints. Nothing to tie me to it. The authorities were supposed to find the truck and suspect the owner." He smoothed the thick mustache on his upper lip. He settled back in the seat and closed his eyes. Something was wrong. Nadja was his contemporary, a counterpart. She was good at what she did, very good. Why would she be sent to bring him in, when he could very well have returned to his own identity and profession with no danger of being connected to the assassination attempt? His mind sorted through several possibilities. No, Ibrahim would have no way of knowing he had deliberately missed the target.

He had worked with Nadja, not her own name he knew, in the past. She was a Muslim from the former Soviet Union State of Georgia. He knew little more about her, except that she was the most ruthless killer he ever encountered. She was also very beautiful. The combination was lethal. He did not know what motivated her, she seemed to care for nothing.

He himself, in the early years, had no compassion for those who had been his targets, or those who got in the way. He had started very young, fired with patriotism and religious zeal. One thing led to another and later, the chance to make a good deal of money was the draw. He worked hard and was faithful to his ideals, at the same time earning a medical degree. He was considered an expert on Middle Eastern and African diseases, often asked to speak in various parts of the world. A perfect cover for his other activities.

Unfortunately, his rash youth and hard line religious training had put him with people who had no qualms in creating terror. He had tried before to break away, never with success Not often, that would have been fatal. Where he called home now was such an attempt. He had been very circumspect, very careful, not to give anyone any reason to look for him. Still, they found him. Ibrahim, and whoever employed him, took full advantage of Ahmed's past. His son would be safe only as long as he obeyed their dictates. He was neatly trapped.

He began to take notice of his surroundings. The exit to Carthage flashed by then the first of many crossings of the Caney Fork River. Somehow, he had to get away from Nadja. His opportunity came when they passed the ramp to a Rest Area. A huge eighteen wheeler pulled back on the interstate in front of the car. Nadja slammed on the breaks and swerved to the right to avoid the heavy traffic. Ahmed opened the door and rolled out on the grassy road side. Shrubbery broke his fall, but he felt something sting his left arm. Cars behind braked and veered right and left. Horns honked and Nadja was forced to speed up again.

Ahmed knew he only had a temporary reprieve. He stumbled to his feet and grabbed his arm and made for the underpass. A car dodged him as he crossed, then a truck's horn blared. He dove again, crashed through bushes, rolled down the bank to the river. Stunned by the fall, he lay dazed, half in, half out of the shallow water.

A hand reached for him. "*Señor!* Are you living? Wait, wait, you are hurt! I go get help."

"No, no, I'm okay. Just help me up." The hand took his good arm and he managed to stand. His new suit was ripped and blood dripped from his right hand.

The man, with long gray hair and an even longer mustache, spoke accented English. An old station wagon was pulled to the side of the entry ramp. Ahmed switched to Spanish and began to swear. "Bitch, I should never let you drive!" He shook his fist at the receding sedan. "My girlfriend," he grinned sheepishly. "What a temper! She will turn around and come back for me. I would like to teach her a lesson. Would you take me to the nearest town, *amigo*? To a doctor? I can pay you very well."

The man looked dubious, but nodded to the old car. "Come, I am going to town. There is a small hospital there."

* * * * *

Jeff Fischer left Smithville and drove to Oak Ridge in record time, only to be turned away by a National Guard blockade at the Clinch River. He back tracked to I-40 and continued into Knoxville. His nerves were stretched tight as a tennis racquet string before he reached Karen's apartment complex. She had to be okay, the explosion was early, before she went to work. Too much depended on the time he had spent with her. This wasn't in his plans. He needed more information. He felt their relationship was finally to a point where she would open up to him.

The sight of police cars in front of her building was not re-assuring. He calmed his breathing. Okay, they were probably only questioning her about the explosion at Oak Ridge, then he saw the yellow tape across her entry porch. He left his car out in the middle of the road, and ran to the building. A uniformed patrol officer stopped him. "Sorry, sir, you can't go in."

Jeff pushed by the cop, but the man grabbed his arm and held him. "What happened?" Jeff was surprised to hear his voice high and tense.

"A woman was killed. That's all I know. The Detective is in there now; the Coroner is on the way."

Jeff started to argue, when a man he knew came out the door. It was one of Karen's co-workers from Oak Ridge. "Roger," he yelled. The man recognized him and came over.

"Sorry, old man. I know how you felt about Karen."

Jeff sagged against the policeman. "How did it happen?"

Roger hesitated and looked at the cop, "I don't know how much I should say. There's not much I can tell you anyway. I was worried for her, after I heard about the explosion at the lab. You know she often worked at night. She didn't answer the phone, so I came over. When she didn't answer the door, and I could hear water running, I went to the office. A maintenance man let me in. She was… Er, wait a minute." He went back to the door and spoke to the policeman inside, then gestured for Jeff to join him.

Jeff made himself move in that direction, sick to his stomach. Months wasted. Now what was he going to tell Houston? If it didn't go right, he might have to take his brother's offer. The thought created even more panic.

Inside, it was a classic murder scene, straight out of a made for TV movie. Photographers finishing up and technicians working to retrieve finger prints, carpet fibers, DNA, or any evidence that would lead to the killer. The uniformed cop led them down the hall, past the bedroom to the bath. Her body was still crumpled in the shower. The water had recently been shut off; she was still wet. There was hardly any blood, the shower would have washed it away. A black hole showed through the wet hair on the side of her head. Jeff couldn't see the other side of her head, she was leaning against the opposite wall. He thought it was a good thing, just this much made his stomach roll. "Oh, God," he said, putting his hand over his mouth.

The detective sergeant let him take a good look. "I'd say it was someone she knew, no sign of forced entry." He took Jeff's shoulder and turned him away from the shower enclosure. "Let's go in the other room. Your friend here, says you knew her."

Jeff swallowed the bile that rose in his throat. It wasn't seeing a dead body, it was seeing Karen. He didn't love her, but they had been intimate. It made a difference. He nodded his head, unable to speak through his stinging throat, the acid rising from his stomach to scorch his mouth. He rushed to the kitchen sink and threw up the contents of his stomach.

The police sergeant waited patiently, obviously used to this kind of reaction. Roger found a paper cup in the cabinet and filled it with water. Jeff washed out his mouth and spit down the drain, then took a sip of the tepid liquid. After a moment of hanging his head over the sink, the water stayed down and he felt his stomach settle. He turned to the policeman, "How long has she been dead?"

The man gave a non-committal gesture. "Hard to say. The shower running with hot, then cold water would throw her body temp off. The Coroner will know for sure. Oh, oh, here comes the Feds and Immigration. Feel like answering a few questions?"

Jeff was beginning to get a hold on himself. He found his handkerchief and wiped his mouth and face. "Yeah," he looked at the Sergeant. "Sorry for that. It's quite a shock."

"How well did you know Dr. Fielding?"

"Depends on what you mean by well."

The policeman pursed his mouth. "Mr. Todd," he pointed to Roger, "said you were fucking her."

Roger looked slightly embarrassed, but stayed put. The agent from the Immigration and Naturalization Service, and a female FBI agent joined them. Jeff decided there was no point in trying to avoid the questions. "Yes, though I would prefer to say I was in love with her. I knew she would return to Israel when this project was finished. I even made some plans to accompany her." The INS agent nodded, confirming that she was a foreign national.

"Do you know what the project was?" The question from the FBI.

Again, no point in beating around the bush, they might find the logs at the lab and know he had checked in on several occasions. "Not much. I know it had to do with alternative fuel, or something like that. She never talked about her work."

"Did she ever mention a man named Ibrahim Hassim? Or talk about her past?" Again from the FBI.

Jeff looked at his shoes, thinking of some of the discussions he had with Karen. More like arguments, really. Jeff moved his head slowly from side to side. "She talked of her family some. She had a few relatives here in the States. Her mother and father were dead. She didn't seem to want to talk much about her parents or her life in Israel. She never mentioned an Ibrahim Hassim, that I remember."

The Police Sergeant made notes on a spiral pocket pad. "When was the last time you were here in her apartment?"

"Uh, yesterday, no, two days ago now. Look, I've been out of town on assignment. My editor sent me to Carthage to cover the town hall meeting, so I was there when the attempt was made on the Vice President. So much was going on, I stayed over night with a friend. I need to get back to my office. I only stopped here because I wanted to make sure Karen was all right after I heard about the explosion in Oak Ridge." Jeff stopped and mopped his face with the handkerchief still in his hand. "Could we talk later? I work at the Knoxville Chronicle. Ben Parry will vouch for me."

The policeman continued to make notes. "Don't leave town again. I'll get back to you. I'm sure there will be quite a few more questions," he glanced at the other law enforcement officers.

After giving his full name, address, and phone numbers to the agents, Jeff breathed a sigh of relief. He left, accompanied by Roger Todd. "What did happen in Oak Ridge?" he asked the man.

"Nothing left of the National Laboratory. Years of work destroyed. Not just our project. The bio-meds, everything gone. Fortunately, the reactor held, but some radiation leaked. Everything is sealed off until it's cleaned up."

Jeff whistled his disbelief. What was he going to do now?

When Roger drove away, Jeff stopped at a pay phone outside Karen's apartment building and put a call to David Middleton on his phone card. He left a message for David to call him at his home number. If the police wanted an alibi, he had one for them.

* * * * *

David was in the Sheriff's office when a deputy stuck his head in the door. "Sorry to interrupt, sir. Gun shot wound treated over at the hospital. Not serious, flesh wound in the upper arm. Man said his girlfriend was mad at him. He didn't want to press charges."

"Go take a statement and make a report, Scott." Steve brushed off the information, without asking who was injured. Domestic disputes were not high on his agenda at present. He turned back to David. "Maggie Lewis is coming in to look at your client. I don't know what good it will do, but she was the one who spotted the truck."

"I don't know if it will help," David responded. "She swears the man who was driving it in Carthage is the same one who left the dress in the campground a few days ago. What a mess this has turned out to be. How did the search go at Center Hill?"

"Nothing else turned up. The body is down at the mortuary. We are trying to identify the girl. None of the missing person reports match up." Steve stretched and yawned. It had been a long night, with only a few hours sleep. "This Buddy Adams your client says is his cousin, hasn't shown up. Can you stay around for a while? I've had so much coffee I'm floating. I need to go home for a good meal and shower."

David nodded, "You say the FBI took the guns to run tests?"

"Yeah, with the overalls and boots for mud samples. Jennifer Smith, the TBI terrorist expert has talked to your client, WITH the permission of his mother. That'll teach you to sleep late." Steve rubbed a hand over his tired eyes. "Sorry, David, I'm so tired I'm not thinking straight. The kid agreed to see her. I think he told her the same story he told you and me."

David grimaced. "Steve, you should have called me." He was not happy to have his client questioned without being present. "You said the mother was on her way here?"

"Umm," Steve yawned again. "She was upset, of course, when I talked to her on the phone last night. Said she needed to get hold of his father. Construction worker, out of town most of the time on highway jobs. One of them should be here sometime today. Look, David, I'm bushed. When Scott gets back, tell him to take over for a few hours."

"Sure," David levered himself out of the chair, "I want to be here when Maggie comes in, so I'll stick around."

"She can take a look at the kid in his cell, if you don't mind. The FBI took over the conference room. With the TBI already here, it's getting crowded." Steve was standing, car keys in hand.

David left the room, looking for Jennifer Smith. He wondered if a Public Defender could swing some weight with the Tennessee Bureau of

Investigation. It was necessary to his defense to know the type of discussion she had with Orville. He found her at a small café across the street.

The news media had been warned to stay clear of the Sheriff's offices and the County jail, but David noted several reporters on benches around the courthouse. Evidently they hadn't gotten wind of the new developments with the truck and guns. They looked bored and unhappy, sitting in the sun on what was a warm day.

Pete Stryker was coming out the door as David tried to enter the lunch room. It was a heavy wood and glass door that said PULL, and he had just managed to wedge himself in the frame; something difficult to do when you had to use your hands to help walk. Stryker, a rural postman on the Center Hill route, was anxious to talk about everything going on. David begged off, inviting the postman to come by his office later for a full update.

Looking around the restaurant, he didn't see anyone who filled the bill for an expert, especially one on terrorism. The only stranger he saw was sitting by herself at a wall booth. He made it through the crowded cafe and introduced himself.

The woman was probably no more than forty-five, a few gray sprinkles in dark hair pulled back in an attractive style. She was plump, the kind called pleasing, with a fair complexion and rosy cheeks. She looked like everyone's favorite aunt. A ruffled apron and the scent of sugar cookies would not be out of place with the plain shirtwaist dress she wore. The kid had probably spilled his guts to her.

"Please, sit down," she invited David, daintily wiping her mouth on a napkin. "I was hoping I would get a chance to talk to you."

The harsh words he intended to say suddenly left him. He lowered himself into the seat opposite her. He watched her take her time looking at him, the same expression on her face that he got from most strangers. He gave her his extra charming smile. "Yes, I have a prosthesis, but I prefer not to wear it except for certain occasions. Actually, it gets in my way."

She patted her face again with the napkin, not in the least flustered. "That gets that out of the way, doesn't it?" Her soft laugh hinted at an easy going nature. "Okay, satisfy my curiosity."

"Army, Kuwait, land mine. Enough?" David was ready to laugh too, by this time. "You don't pull punches, do you?"

"I found out a long time ago the best way to get answers is to ask questions."

"Which brings me to the problem. Orville Wright, my client, is a juvenile. Nothing he said to you can be used against him."

She folded her hands in front of her plate. David noted the pink polish on the well-manicured nails and the absence of a wedding ring. Despite the apple cheeks and rosebud mouth, there was a shrewdness to her eyes.

"What do you think of your client?

"I'm a Public Defender. I'm not supposed to think."

"You were in Carthage. I read your statement. Do you think the shooting was intended to kill the Vice President?"

"What kind of a question is that? Why would anyone fire into a crowd unless they intended to kill. It was the bad angle, bad elevation, extreme distance for that rifle, that..." David trailed off, looking at the woman.

She nodded. "You get the idea, don't you. I have a full folder on you. Army sharpshooter, expert marksmen medal. Just what did you do in Kuwait, Lieutenant Middleton?"

David was silent, remembering back to the war. "That was a long time ago," he finally said. "What's the point of all this? I came to discuss my client."

"Relax, counselor. I only wanted to see if your boy matched any of the profiles for this area. I never questioned him about his case. The sheriff was there for most of it, he will vouch for me. I will tell you, though, and it is in my written report, I'm recommending the State take custody of the boy. Buddy Adams is not new to me. He's as sorry a loser as I've ever seen." Ms Smith slowly chewed the last of her sandwich.

David sat back and swallowed the uneasy feeling that she would somehow interfere in his defense of Orville. Now was not the time, though, to argue. If one of Orville's parents didn't show up and it came to a choice of the State or Adams, he himself had questions about Buddy Adams.

Ms Smith waved and the waitress found time to come over with her check. "I didn't ask if you wanted lunch. We can talk some more, if you like. I'll have some dessert."

"No, let's go. I told Sheriff Milloy I would stay around for a while. I need to call my office, too." He rose from his seat and fastened the crutch cuffs, as she went to pay her bill.

"Will I see you later, David? Roast beef and apple pie for supper tonight." The cashier made a big deal out of slowly counting change to his companion, openly flirting with David.

Outside, Ms Smith kept pace with him as he swung across the street. "One more question, counselor. All I've been hearing since I came to this town is, David this, and David Middleton that. Everyone I talk to swears by you. Ever think about running for congress?"

One of the reporters lounging on a bench overheard her. He whipped out his recorder and ran over. "You're Middleton? Did I hear you say you're running for Congress? Hey, Charlie, he's the lawyer from Carthage," he called to another man. "He's running for Congress, next election. What's your party affiliation, Mr. Middleton?"

"Oh, hell," David glared at his companion, and stumped through the door to the Sheriff's Department.

* * * * * *

Bobbie was upstairs, washing the coffee pot and cups when the phone rang. She had finally given up and retreated to the second floor when members of the press kept pounding on the front door. The office line connected to the living room telephone, she could answer it here if need be.. She dried her hands as the answering machine picked up the call. A man's voice, rather frantic, asked David to call and left a number. She recognized Jeff Fischer. She took down the number and went downstairs to find David's pager number.

* * * * *

David's pager beeped, and he glanced down at the number. His office, so Bobbie must need him. He made a mental note to call as soon as he talked to Orville.

A couple of drunks, local types, were giving the boy a bad time about his shaved head, but they were in other cells. David could only hope the jibes would knock some sense into Orville. He made his way back to the cell block, wanting to know more about the Nazi, Militant, or White Supremacist group.

Orville was sullen and quiet. No telling when his pa would show up, and his mother could never make a decision by herself.

David asked about his shaved head and the tattoo. A spark of irritation came into the boy's eyes. "Why does everybody get upset by the way I look?" World War II and Nazi's didn't mean a thing to him. It was just a way to fit in and have some friends. Buddy had already bawled him out over it.

Orville paced the small space of the cell, while David sat on the bunk. David let him talk without interrupting, then turned the conversation back to Buddy Adams and was told again that Buddy was kin. Would David call Adams and ask why he wasn't here to get him? Buddy must just be busy. Buddy was cool, he would have a good reason why he couldn't come right away. Hey, maybe the Judge would let him go live with Buddy. He was going there when he got stopped. David told Orville he would ask, but didn't promise anything.

David steered the conversation back to the swastika tattoo. He laid it straight out to Orville, it could cause serious trouble. He needed to know what kind of organization it was and who headed the chapter and where they met. Orville said he couldn't tell, he was sworn to secrecy.

"Orville, you left out a lot of what you did yesterday. For one thing, where did you go between the time you boosted the truck and got here? I need the truth this time." David added a few things about some of what might happen if he was tried as an adult and went to prison. He left Orville to think about it.

* * * * *

Ahmed left the hospital in Smithville in the company of Jose Deguiro, the elderly man who owned the old station wagon. He told Deguiro to go on, that he would make his own way back to Nashville, but the old man seemed to think he had taken on a new responsibility and was sticking tighter than glue.

Ahmed was impressed with the small hospital's facilities. It was a modern building on the outskirts of town, the ER doctors and nurses efficient. Efficient enough to immediately report the gunshot wound to the authorities. A deputy from the Sheriff's Department had come in to question him about the incident.

He stayed with his story, but changed it enough to fit the new circumstances. He had to show the hospital his international drivers license permit with his correct identity, and his credit card to guarantee payment. His friend, Yvette had brought the gun along. It seemed that in Tennessee almost anyone could get a permit to carry a concealed weapon. They had argued, the gun went off, and he fell from the car. No, no charges. It was as much his fault as hers. He quickly made up a Nashville telephone number for Yvette, hoping it was standard enough to pass. She lived in some apartment complex, but usually met him down town. He gave them just enough information to let them think she was a call girl, grinning sheepishly as he spoke. If there were further questions, he could be reached at the seminar at Vanderbilt University. Yes, his friend, Señor Deguiro, would see him back to Nashville. Finally they were permitted to leave the hospital.

The friendly gray haired man, who seemed delighted to have someone to talk to and something to do, insisted Ahmed accompany him to his house for a good meal. Keeping an eye on the deputy, who was leaving at the same time, Ahmed obligingly got in the old car. Why not? Nadja will not give up easy. This is as good a place as any, and he could fit right in with the Mexican population that worked the huge plant nurseries and farms in the area. He needed time to think. What had he done to deserve this fate? One thing he knew for certain, it would take all his wits and skill to survive.

* * * * *

Jeff Fischer went to the newspaper office from Karen's apartment complex. At his desk, he brought up his computer and started writing an article dealing with the attempted assassination. His memory was clear on what he had seen, but he was having a hard time concentrating on the task. Then he remembered that his pocket recorder had been running. He fished the machine out of his jacket and hit rewind. Nothing happened. The batteries had gone dead. Searching his desk, he found replacements and stuffed them in the machine. He punched rewind, then fast forwarded through the beginning of the tape, until he heard Liz Tidwell's voice. Listening to the tape was like reliving the fifteen minutes of recording. The distant echoes of gun shots, the confusion with people screaming and running for their lives, the close up gun shots as the police returned fire, was all there. For a few minutes, he let his mind go back to Saudi Arabia. He let the tape run to the end, then rewound and listened again.

At the end, he heard his own voice, then that of Maggie Lewis. There was another voice, in the background. He couldn't quite make out the words. Seemed like a one sided conversation. Someone on a phone? Then he recognized the voice. What the hell was he doing there?

Before he could play the tape again, Ben came in the room. "You took your own sweet time getting here. We missed today's deadline, I had to use what the wire services put out. Hell of a note. One of my reporters on the scene and I had to get the information from Associated Press."

Jeff could see, as usual, his boss was not in a good mood. "I tried to stop by Oak Ridge, only got as far as the Clinch River. They got the whole area cordoned off. Then I went to see if Karen was all right, I mean the explosion and all." His voice fell almost to a whisper. "She's dead, Ben, somebody shot her."

"Do you mean murdered? Oh yeah," Ben stepped back and tapped his fingers on the back of a chair. "The call was on the police radio. I sent Shawn Williams to cover it. He didn't stay long, said it was some foreign dame. Immigration already had someone there, and it was hush hush. He couldn't get a foot in the door." Jeff's editor was by no means a sentimental man, but his bark softened to a growl. "That the woman you been living with? Worked out at Oak Ridge, didn't she?"

Jeff nodded, swallowing hard. "We never lived together. I did think she might love me."

"Write your article, boy." He slapped Jeff on the back. "You gave me enough on the phone for the headlines. All the newswire services are in on it now, but we got the scoop here in east Tennessee."

Jeff sat slumped, shoulders drooping. Ben sat down in the chair. It wasn't late, but most of the day crew had gone home. In just a short distance, Jeff had lost an hour of time from Central to Eastern time zone.

"Write another one about your girl. Put in everything you know about her in it. They are being close mouthed about Oak Ridge, but I understand there was considerable damage to the National Laboratory. Do you know what they were working on? I mean, did you know what your girl was doing out there? Does her murder tie in with it?"

Jeff perked up. He hadn't even thought of that. Maybe everything wasn't lost. The money and deal his brother offered was peanuts compared to what he could do now. If he could make the Houston backers believe Karen had confided in him, even left him her notes for safe keeping, he could sell them the information.

"Okay, give me until tomorrow."

"Good boy. Make it smaltzy, put down what you are feeling now. The public gobbles up that stuff. Sizzle up what she knew about Oak Ridge. It sells newspapers."

Jeff flinched as Ben clapped him on the back again. "Sorry to hear about, er, what was her name?" Ben said from the doorway on his way out.

"Her name was Karen, Karen Fielding," Jeff said to the empty hall. Not that it matters. She's dead.

Jeff clicked *new* on the computer to start his article on Karen. He had used her, never intended to make a commitment, but somewhere along the line, maybe he had started to care.

No, stop it. Keep the emotions locked up. She was only a means to an end. But what an end! The mock up for the automobile of the future was destroyed, but they would have a safeguard, wouldn't they? But what? Backup computer disks? Tapes? Presumably, the safeguard would be at a different location. It was a government project, wasn't it? Maybe the Houston corporation would up the ante if he could get his hands on the backup information or make them believe he could. Stop, think now. How could he word this to make them believe he knew everything about the little moon buggy. He tapped words into the keyboard, letting his mind roam back to Karen and everything they had discussed. The article on the Vice President could wait.

CHAPTER EIGHT

David was headed back to use Steve's office phone when he saw Maggie Lewis come in. He beckoned for her to come to the back with him and asked the deputy at the cell block to pass both of them through. At the door to Orville's cell, he introduced her to the boy. Orville slouched on the bunk, disappointed that it was not his mother, but had been taught enough manners to stand and acknowledge his visitor. Maggie asked the boy if he was all right. She had the presence of mind to chat a moment with the youth, just asking where he lived, and about his family. She told him she lived in Nashville when they were not at the campground. She would call his mother herself, to let her know he was okay. He nodded, then turned away.

Back outside the block, Maggie shook her head. Orville definitely was not who she saw driving the truck in Carthage. She was positive the man who drove the truck in Carthage was the same man who drove a green automobile into the campground a few days ago. David thanked her for coming in and walked her to the front door, as Scott returned from his rounds. He had his clip board in his hands and was pulling loose his report from the pad.

At the desk he called to the sergeant on duty. "Hey, Sarge, that gunshot wound at the hospital was a strange one. Some foreigner said his girlfriend had a permit to carry a concealed weapon. They got into a fight driving on the interstate. She shot him as he bailed out of the car."

"Some temper, huh? What was she, Mex, or something?"

"Nah," Scott answered. "The man spoke good English, but the name was Arab, or Egypt maybe. Said he was a doctor. He rented a car for a ride to see some of the country before he went to a meeting at Vanderbilt." Scott checked his log, "Name was Dr. Ahmed Faziz."

Maggie stopped dead in her tracks. "That's it! I knew there was something familiar about him. The man I saw in the campground is a Turk!." She grabbed David's arm. "John and I were stationed in Turkey back in the seventies at Incirlik Air Base. I was working at the base hospital when there was a dangerous hepatitis epidemic. The Turkish government sent some young interns to train with the military doctors. The name Faziz is familiar. I'll bet he was one of them." She stopped and tapped her forehead with a finger. "Yes, that's it! Ahmed Faziz!"

"Maggie, can you be sure?" David was excited, this could give his client a real chance.

"Land sakes, David, it's been at least twenty-five years ago, but when I talked to the man in the campground, he never moved his head. Never moved at all. Kept his hands still, too. Turks and most Arabs don't use body language or shake their head yes or no. They blink their eyes for no, but he had on sunglasses. It was so odd, I mentioned it to John, just after the man left the campground. I would have to see him again to be sure, but I'd give you odds he is the same one."

Jennifer Smith appeared at the door of the next room. She looked at Maggie, "If I bring up some pictures on the computer, do you think you could recognize him?"

David quickly introduced the two women. Maggie agreed to look at the pictures and went into the interrogation room where the equipment was set up. Ms Smith tapped into a direct line to the TBI mainframe. "It will take a minute," she said, "this info comes from Washington, but it won't take as long as asking them to fax the stuff."

The laptop beeped, and began bringing up the information. The first picture of a man appeared on half the small screen, with ID information on the other half. "Nope," Maggie said, with a chuckle. "Honey, I'm sixty three years old. Do you think you could make it bigger?"

The TBI agent refrained from making a comment, just adjusted the screen so that the picture filled the entire area. Maggie said no, and the next frame came into view. They went through several photos, Maggie still negative. Scott came in the room, a cold drink in his hands. It was hard for all of them to crowd behind Jennifer, to see the small screen. Scott suggested they move to the Sheriff's office and use his computer. It connected directly to a modem that had a private line; he had used it before.

The transition was made, and the larger screen allowed much clearer images. A couple more pictures, and it was Scott who whistled. "That's the man at the hospital." Maggie was silent, watching intently. "If I may?" Scott unseated Ms. Smith and took over the computer keyboard. He looked up at David and grinned. "I've done this before. You don't think the Sheriff has time to take computer lessons, do you?"

David patted the young man on the back. "Let's see what you can do, Deputy."

The picture on the screen was of a swarthy man with shoulder length hair, glasses, and a stubborn look to his face. Maggie caught her breath. Scott brought up a window, clicked an item and then used the mouse to erase the long hair and glasses. He clicked again, painted a full drooping mustache on the upper lip, age lines around the eyes and nose, then sat back satisfied. "That's him. Dr. Ahmed Faziz, now with a little gray in his hair, and a bullet wound in his upper left arm. This the man you saw, Mrs. Lewis?"

"The first, before you changed the picture, looked like the man I remembered, but it has been a long time ago. Can you put a beard on him now?"

Scott painted a beard, then paused. "Not so long," Maggie used her finger on the screen to show Scott what she wanted. "It was a nice tidy beard. Looked soft, not bushy, straight hair, not curly."

Scott adjusted the picture, and Maggie chortled. "I told John I wasn't crazy. It's him. After all these years, Ahmed Faziz. He did get to be a doctor, you say? He was about one of the best I've ever seen in all my years of nursing. Funny duck, though, if I remember right."

David was beginning to see a ray of hope for Orville. "Let's see what else the TBI might have on file."

Agent Smith took over and brought up the remainder of the file on Ahmed Faziz. Five foot ten, stocky build, one eighty pounds. From known information he was approximately fifty eight years old and unmarried. Born in a mountain village near Gaziantep, Turkey, he was sent to an uncle in Iran at the age of eight for his basic education and religious training. College at the American University in Beirut, Lebanon; medical training in Paris, interned at the state run hospital in Ankara, Turkey. Spoke excellent English, French, Spanish, Arabic and Greek, along with his native Turkish. He had specialized in communicable diseases, worked in many remote areas of the world, including trouble spots and local wars. In the later years he had gained a reputation as a speaker, and was asked to medical seminars in varied locations.

"My, my," Maggie mused after they read that far. "How on earth did he ever get on a list as a terrorist?"

The group of onlookers was silent as they read. What had been drilled into the man to form the unusual combination of humanitarian and terrorist? The computer went on to list The Turkish Liberation Army, the Issadd, and several fanatic religious groups with whom he worked in the capacity of medical doctor. It noted incidents where he was in the area when acts of terror and violence occurred, some of which were the assassinations of prominent leaders. Too many to be mere coincidence; nothing substantial enough to bring charges, but he had made Interpol, the KGB and CIA lists.

Scott left the room to put out an APB for one Dr. Ahmed Faziz. Agent Smith keyed the commands to print both pictures, one with a beard, one without. The information would print, too. David walked Maggie to the door, and made arrangements for her to make a written statement tomorrow.

"I hope it helps," she said. "I'll tell John, in case he can remember more." She spoke to the deputy at the front desk, then stepped out the door.

David turned to the back, intending to talk to Orville again, then remembered he needed to call Bobbie.

Buddy Adams was waiting for David outside the Sheriff's office door. A small man, with a definite overbite made more obvious by a wispy mustache of reddish hair, was pacing the hall. The minute he saw David he began a tirade of four letter words, to the effect that the law had no reason to hold his cousin. "I should'a known a gimpy lawyer wern't good enough to get some bail," he ranted. "Probably gave you a job 'cause they was sorry for you. You go get my boy out of that cell right now." He stopped long enough to draw in a breath, and wipe a perpetually running nose.. "You can't hold him 'cause the only thing you got right now is that truck!"

"Hey, wait a minute!" David could feel his temper rising. "I'm on your side. I took an oath to do my duty when I accepted the Public Defender job. Settle down and let's discuss the situation."

David pointed to the Sheriff's office. "We can use this room. Space is limited, what with the TBI here and the FBI sending a team. Now, please tell me how you are connected to Orville."

Buddy sat in the visitor's chair before the desk. He snuffed this time instead of wiping his nose, and used his thumb to rub his protruding upper teeth. When he spoke his voice was calmer and quite clear of the red neck accent he had adopted earlier. "The boy's my cousin. Second cousin really, his mama and I are first kin."

"Orville obviously thinks a lot of you. You are the one he called, not his parents."

"Old man's never home, and their mama works so much, the kids were running wild. I took an interest in Orville. He's a good kid and bright, too. Just needs a man's influence."

David kept his opinion to himself of what kind of influence Buddy Adams would be. "The mother and father, are they divorced?" When Buddy indicated no, David continued. "I need to know about Orville's home life, as much as you can tell me. They have him dead to rights, driving a stolen truck, and if the guns check out as those used on the Vice President, it's big trouble. Orville told conflicting stories at first. He said the truck belonged to you, then changed it to seeing a bearded man park it. Trouble is, no prints were found except the owner and Orville."

Buddy sat, continuing to massage his teeth, looking sullen and unhappy. David gave him a moment, then when he remained silent continued. "Tell me more about the family. Drugs, alcohol, money? Highway construction pays good money. Does the father take care of his family? Orville's clothes were good and he had eight dollars, plus change on him."

"His pa is never there. Works out of town most of the time. Yeah, he sends money, but it's spent as fast as they get it." Buddy had relaxed and taken his thumb out of his mouth. He had watery blue eyes, and a complexion that looked like he would cook if out in the sun for more than ten minutes.

David was absorbing this information. He didn't know what to make of Buddy Adams. He had been prepared to dislike the man, and the opening tirade didn't help. Now he wondered if that scene had been for the benefit of anyone watching. Buddy seemed more than willing to help his young cousin. "Tell me about his family."

Buddy snuffed loudly, then continued. "Not much to tell. Guess I'm about the only living relative they got. Orville's ma works all the time. Bought a little house out in the suburbs. It takes everything she earns just to make ends meet."

"How do you fit in with them?" David was having a hard time believing what he was hearing. Buddy might as well be describing almost any blue collar American family with teenage kids. Both parents working, kids mostly unsupervised.

Buddy shifted in the chair, and rubbed his teeth before going on. "Sorry," he said, putting his hand in his lap. "I quit smoking a while back, I still miss it. I worked up north for several years, then decided I wanted to come back south. Had a job offer in Sparta. Car dealership; I'm a pretty good mechanic. They let me sell, too, used cars on commission. I got in touch with my family. Like I said, Orville needed some adult supervision. That shaved head and tattoo came from school. He hangs on to the image, but I don't think he really believes that junk."

David managed to keep his face noncommittal while he silently cursed. A Neo-Nazi chapter in the high school? Orville had enough trouble without this clincher. After all the high school shootings going on around the country, no judge or jury would be inclined to go easy on Orville. If the guns checked out, David might as well lock the cell door on his client himself.

David looked for some note paper on the desk, found a pencil and scrawled a few lines on the pad. When he looked up, Buddy was watching him intently. Why the sudden turn around? Out in the hall, the man was a raving maniac. It was like the phone call that had settled down Orville. David's guts told him there was more to this little used car salesman than he wanted to know.

"Have you seen Orville?" David paused from jotting his notes.

"Yeah, I told him to be cool and sit tight. When will you know about bail?"

"Juveniles don't get bail. They are released in the custody of their guardian, or a responsible adult. I'll try to catch Judge Jenkins in the morning." David handed Buddy one of his cards. "Call me tomorrow."

The little man stood up, pulled a soiled handkerchief from his pocket and blew his nose. To David's relief he didn't offer to shake hands. After looking David up and down for a moment, Buddy went through the door.

* * * * *

David dialed his office number, and Bobbie picked up after she heard him on the answering machine. She sounded good to him on his phone. He was glad to hear a calm voice after the day he was having. He asked why she paged, and she gave him the information. He jotted the number on Steve's desk, wondering why Jeff Fischer had called so soon. He told Bobbie to stay put a while longer when she complained that news personnel were still camped outside his door. He had one more chore, then he would take her to dinner. She said for him to come on home, she was all ready cooking supper. She hung up the phone with a kiss.

He dialed the number in Knoxville and let the phone ring until answered by a machine. He left a message to the effect that he would be unavailable until later in the evening. If it was important, Jeff could call back.

In the cell with Orville, he made one more try to convince the boy to tell the truth and all of it. He pointed out the missing hours, from about 5:00PM in the afternoon until he was stopped at 10:00PM. Just riding around, Orville insisted. No, he didn't go home. His ma was on swing shift, but his sister would be there.

"Weren't you afraid someone would recognize the truck?" David asked.

"You don't think I'm dumb enough to stay on the interstate, do you? I didn't even go any place near there." Orville looked at David like he was the stupid one. "I went to...," then realized that would be the answer David wanted. "Oh no, that dog won't hunt. I told you I swore an oath." The boy hung on the bars with his hands, looking defiant and angry.

David used his crutches to help stand from the low bunk. "If that's the way you want it," David shrugged. "I'll do what I can, but it won't help much." He called to the cell guard, and left Orville to think a while longer. He did not show the boy the picture of the bearded man. He patted his jacket pocket to feel the folded paper. He had asked that Buddy Adams be kept in the dark, too. At least until he could make a little sense of this. Right now, he didn't have the foggiest idea what to do.

* * * * *

Bobbie watched for David from the upstairs window. Their supper was keeping warm on the stove. She had found chicken in the freezer and fresh vegetables in the 'fridge. The ingredients for a pan of cornbread were in the cabinet, and she mixed up a batch. David had a good supply in his small kitchen. She knew he often spent much of his time alone. Evidently he enjoyed cooking, from the array of spices and marinades she found in the cupboard. Like the elegant touch of oriental rugs in his offices, he possessed an excellent set of cookware, along with fine china and cut glass crystal. The sudden knowledge that he surrounded himself with beautiful things to blot out the hurt of being physically less came to her. She thought of her apartment, knowing its stark bareness meant little to her. She spent almost no time there, but this was where David lived, spent his time away from what could hurt him. The fact that he had finally opened up to her was immensely satisfying.

David came into view, swinging on his crutches. She admired his graceful gait, almost like a gymnast on parallel bars. He used the hip high metal rods, fitted with handholds, like another leg, moving them to take a step, then his arms supported his weight on the rods as he moved his one leg forward. Sometimes he fastened the clamp like cuffs to his wrists. That gave him the freedom of using his hands without putting down the crutch. Bobbie ran down the stairs to open the door for him.

Immediately reporters piled out of parked cars. "Here he comes. It's Middleton. The lawyer who saved the Vice President yesterday. Did you hear, he's running for Congress. The VP will endorse him!"

Bobbie couldn't believe what she was hearing. Congress? And who saved who? She opened the door, as David pushed through the reporters, shaking his head. He was trying to talk over the babble, gave up and shouted, "NO COMMENT!"

"What's this about Congress?" Bobbie took the jacket from under his arm, as he used his shoulder to close the door.

"Not you, too," David groaned. He leaned down to kiss her. "Come on, let's go upstairs. Maybe they will get tired and leave."

Halfway up the stairs, he stopped and sniffed. "Is that cornbread I smell?"

"You know it is." She pushed him up again, ahead of her.

His smile could have turned heads in Hollywood. "Smells just like Mom's. You know, lil'bit, I think I really will marry you."

"If you don't go on up the stairs, it will burn before we get there. You've got some explaining to do, mister. I want to know all about Congress!"

David sat back and patted his full stomach. He had eaten almost the full skillet of bread, along with chicken and vegetables. He raised a crystal goblet of good German Rhine, and toasted the cook. "I haven't had a meal that good since ...," he looked at Bobbie, "well, for a long time."

Bobbie gave a contented sigh. "Not since we were over at Aunt Ellen's three Sundays ago. Keep it up, though. It may get you another pan of cornbread." There was a rapport developing between them, almost like the last nine years had disappeared. They had an understanding, but that didn't begin to say enough. She liked what she saw when she looked at David. His usual somber, noncommittal facial expression was broken by an absolutely beautiful smile, little used laugh lines crimping his mouth and warm brown eyes. This was the David she knew, loving and teasing. She would never love anyone else the way David affected her, but she refused to live her life locked away from people. She would no longer let him hide from the world. Congress was beginning to sound like a very good idea.

Bobbie stood and started stacking the dishes. "I guess I need to go on home, David. We can see Aunt Ellen tomorrow." She looked down at her uniform, "I thought I would be going to work today, so this is all I have to wear. I need to change clothes."

David was up and put his arms around her. "I'm glad you didn't go to work. I want you here all the time."

"Hah, you just like my cooking. Let me put the dishes in the dishwasher," Bobbie slipped from his grasp and carried plates to the sink. In one hop David was behind her, reaching an arm on each side around her to balance himself on the cabinet. His grin was delicious. "Well, there's the cooking, too." As she turned to him, he found her mouth with his, and all the years of pent up frustration melted with her kiss. She raised her arms to circle his neck and David knew he had made the right decision. God, she made him feel good. She was what he needed to be whole again.

Bobbie broke the kiss with a sigh. "Much as I love you, David, I need to go." She ducked, slipping under his arm. "My car is out back. Maybe I can get away without being seen."

David caught her arm. "I'll go with you, honey. I'll draw off the press, then I can make sure you get home safe. First I want to thank you for that delicious supper." He tucked his head and kissed her again, this time pulling her closer, feeling her mold herself to him; this time putting all the emotion he was feeling into the kiss. It was David who finally pulled away. "Bobbie," he whispered into her hair, "stay with me tonight. Make love to me. We've wasted so much time, I don't want to wait any longer." His chuckle was deep as he admitted, "I...I'm in a bit of trouble here. I don't think I can wait." His fingers began working the buttons on her shirt. "Honey, I know you want a wedding, and we will have that, only..."

Bobbie raised a hand to his cheek, then silenced him with her own kiss. She deftly unbuttoned his shirt and slipped her hands inside to skim the hard muscles of his shoulders and chest. She could feel the calluses on his fingers and palms as he pushed her shirt from her shoulders, and stroked her back. The effort of walking with crutches had left its own scars, but given him superior upper body strength. His arms lifted his own weight with every step, she realized. This was the David she wanted. Now, with no reservations. She squirmed closer to him, feeling the part of his anatomy that was giving him trouble. She intentionally rubbed against him again, looked up into eyes that were looking at her with a heartfelt love. She said nothing, didn't have to. She started for the bedroom.

David reached for his crutches.

* * * * *

It was close to midnight before Jeff was satisfied with the story on Karen. He made a copy on a floppy and printed out a hard copy for himself, filing it in his desk drawer. The disk fitted between several used X'ed out disks he kept in a cardboard box. He threw it in a bottom drawer. He then clicked *send* and forwarded the article to Ben's computer for approval in the morning.

No one saw him enter the lobby. The night crews occupied the lower floors. There was a phone booth on the wall by the door. He stopped, fished out a prepaid calling card, dialed all the numbers and waited. The line was answered and he quoted part of the article he had just written, then promised to substantiate his information with back up material. He knew he was talking to a computer that would record the information. He just hoped that it was enough to keep Houston thinking Karen had confided in him. He should get a confirmation call in a few hours. He let himself out of the front door of the building, found his old Mustang in his assigned parking spot, and drove to his apartment.

He had to park down from his entry, feeling tired and dirty as he walked toward his building. He would miss Karen, she had been company. They had always made love at her place. His complex was old and run down. He didn't see the men step from the untrimmed bushes until they had his arms pinned behind him. "What the...?"

"Jeffrey A. Fischer? You have the right to remain silent," one of the men read him his rights, then cuffed his hands behind him. The men took his arms and hauled him upright. Jeff struggled instinctively, but he was dragged along.

"I'm being arrested? Why? What's this for?" The cop pushed his head down and into a car.

"For the murder of Dr. Karen Fielding. Just shut up, lover boy. You can yell all you want in a cell."

* * * * *

After seeing Bobbie to her apartment, it was past midnight when David parked his Durango in the shed back of his building and went in by the back stairs. Whistling a tune of his own making, he felt happier than he had in years.

The press corp had apparently given up for the night. There were no cars parked on the street, or around the square. Upstairs, he routinely checked his answering machine. This time the call from Jeff Fischer spelled disaster. The man had been arrested for murder. He begged David to confirm that he was in Smithville the previous night. Come to Knoxville, the desperate voice continued, I don't know another lawyer. It was all circumstantial. If David would only come and set it straight, it wouldn't take long.

David sat in the arm chair beside the telephone table and listened to the long taped message again. He suspected this was the only call Jeff was allowed to make. Tapping his fingers on the machine didn't help him make up his mind. The memory of the empty couch at 2:00AM was sticking in the way. He had taken a sleeping pill about 10:00PM, and slept until the telephone call from the Sheriff awakened him. Slept like the dead. He always blacked out early after one of those pills, becoming more alert toward morning. Jeff could have left anytime after he went to sleep, and returned before he got back home around 7:00AM. Come to think of it, he had been so tired, he didn't check the living room when he came in. Came in the back door and gone straight up to bed.

What a dilemma! Whatever happened to the quiet, peaceful life he had built for himself? Jeff could wait until morning, then he would call. Surely one of Orville's parents would show up tomorrow. Heaven forbid if the Judge released the boy to Buddy Adams. Steve would need to formally charge the youth with car theft, if nothing else. David needed time to think about Jeff Fischer.

The bright side of this whole mess was Bobbie. Making love to her was everything and more than he dared hope. The act of sex had been too long put off for him. He had not even tried to conceal his urgency. Instead, he had behaved like a pimple-faced kid his first time. Good thing she wasn't a virgin, he had all but attacked her. Bobbie hadn't complained. She was almost as eager as he, and was quick to respond. The second time she straddled him and set a slower, gentle rhythm that drove him crazy. When the climax came it left them both shaken and satisfied. He hoped with every fiber of his being he had gotten her pregnant. To have her always with him, always in his bed, the mother of his children, his lover and companion, made David want to fall to his knees, as if he had two, and thank God. They would marry right away. No more waiting, and somehow, someway, he would see that she was safe and protected.

David quickly stripped and used his arms to help haul himself into his shower. While the water washed over him, he decided to go to the gym in the morning. Exercise helped him think. Tonight, he was going to go to sleep and dream only of Bobbie.

* * * * *

A computer in Houston, recorded the incoming message from Tennessee, downloaded to the specified save location, then blinked the *new message!* button on the screen. The building that housed the computer was located in the high rent district. Sleek and modern, with blue neon lights running around the cupola on the summit, the building stood out among the other office towers on the Houston skyline.

The night technician on duty was too busy to stay at the computer station and missed the alert. He was in the break room with a cup of coffee and a good looking college summer intern.

CHAPTER NINE

In a perverse kind of way, Ahmed was enjoying himself. It had not been difficult to become one of the Mexican laborers at the New Mountain Nursery. Carlos, the son of his host Señor Deguiro, supervised the workers for the farm. He was asked for a green card, but when he hung his head and didn't answer, he was told to pick up a hoe and go with the crew that was leaving for the fields.

Acres and acres of young trees, all six to eight feet high, surrounded the open truck as it followed two ruts into the field they would weed today. The sun was bright, the humidity down, and Ahmed was beginning to feel hopeful. There had been no sign of Nadja in the two days he had stayed with the Mexicans. Now he needed to make plans to leave the country. The Deguiros had accepted his story of a woman who would kill him. They would help him cross into Mexico when the bus loads of migrant seasonal workers returned, but that was several weeks off. He had to think of something else.

There had been a bad feeling from the beginning. Ibrahim had rushed him, with little information and almost no time to prepare. He was never told until the last moment the government employee he was ordered to eliminate was the Vice President of the United States. I should have smelled a rat, thinking of Ibrahim's narrow face. He laughed at his own joke, his mind going back to what had gone wrong at the shoot. I knew the equipment was inadequate for the distance and terrain. I should have checked the scope and test fired for accuracy. My own arrogance is to blame. Nadja is right, I am too old for this line of work, and I have become careless. I was out of the game. They should have left me alone. He cursed under his breath as the truck stopped and the tailgate lowered. The men spilled out to begin work. Ahmed grabbed his hoe and attacked the ground around the trees, taking out his anger on the weeds.

The morning was half gone when Carlos came to check on this crew. Ahmed had worked down several rows of young Bradford Pears when he saw Carlos.

"Amigo!" Carlos hailed. "What's this?" He indicated the blood seeping through the bandage on Ahmed's arm. "I told you to take it easy, now you must come with me."

"It is nothing," Ahmed answered in Spanish. "I have been getting soft, the exercise feels good."

"It will not feel good if you get a fever. Come with me to the dispensary." Carlos spoke briefly to the crew chief, then motioned for Ahmed to get on the ATV behind him.

A rude sort of medical facility was housed in the same shed like building that contained barracks for the single men. If they were lucky some of the migrant workers who traveled with their families lived in a row of one room mini-houses. The others used the tents they brought with them. Most of the women worked along side the men out in the fields, leaving other women to cook and care for the children.

The compound area looked like a small village under the mature trees of hickory, walnut and southern oak. A common cooking area was set up under a plastic tarp in the center. The smell of beans and tortillas came from a fire watched by an old woman. More women tended a thriving vegetable garden. A clothes line with white, billowing sheets stretched between the trees. Carlos, a naturalized citizen of the United States, and his family lived year round in the large farm house by the highway.

Ahmed let Carlos bandage his arm, seeing the tall, muscular supervisor was the only one in the building. "You have no nurse?" No, he was told. A doctor from the hospital came out once a week for sick call.

Carlos finished a neat job, then when Ahmed started for the door, he placed a restraining hand against Ahmed's chest. Ahmed felt his heart rate pick up.

"No, stay and rest awhile. I must go back to work." Carlos tanned, Latin face looked concerned.

Ahmed put a hand to his chest, he could feel his heart pounding. Carlos had thought he might have a heart attack, not that for a moment Ahmed believed he was being detained. "*Gracias, amigo*," he said and sank in a chair.

The supervisor was hardly to the door when he heard the women scream and children yelling. A young woman ran toward them with a child in her arms. Carlos ran to meet her and took the little girl from her. Through incoherent tears, she was pleading, "My baby! Someone help! My baby is dying! *Madre Dios*, help her!"

Carlos put the child down on the examining table and ran to the telephone. He dialed 911, called for help, then remembered to speak English to ask for an ambulance.

Ahmed was standing over the child. The little girl's skin was mottled red, her face swelling as he watched. Her lips were white, with a bluish tinge. He put his mouth over her mouth and nose, one hand on the small chest. Gently he blew air into her lungs, then pressed to expel it. Again, and again, but there was no movement. There was nothing to do but reveal his medical knowledge. He motioned for Carlos to keep the frantic mother away, and another woman took her place to hold the child's head. Ahmed found the sternum, followed the line of bone and placed one hand over the small heart. With his other hand, he struck hard. Once, twice, again. He was sweating now, willing the child to live. "Come, little one. You are too young to die." He didn't notice that his words were from his native language.

Another blow, and he felt the tiny flutter. He would give anything for adrenaline, for any heart stimulant. He kept his hand over the child until she pulled in a ragged breath. Then he went to the medicine cabinet. It was locked, one look of apology to Carlos and he picked up a towel and smashed the glass front. Ah, a small box of Epi-Pens, bee sting kits, was on a bottom shelf. He broke the round cylinder open, too much for a child. Barely depressing the plunger, he half emptied it, then held it against the child's leg and injected the epinephrine solution.

The women crowded around, watching anxiously as the child finally took a deep breath. A flush was replacing the blue tint of her face. Ahmed picked up her little hand and looked at the grotesquely swollen fingers. In Spanish he asked the mother, "Was she bitten by a bug?" Yes, all of the women replied. The children were playing in the clover patch when she started crying. It was a bee, or wasp, they didn't know which.

Sirens wailing brought Ahmed to attention. Carlos was outside waving the ambulance to the door. Ahmed caught his arm. "Tell them it was anaphylaxis, and she has had .01 mg of epinephrine." Then he disappeared behind the building.

Carlos was too busy to think of it then, but when the child was transported to the hospital for further treatment, the paramedics verified the diagnosis. When they asked about the doctor who knew to inject epinephrine, he wondered, too. Who was this man his father had befriended?

* * * * *

Bobbie had completed part of her morning route, when she got the call. She had left the first campground on her way to the next when Steve's voice came over the radio. "Hey, lil'bit, come back to the office. I'll tell you what for when you get here."

With everything going on in the area, she didn't question the call. She acknowledged the transmission and her position to the dispatcher, estimating twelve minutes to arrival. On the dot, she parked at the side of the building, making notes on her log, and went in the building. Steve was in the hall, using words the local preacher would never condone.

"Now the f------ FBI took my office. How the hell am I supposed to work? You'd think all I did is sit and whittle before the Vice President got himself shot at."

Bobbie touched his arm before he could dig himself in deeper. "You sent for me, sir?" she said professionally.

He jerked her into the interrogation room occupied by the TBI, empty at the moment. "You're a woman," Steve said unnecessarily. "The little black girl, a Mrs. Hayes is here, might be her grandma." He grabbed up the plastic bag with the pink dress inside. "She says this looks like one that belonged to her daughter-in-law. Take her over to the Funeral Home to look at the body. Make sure it's a positive ID. If the Coroner is through with the body, maybe you can release it to her. You know what to do." Steve wiped the sweat on his forehead with his shirt sleeve, patted Bobbie's arm and went to answer the page blaring his name all over the building.

Bobbie picked up the little dress, wondering what being a woman had to do with it, but feeling guilty for not finding the body herself. She had only half believed Maggie. The least she could do for the unfortunate girl would be to help her grandmother.

Bobbie found the woman in the break room, her round bulk almost filling the tiny space. She overflowed a folding chair, fanning her face in the closed room, perspiration turning her dark face shiny.

"Mrs. Hayes?" Bobbie looked at the paper in her hand. The woman lumbered to her feet, pulling down a flowered rayon dress, and clutching one of the biggest handbags Bobbie had ever seen.

"Yes," she said softly. Are you going to take me to my girl?"

"We need to make sure it is your granddaughter. Come with me, we'll take my car. It's several blocks down the street." Bobbie smiled, trying to put the woman at ease.

In the car, the quiet dignity of the woman was a surprise. She shed no tears, asked no questions, simply took in her surroundings. Smithville was an old town, many of the beautiful old houses restored to pristine vintage. The funeral home occupied one such house on the edge of the business district.

Bobbie waited patiently as the heavy woman extracted herself from the patrol car. They were met at the door by the funeral director. This way, he indicated.

It only took one look. Mrs. Hayes nodded yes, then covered her mouth with her lacy handkerchief. She backed away from the slab and tears overflowed her eyes. The massive shoulders shook, but she made no sound. Bobbie could feel the torment of sorrow now confirmed, tears held in check finally released. The woman had known even before she saw the girl.

She guided the woman into a chair in one of the side rooms and brought a paper cup with water. Mrs. Hayes was rocking back and forth, but had stopped crying. Bobbie gave her some tissues and she blew her nose. The funeral director hovered in the background.

Bobbie squatted before her. "Are you all right?" When the woman nodded, Bobbie hated herself but she had to ask. "You are sure the girl is your granddaughter?"

"She is my granddaughter." The soft, well-modulated voice was strong. "I cared for her from the time she was born, until her momma came back for her. She's my son's baby. He got his self killed in the army." Her face screwed up again, but she continued. "The court said I couldn't keep her, so her momma got custody. She was about ten years old then. The court said I could see her now and then, but they moved away and I never did, until now."

Bobbie found a chair and pulled it up. She reached over to hand Mrs. Hayes more tissue. The grandmother continued, "Her momma called, wanted to know if Shemisha was with me. That's when I asked the police to find her."

Bobbie encouraged her to talk, making mental notes for her report. No, the grandmother had not called the mother. The story was one of the tragedies of drugs. The woman was never married to her son, so the army did not owe her or his child any support. Mrs. Hayes had filed and collected Social Security for the infant. The mother got it when she took the little girl, but the small amount of money was never enough. She was influenced by the wrong people, weak enough to listen to a female friend who led her back into drugs and prostitution. Mamie Hayes would never forgive herself for not fighting for her son's child. An all too often told story, Bobbie thought, her sympathy going out to the grandmother.

When Mrs. Hayes was silent again, she went to find the coroner. She was distressed to have to tell the grandmother the body could not be released just yet. Not all of the reports were in, it would be another day or two.

Mrs. Hayes took the information stoically, she would stay until Shemisha could go home with her. Bobbie did not have the heart to tell her that since the girl was underage, it would be the mother who could claim the body, unless she signed a release.

When they rose to leave, the grandmother asked, "Could I see her one more time?"

The funeral director graciously again sent for the body. The girl was so small, you could easily imagine that she was still ten years old. Her hair was in little braids covered with white beads. Some cosmetic work had been done after the autopsy, and Bobbie was thankful that she looked peacefully asleep.

When they left the funeral home Bobbie never even asked where Mrs. Hayes intended to stay. She headed to her apartment. She enforced the laws, but justice did not always prevail through the Courts. Maybe David could do something about that when he was in Congress.

After seeing that Mrs. Hayes was comfortable in her spare bedroom, Bobbie checked her answering machine. David had left the message that he was going to Knoxville, he would explain later.

* * * * *

While working out at the gym, David had decided to talk to Jeff Fischer. As a lawyer, he knew jumping to conclusions was dangerous. He could at least give Jeff the chance to tell him where he was at 2:00 AM on the night in question. A phone call to the Knoxville police told him where they were holding Jeff. Besides, there was not much he could do for Orville today. When he had gone to the jail, Steve informed him that the guns found in the truck were the same guns used in Carthage. The State would take custody of the boy, since neither of the parents had shown up. It was still to be decided if there was enough evidence to bring Federal charges against the boy. Buddy Adams was strangely missing, too. David had given Orville a pep talk, told him to cooperate as best he could, and David would be back tonight. Orville was sullen and unresponsive and David knew that being locked up was beginning to tell on the boy.

David felt like King Solomon, only he was the one who needed to be divided in two. With Ellen in the hospital, and no one else trained to handle legal matters, he needed to be in two places at once. His good morning telephone call to Bobbie had ended in their first disagreement. She was going to work this morning. Wonderful as last night was, he still did not need her to sit and do nothing in his office. She was a deputy and the sheriff needed her and that was that. Rather than continue to argue, David backed off. Most of the media attention had cooled or taken up the explosion at Oak Ridge, so he couldn't use that excuse again, nor could he honestly claim he needed her at the office. Better to make the best of it until later. Driving on I-40, he picked up his cell phone and left her the message that he would be in Knoxville today.

Traffic through Knoxville was always at a standstill. What seemed like perpetual construction on the major thoroughfares threw traffic on alternate routes, streets that were never meant to handle the volume of cars and trucks. Making his way to the Justice Center, he wished he had taken the army up on a handicap sticker. He finally found a place to park and hurried into the building that housed the precinct.

If he had been annoyed before, he was exasperated now. Shuffled from one desk to another, he was finally led to a small conference room. After a ten minutes wait, Jeff Fischer was brought in. David asked that the handcuffs and leg chains be removed.

When the door finally shut, Jeff sat opposite David at the small table. "Wouldn't have a cigarette on you, would you?" The small hang-dog smile made it a joke. "No, you don't smoke, do you?"

"Ah, no, I didn't think to bring any." Jeff just shrugged, so David got right to the point. "Where did you go at 2:00AM?"

"That what time you went out?"

David nodded. He had his tape recorder in his hands. Jeff was watching him intently, but keeping a half smile on his face.

"Look," Jeff made the effort to sit erect, "you don't owe me anything, just tell them I was with you in Smithville. That's the truth, isn't it?"

"You haven't answered my question. Before I tell them anything, you have to convince me it is the truth. If not, you can rot in here for all I care."

Jeff slumped again, holding his fingers like he had a cigarette in them. He moved his hand to his mouth and sucked in a breath. "My kingdom for a Camel. I tried to kick the habit once. Couldn't do it. I woke up around midnight and went out back to smoke. Only had two left in the pack. I sat on your back steps and could see lights down the street a couple of blocks, maybe. I thought it might be an all night market, so I walked down there. Sure enough, I bought a couple of packs. You can ask the clerk. He'll remember. He was closing up and thought I was going to rob him. It was almost funny." He turned his head to look squarely at David. "Come on now, I wouldn't lay a snow job on a fellow veteran, especially one who's a lawyer." Jeff's grin was on the cocky side now.

David snapped off the recorder. "Sorry, I just had to ask. Now tell me why you are in here." He pushed the on button again.

Jeff told him about Karen, the work she did, their relationship and was honest about trying to get a story out of her. He went even farther back, to a divorce that had cost him his family. He had come back from the Gulf War with what they called a syndrome, but was as real as any sickness there was. He couldn't work, eat, keep his mind on anything for more than a few minutes, or control his temper. Finally his wife had enough, took their three kids and split.

David let him ramble on, getting the mental image of a man who was his own worst enemy. It made David angry to think of those, including himself, who had given much more to their country. This man just whined, using it as an excuse and refusing to get the help that was available. Still, if what Jeff claimed was true, he couldn't let him go to prison. He agreed to represent Jeff, and went to file the papers. After he telephoned the market in Smithville, he would alibi Jeff and get him out of here.

The block warden came to get Jeff and took him back to the cell. Jeff knew it would not be for long. What he told David was the truth, most of it anyway. He only left out the calls he made from the pay phone at the market.

The telephone call to the Smithville market verified Jeff's story. The manager put the night shift clerk who was in early to collect his paycheck, on the phone. Yeah, he remembered the guy. Tall, stringy man in a rumpled tan suit. Light hair and tobacco stained teeth. Looked like a bum, the clerk had been afraid of him, but the guy just bought some cigarettes. David asked if the clerk remembered the brand. Yes, the man answered, Camels. Don't sell many of the straights anymore. Younger people want filters.

David was convinced, thanked the store manager when he came back on the telephone, then went to rescue Jeff. He was met in the hall by a deputy prosecutor. The man introduced himself as on the Fischer case, and led David to an empty office. "Mr. Middleton, is it? You wouldn't be the Middleton who played football for Tennessee back in '90, would you?"

David had thought the handsome African-American was familiar. He searched his brain and it finally clicked. "Josh? Josh Petry?" The two men shook hands. "At the risk of sounding like a cliché, look at you now!" David remembered the skinny kid who served as a gofer for the football team. David was a senior when they met last, Josh in his freshman year.

"Man, what a running back you were. Scouts from the NFL were at all your games. I never did catch up with you. I tried, you know. Wanted to be just like you. I never did make the team." The man motioned for David to sit down without making any reference to David's disability.

David appreciated his consideration. "I expect you asked me in here to talk about Jeff Fischer."

Pulling a file folder from his briefcase, Josh nodded. "I hate to blow your case, counselor, but we have an eye witness who will swear she saw Fischer at Dr. Fielding's apartment at 4:00 AM. The coroner says that is about when she was shot."

David did some mental arithmetic, keeping his face blank. He swore to himself he would never take another one of the sleeping pills that literally knocked him out. A freight train could have come through the building without waking him up. He could verify that Jeff was still in Smithville at 12:45AM, from the phone call to the store. He himself knew the couch to be empty at 2:15AM. Not much to go on. Jeff could have sat out back to smoke again. It nagged at him, though, that even taking in the time zone change, there was still plenty of time for Jeff to have driven to Knoxville and be at the apartment before the woman was killed.

Knoxville's Deputy Prosecutor gave David the computer print out with the alleged charges. Capital murder. Murder one, no matter how you looked at it. Jeff would be held until the hearing when the charges would be brought, then bail set, if granted. What have I gotten myself into, David wondered. He needed to find out everything he could about Jeffrey A. Fischer. If he had ever needed Ellen, it was now. He thought about Bobbie again, speculating what she would do if he asked Steve to relieve her of duty for a time. She didn't have the legal training Ellen did, but she could do the leg work. Leg work, he muttered. I could sure use another leg or two right now.

He swung up on his crutches, and thanked Josh Petry for the information. The two men made plans to have lunch on the day of the hearing and exchanged business cards. David asked to speak to Jeff again and was escorted to the same conference room.

Jeff came in again, not in chains this time, and slumped in the opposite chair. He looked like he just awoke from sleep. David didn't think he could have napped so calmly, had he been in Jeff's place. David didn't mince around. "The charges against you are Murder One. Premeditated. There is a witness that will swear you were at Dr. Fielding's apartment the morning of the murder. Anything else you care to tell me?" David didn't bother to conceal the sarcasm in his voice.

Jeff visibly blanched. "That's not possible. I told you the truth. Call the market, they will tell you I was there!" He was sitting stick straight now, wide awake.

"I called," David looked the man direct in the eye. Jeff slumped back in the chair, like the life had gone out of him. "I did the arithmetic," David continued. "You had time to go to Knoxville and return before I got up. I came back to my house a little before seven. I was tired and went straight to bed. I didn't check the living room couch. It would still have been enough time. What's it take to drive to Knoxville from Smithville? Hour and a half, two at the most. That is if you obey the speed limits. Figure it out yourself."

Jeff sat tapping his fingers on the table. "If you won't bring me cigarettes, could you bring some gum or something?"

The frustration that had been building up in David all day, came boiling out. "You want to plead guilty? Save us all a lot of time."

The hang dog look was back. Jeff grinned that sheepish smile. "With my luck I might as well, when my own lawyer won't believe me. Honest to God, David, I'll swear on a Bible I told you the truth. I don't know who thinks they saw me. I wasn't there." He simply folded his hands and sat back.

David nodded curtly. "If you can't convince me, how do you think we will convince a jury? I've got to go now. Think of everything that happened that night, even if it is trivial it may help. Think about the woman; who else would she let in her apartment late at night? Who might want her dead? I can only represent you Jeff. I will be your advocate, tell your side of it, but you are the only one who can save yourself."

David stood, adjusting the crutches and settling the strap of his briefcase over his shoulder. He went to the door. "Hang in there. It's not over yet."

David drove out of Knoxville before he remembered he missed lunch. His usual skimpy breakfast was fading fast. He pulled off I-40 at a truck stop that included a restaurant. When seated in a booth, he ordered the Drivers' Special from the friendly waitress. She brought his coffee, then picked up a newspaper from the opposite bench. "This belong to you?"

It was the Knoxville Chronicle. David could see the headlines and date. It was today's paper. He used his best smile on the girl. "No, but I would like to read it. Think anyone would mind?"

She grinned back. "Naw, some driver must have left it. You're welcome to it."

The abundant food came, hot and steaming, and David dug into the mashed potatoes and country fried steak. He spread out the paper so he could read while he ate. The headlines dealt with the assassination attempt on the Vice President. The Vice President had issued a statement to the effect that he would not be scared off any of his stands, and would keep his schedule of appearances. He was due to speak at a dinner to raise funds for the Democratic Party to be held at the Opryland Hotel in Nashville, however no date or time for the event was printed. All the usual rhetoric by the major political players was also given space. An article giving a personal, first hand account was by-lined by Jeff Fischer. David was impressed. Jeff knew his business.

The other front page article was a short reference to the explosion at Oak Ridge It stated that radiation was suspected in the area and it would be closed until further notice. Residents who had been evacuated could go to their homes for short periods to get articles they would need. Call the indicated telephone number for additional information. A related article on the fourth page was referenced.

David flipped the pages between bites of steak. Half the newsprint on the fourth page was the article, again by-lined by Jeff Fischer. It dealt with the death of Karen Fielding, almost the same story Jeff had told David this morning. Somehow, seeing it in print made a better impression. For one thing, Jeff was an excellent writer. There was emotion to the piece and a sadness that told David that through writing, Jeff was able to own up to more of his feelings than he could vocalize. This morning, though, Jeff had only partially included what he knew of Karen's work. Now, in newsprint, you could believe he was her confidant, almost a cohort in the development of a new power plant that would eliminate the worlds' need for massive oil reserves.

David's fork scraped his plate, and he looked up to see the waitress filling his coffee cup. "Finished with that?" She took the empty plate without waiting for an answer, and moved to the next table. David had been so preoccupied with the newspaper, he didn't remember eating his food. Now I have two mysteries, he thought. And two mysterious clients. A teenage kid who refuses to rat on his friends, even to save his own neck, and a down and out reporter who hasn't begun to tell me what he knows. The thought crossed his mind that neither client would be able to pay him the first penny. The open and shut case against Cal Snead and the cow was looking awfully good.

CHAPTER TEN

The well-dressed man in the tower suite seemed preoccupied with viewing Nashville from the small balcony. For a span of ten minutes he watched the traffic on the Cumberland River. Barges laden with sand and gravel being pushed down river by powerful tugboats that would deliver them to the Ohio and Mississippi. Sleek, fast river taxis headed up river to the Opryland complex. In the distance, around the bend, he could hear the deep throated whistle of the General Jackson showboat as it headed out for the breakfast run. Inside, on the desk behind him was an opened Knoxville newspaper. With a heavy sigh, he returned to the desk and picked up the phone. He dialed a number in Houston. When the call was answered, he listened to the recorded voice and punched in an extension number at the proper time. The voice mail came on. He almost hung up before a human voice interrupted.

"Good morning, this is...,"

"I know who you are, you little slut. Put your boss on, and get the hell out of there," the man in Nashville said softly, his voice loaded with menace.

A male voice came over the phone. "You're pushing your luck, old man. What is it you want?"

"Send your secretary, or should I say mistress, out of the room."

The younger man acquiesced. He turned away from the phone. "It's okay, we'll continue later. Would you give me some privacy now?"

The Houston man came back to the phone call. "She's gone," he drawled. "Now, what's your problem so early in the morning? You sound like you got a burr under your saddle."

"It's the same time in Houston that it is in Nashville, so don't give me that Texas crap. I am going to scan an article from the Knoxville newspaper and send it to you. It would seem our little bird did some singing before she was out of the cage."

There was a moment of silence on the line. "I think I all ready know what is in it," an audible sigh came through with the words. "My secretary," he made a point of using that word, "just brought me a print out of a computer recorded telephone call that was overlooked yesterday. So? I understand from the TV news the reporter has been arrested for her murder. You can take care of it, can't you?"

"Birdbrain! Read the damn thing! He has the right to an attorney. If he talks before we get to him..." The threat was left hanging. "I've kept my part of this bargain. I'll see to my end of the deal. How are you doing with assembling the data?"

The younger man hesitated. A sound, suspiciously like he was searching through papers on his desk, came through the phone. "It will take a few days. Until then we can only hope we have everything. I'll let you know then."

In Houston the telephone line went dead as the man in Nashville hung up. The Texan grimaced as he kicked his desk, then punched the intercom button. "Tell Honeycutt to get his ass up to my office, NOW!" He slammed the receiver down, sat, and wadded up the computer print out.

* * * * *

David returned to Smithville in time to join a combined conference of the FBI and TBI. To his surprise, Jim Orson was present to represent the Secret Service. "Didn't expect to see you here," David shook hands with the man.

"I asked for this assignment. Didn't want to go out with the shooting hanging over my head. It happened on my watch." Orson looked like he would rather have retired two months ago, instead of two months from now. The meeting got off to a start with Orson presiding as an informal moderator. He informed the group wanted posters were already printed and a nationwide manhunt in progress.

The FBI presented their current photograph and the information that had accumulated over the years. Most of it had been compiled by the CIA. Though responsible for information regarding known terrorist, they had not kept tabs on Dr. Ahmed Faziz's recent whereabouts since nothing of consequence had occurred in the last few years. In the early 90's he had gone to Niger in northern Africa where he set up a small hospital in Djado, a town on the edge of the Sahara Desert. He bought a small house where he lived with his aged mother. He accepted speaking engagements from time to time, but there was no known connection to a terrorist group at the present.

After frantically digging through their files, the CIA had turned his folder over to the FBI. This was a domestic occurrence; the CIA should really keep out of it. In fact, they advised the FBI to turn the matter over to the INS. They were the agency who should know the intentions of those to whom they issue visas for entry into the United States.

David might have been amused, had it not been a case of somebody's life. A typical government shuffle. The top brass handing blame down to the next level and so on. He wondered where it would end and who would be the last rung down the ladder.

Jennifer Smith represented the TBI, along with an older man she introduced to David as Captain Strickland. She confined herself to several comments during the meeting, but took copious notes. Several times David caught her looking at him as if he had the answers tucked away in his shirt pocket. Finally he smiled back at her, giving a noncommittal shrug.

Other than the usual bickering, the meeting did present some interesting thoughts. The theory was that the shooter acted alone. The aging Dr. Ahmed Faziz was named the chief suspect. Why now though, after being inactive for so long? Perhaps to reinstate himself with one terrorist group or another? Again, pointing to the older man was the equipment used. Why choose a hunting rifle, when better target guns were readily available. Perhaps to throw off the investigators, even if it meant a failure to hit the mark? Another puzzling aspect to the shooting, besides the obvious, was the scope on the rifle. While an excellent piece of equipment, its calibration was slightly off. Any professional, especially one with the reputation of Ahmed Faziz, would know his equipment. Could it be the assassination was not intended to succeed? Was more involved than the life of the Vice President of the United States?

The meeting continued with input from everyone except David. Like a think tank, they tossed out ideas to be discussed, compounded, and dissected. The main question was, why the Vice President? An attempted assassination of the President would make a much bigger statement for a number of reasons. The favorite scenario that finally emerged agreed that the Vice President would be scared off one or the other of his stands in the upcoming election. That it might be a warning of more dire things to come, as one of the hate groups indicated in claiming responsibility, could not be dismissed either. After all the rhetoric, the questions that remained unanswered were the same as when they started. Why, and who was behind it?

David had only half listened, as it was unlikely that federal charges would be brought against Orville now that his school had verified his attendance of the afternoon classes. He had turned his mind to Jeff Fischer, then a rather far-fetched thought tickled his mind from something Jeff had told him. He spoke up just as the group was gathering up their notebook computers and paperwork.

"What if the attempted assassination of the Vice President was part of a larger plan? What if it didn't make any difference whether it succeeded or failed? Maybe it was only a smoke screen, meant to draw attention away from the real issue? Has anyone bothered to check beyond the political scene?"

One of the FBI men jerked his head up and snorted. "Are you suggesting it might be a personal vendetta of some sort? Who, in their right mind would hire a bumbling, has been hit man for that?" He didn't laugh, but his attitude plainly said this small town lawyer was only here at the request of the TBI. Nobody bothered to answer.

David gladly left the room and went to find his client. Maggie left after she signed an affidavit stating that the man driving the truck in Carthage was alone when she saw him shortly after the shooting. Orville was shown the pictures and identified the bearded man as the one he saw park the truck in Mt. Juliet.

David was festering with guilt. He or Ellen should have been present with both Maggie and the boy. He had tried to withdraw from Orville's case, but was told that the charge of vehicle theft would be left for the State of Tennessee. No state lines were crossed. It was not a Federal matter. Maybe Boyd could take it pro bono, he thought, naming the other lawyer in town. He would see Judge Jenkins tomorrow. There was not much he could do for Orville, anyway, except try to see that he was charged as a juvenile. There were still the missing hours to consider, but now that Orville was no longer a suspect in the actual shooting, it didn't matter that much. David admitted to himself, his curiosity was not appeased, but he had more to think of now.

He entered the detention block to find Orville pacing the confines of his small cell. "Where have you been?" the boy's voice was belligerent and tense. He stopped and stared at David.

"It's really none of your business," David said mildly, "but if you want to know, you are not my only client."

The boy stood there, twisting his fingers together as the cell door was unlocked.

David unhooked his crutches and lowered himself to the bunk. Orville assumed his favorite stance, hands above his head, hanging from the bars behind him. His face screwed up and for a moment David thought he might cry. The image of a child, teetering on the verge of adulthood, confused and scared, crossed David's mind.

"I have taken another case. A very important case. A man has been accused of murder. I don't know if I will have time to work on your problems. I will try to get another lawyer to help you."

Orville released the bar and walked as far as the back wall allowed. He turned around but kept his face averted, so David could not see his eyes. His voice was strong, but wavered. "My mama's not coming. Did you know that? Mrs. Lewis called her. Ma told her I deserved to be in jail. She called my Pa. He won't come either. They give up on me." The bitterness came back in his voice and he turned away again. "Even Buddy hasn't shown up again." He ran his hand through the dark brush of hair sprouting from his head.

David felt like he had been hit in the pit of the stomach. He had known, since he was told the State had taken custody of Orville. What he had not known was how it would affect Orville. Now he was telling the boy he would abandon him, too.

Orville turned to face him this time. "Guess I'm not important, now they believe me about the man with a beard parking the truck."

"Is that what this is all about? You stole the truck because you wanted to feel important?" David cleared his throat. "Vehicle theft is the same as grand theft. It is a serious charge, whether you are tried as a juvenile or an adult. Serious jail time either way. You are important to me, it's just that this other case came up..." David didn't know when he had felt so lousy.

The dim light in the cell kept him from reading much emotion on Orville's face, but the boy came to sit beside him on the bunk and patted his arm, like David was the one who needed consoling. "It's okay," the youth said, then stood and turned his back on David.

David left the building heavy in heart, knowing he needed to assess his priorities. It was only business; he could not afford to get emotionally involved with a client. Resolutely, he turned his thoughts to Jeff Fischer as he drove the short distance to his office, parking in the shed behind his building. He stopped a moment after climbing the six steps to his back stoop. It wasn't big enough to call a porch, but afforded a place to stand while unlocking the door and protection from rain with a small roof jutting overhead. From where he stood, he could see all the way down a couple of long blocks to Broad Street. It was deep twilight, dark enough for the street and market lights to catch his eye. At least that much of what Jeff told him was plain to see.

He put his key in the lock, shoving his briefcase inside as he opened the door. Flipping a light switch, he maneuvered himself in the door, glad to be home to a little peace and quiet. Lord, he hoped he did not have to go out again tonight. He needed to get on his computer, send e-mail, and fax hard copy requests for Jeff's army records, previous employment and anything else he could get his hands on. He really wanted to believe the man, still the time element nagged at him. Maybe Jeff could think of something else. Another trip to Knoxville was in order. He had made an appointment to speak to Ben Parry, Jeff's editor. He wanted everything he could get on Dr. Karen Fielding and the Oak Ridge project, too. Most of all, he needed some time just to sit and think.

Sipping a cold drink from the can, he scrolled down a list of government office addresses from the internet. A wealth of information was available, but even at the speed of light it would take a while to sort through the jumble. David resigned himself to a long evening.

The old fashioned door bell on the front entrance emitted a shrill buzzing. David pressed an intercom button. "Sorry, I'm closed," he said, without taking his eyes off the computer screen.

"David, it's Bobbie."

Well, at least she didn't sound angry, he thought as he reached for his crutches. The springs on his old chair creaked as he levered himself up and went to the door. He switched on the hall light and unbolted the front latch. Bobbie was standing at the door, and looming behind her was an immense woman.

David swung the door open wide, shuffling on his crutches to get out of the way and invited his visitors in. Bobbie stretched up to kiss his cheek and pushed a strand of his dark hair back from his forehead.

The very large black woman squeezed past them and stood self-consciously in the hall. David glanced at her, then lowered his head to speak to Bobbie. "I thought you might be mad at me."

"I am," she smiled sweetly, "but that doesn't mean I don't love you. David, this is Mrs. Mamie Hayes. Mrs. Hayes, David Middleton, my fiancée. He is also an attorney," she added like an afterthought. "Maybe he can help you."

David managed to remember his manners, acknowledged the introduction and asked Bobbie to lead the way to his office. Mrs. Hayes was clutching a huge old fashioned pocketbook to her breast as she looked around the comfortable room. "Please be seated," he lowered himself in his chair and propped his crutches against the wall.

Bobbie took the chair beside his desk and looked at the active computer screen, the papers and file folders scattered over his desk and her eyes widened. "I'm sorry to interrupt you," she waved a hand at the desk. "I didn't want to wait until morning."

David laid a hand on her arm, "It's okay, honey. I'll tell you about my day later." He turned to the woman seated on the sofa, "What is it I can do for you, Mrs. Hayes?"

"You can get my girl home for me." The smooth, silky voice seemed incongruous with her bulk. She sat quietly, hands folded over her stomach.

"How can I do that?" David said, eyes on Bobbie for an explanation.

"You see, uh, you remember the other day when I told you about..."

"Bobbie, there is a lot going on, but I am only missing a leg, not my memory," David said, trying to ease the obvious tension, while letting his best smile go to Mrs. Hayes. "Go on," he prodded.

"Well," Bobbie was struggling to find the right words. "Mrs. Hayes is Shemisha's grandmother," as if that was enough.

David didn't say anything this time. Bobbie took a deep breath and continued. "The girl who was found out at Center Hill last week."

David understood. "I'm so sorry Mrs. Hayes, but this is a case for the sheriff and the park rangers. I don't know what I could do."

Mrs. Hayes looked at him with her accepting countenance. "I know she's dead, Mr. Middleton. I know somebody killed her. I only want to take her home and bury her. Your precious girl here, said you could take care of the paperwork for me. Whoever did this to my baby will have to pay for it when they stand before God, if not before."

"We'll get him, Mrs. Hayes," Bobbie put in. "We have a suspect and will trace it back." She looked at David. "The coroner said she had been dead several hours before she was put in the lake." Then realizing it was a conversation she didn't want to have, explained what they wanted from David. "Mrs. Hayes is not the girl's legal guardian and we have not been able to locate her mother. Do we need permission to release the body?"

David sat back, trying to remember some of his family law. Another child, he thought. Why are our children getting into so much trouble these days? It was enough to make him think twice before marriage. Then he looked over at Bobbie's serious face, knowing she might already be carrying his child. She was worth it. "Hey, lil'bit," he engaged the smile again, "we could offer our guest something to drink, or some coffee. I'll dig in a book for an answer, if you would take care of my lapse in manners."

Mrs. Hayes declined refreshments, but drew out her handkerchief and fanned her face. Bobbie shook her head, "We don't have time right now. We're going to visit Aunt Ellen. Did you forget?" She rose to her feet. "Do you want to go with us, or are we really interrupting something important?" She let her voice show she was annoyed with him.

David sobered then. "I haven't forgotten Ellen, but yes, this is important. A man's life hangs in the balance," he added for the dramatic effect. "Really," he said, looking at Bobbie. "Jeff Fischer has been arrested for murder."

"Oh," she said rather weakly. "When? I hadn't heard."

"Yesterday. That was why he phoned me. That's why I went to Knoxville." David resisted the urge to go into it full length, but couldn't resist telling her, "That's why I needed you in the office today." The minute it was out of his mouth, he regretted saying the words.

Bobbie's eyebrows drew together in a frown. "You didn't tell me this morning."

"You didn't give me the chance." David realized they were escalating into another argument in front of a stranger. He backed off and calmed his voice. "It doesn't matter now, honey, but I will need someone tomorrow if you want me to help Mrs. Hayes. I've got Orville to think of, too."

"I thought we settled this, this morning, but I'll see what I can do." Bobbie said and turned on her heel. She went down the hall to the door with Mrs. Hayes lumbering behind her, handkerchief fluttering like a ship under full sail.

David got his crutches and clumped to the hall behind them. He made one more try. "Wait a minute. I'll go with you tonight, if you will help me tomorrow."

"Don't put yourself out!" Bobbie slammed the door hard enough to rattle the glass.

David picked up the telephone in his office and dialed the hospital number for Ellen's room. She answered the call, sounding her usual cheerful self. After inquiring about her injury, David told her of the new cases in which he had embroiled himself. She was fascinated, thrilled that he could now have a chance to prove himself as a trial lawyer. She promised to be back at work as soon as possible. This was too exciting to miss.

Just talking to Ellen settled David's nerves. She had the knack of making him feel like he could take on the world. He wished Bobbie could understand he only wanted her safe from whoever had started this tangle of events. She was with the Vice President when the shooting occurred. Would the assassin think she might be the one who had seen him? He ended the conversation by asking Ellen to deliver a message to Bobbie when she arrived. "Tell Bobbie I love her," he said.

He hung up the phone, only to have it ring. He snatched it up, more than a little annoyed. It took him a moment to recognize the voice on the other end, Buddy Adams. Adams asked if David could meet him to discuss Orville's situation. David did not feel predisposed to be friendly after the disappearing act the man had pulled on Orville, but fueled by the guilt he felt for leaving the case, he agreed to be at Shorty's in half an hour.

It didn't take that long for David to drive to the one-stop market outside of town. No one was at the fuel pumps out front, but several pickups were parked at the door, and an old battered 1970's muscle car sat to the side. A red neon *OPEN* sign blinked on and off in the front window. There had been stories for years about illegal gambling at Shorty's. Nothing had ever come of it. In a dry county, with not much else to do, he suspected the law knew and kept watch so it didn't get out of hand.

David navigated the swinging door and stood inside until his eyes adjusted. The small market held the usual assortment of economy size items on racks across the front. A game room opened to the back, where pinball and video machines circled two full size pool tables. Over the electronic beeps, bells and squeals of the game machines, a juke box valiantly sang out a mournful country tune. The atmosphere was filled with smoke. The blue haze hovered overhead, obscuring the faces of the players and spectators surrounding one of the pool tables.

Shorty himself was lounging behind the counter at the cash register. David asked for Buddy Adams, and was answered with a thumb pointing to the back as the man never took his eyes off a small television. David could tell without looking twice it was an adult channel.

Moving to the rear, he fought the urge to cough from the cloud of tobacco smoke faintly tinged with the sweet smell of marijuana. He recognized Adams as one of the pool players. The game was obviously going Adams way as he continued to run the table. His opponent was striding beside the table, pushing the watching men out of his way. Adams made snorting noises through his nose every time a ball dropped into a pocket. David found a corner table. Its one short leg, shored up with a saucer turned upside down, threatened to collapse when David leaned against the table to unhook his crutches.

The looser slapped money in Buddy's hand and slung his cuestick on the table. It was picked up by a challenger, but Buddy tucked the bills in his shirt pocket and pointed to David. He picked up a can of beer and came to the corner where David waited.

"How do, friend. Buy you a drink?" He held up the illegal beer.

David shook his head, "Let's keep this quick."

Buddy took a long swallow from the can, then sat across from David. He turned his head enough to view most of the room. "I want custody of Orville."

Even though he didn't believe he heard right, the first thing David noticed was the absence of the southern twang from Buddy's voice. "What are you talking about?" David asked, his own voice rising in pitch. "How could any self-respecting judge award custody of the boy to somebody who..." David bit his tongue when he realized he didn't know the first thing about Buddy Adams. He had only been going on gut feelings.

Adams answered with an easy smile. "Sure you won't have a beer? No? Okay, let's get out of here. He waited until David picked up his crutches and stood erect.

Buddy led the way to the door. "Hey, man, take it easy," he waved to Shorty and was rewarded with a grunt.

It was full dark as Buddy walked to the side of the building to the old car. The corner of the building cut off the overhead light at the door and only the scant light of stars illuminated the side parking lot. Muffled speech, filtered by the short distance, caught David's ear as someone followed them from the market. The air was warm, with heat rising from the asphalt, but David felt a chill go down his back as the hair on his neck stood on end. Like when they say someone walks on your grave, he thought. Buddy grabbed his arm, and pulled him around the corner.

David stumbled on the broken pavement, recovering with the aid of a crutch. "What the hell," he started.

Buddy held up a hand and shook his head. He listened for a moment then peeked around the corner. "You own a red Durango?" he said softly.

David nodded curtly and turned to start back to the front of the building. Buddy stopped him by the expedient maneuver of kicking a crutch out from under him. David wasn't prone to use profanity, but definitely not in the mood for any cat and mouse games. He caught himself on the car and threw a few choice words in Buddy's direction, then stopped cold when he saw the gleam of metal in Buddy's hand.

Buddy pressed the automatic in David's side. "You don't want any trouble, do you friend? Best be quiet about it. Let's go for a ride." He opened the passenger side door of the old car. "Get in."

They didn't call the 70's model automobiles muscle cars for nothing. Tires squealed as they turned out of the parking lot, driving without lights. Buddy went through the gears like a Nascar driver and the big 450 V-eight engine carried them out of range as gun shots rang out behind them. David was pressed back in the seat, speechless as the car picked up speed. When Buddy finally slowed, he still couldn't speak.

Buddy turned on the headlights and swung the heavy car onto a side road. Around the bend, he pulled into the Center Hill Lake access area. He stopped the car on the gravel launching ramp and turned off the lights. Pulling a cigarette package out of the console, he felt around with a finger, then crumpled the empty paper and tossed it out the window. A sliver of the rising moon showed dimly over the opposite bank, streaking the calm water with fingers of pale light.

David found his tongue when it came unglued from the roof of his mouth. "If you would tell me what is going on," he said a little more politely than last time, "I might not kill you after all."

Buddy pulled his hand from his mouth and reached for the glove compartment. The gun was on the dashboard and David was tempted to try to beat the man to it. Buddy's eyes followed David, and he picked up the 9-millimeter and stuck it in a side pocket of the car door. The light in the glove box revealed a smaller caliber gun and a small black leather folder. Buddy ignored the gun and flipped open the leather case to show the unmistakable shape of a government badge.

"So?" David drew in a breath.

"Special Task Force." Buddy answered the unasked question.

"So you're a cop."

"Well, not exactly," Buddy didn't extend the explanation.

David had the marked sensation of curling his fingers around the man's throat. "Would you care to tell me why I'm here, and why the sudden exit? And why the hell was somebody shooting at us?"

Buddy grinned, his prominent teeth showing in the dim light. "The last part is easy. If I had let you go to your truck, those men would have killed you. As to why you are here, it is a little more complicated than that."

David gritted his teeth. "I'm supposed to be an intelligent man. Suppose you tell me. I may be able to understand complicated."

"No need to get sarcastic, friend."

"I'm not your friend." David was tempted to end this right now. The training he did with Jim Ed at the gym had taught him some pretty nasty moves, even on one leg, but shots had been fired at them when they left Shorty's. If he was the intended target, he needed to know why.

"Take it easy," Buddy found a toothpick from somewhere and stuck it in his mouth. "I'm a government agent, for real. Not the usual kind, you understand. There is a group of us who work for--, let's just say our Commander in Chief, straight out. No bureaus to get in the way. I, well, sometimes I get loaned out to various agencies to do undercover work. Right now I'm with Alcohol, Tobacco and Firearms. I'm taking a chance on you, Middleton. You had a high enough security clearance with the Army, but this goes right to the top. You savvy?"

"Yeah, I 'savvy'," David said, with no noticeable softening of his voice. "In other words, you're a spook. I thought they went out with the cold war. Any way you can prove what you say?"

"Not at the moment." Buddy chewed on the toothpick, "Know any reason why somebody wants you dead?"

"Not at the moment," David echoed the words. "What's this got to do with Orville?"

"Orville," Buddy said with an extended sigh. "Orville is the key."

"The key to what? This is ridiculous. I don't know what the hell you are talking about. I'm going home." David opened the car door.

"Wait!" Across a field, lights went by on the road. "Wait," Buddy said, "I need your help. And whether you know it or not, you need mine."

David closed the car door. "Why don't you tell me," David said, resigning himself to the situation. It was a fifteen mile walk back to town. "Is Orville really your cousin?"

"No, but they think I'm a long lost relative. Actually I knew the man, so I took the assignment. Buddy talked a lot about his family and wanting to come back down south. He bought it at Waco. Seemed like I could do the job and pay back some favors at the same time. I really like the kid, tried to help the family, too."

David waited patiently until Buddy number two resumed. "It's the Neo-Nazi Chapter. They're tied hand and foot with the hunting club in Sparta. Did you know they are actually training for a war up there? That's where I come in. At first anyway. The ATF knows about the stockpile of guns now and is watching the compound. They got the usual run of the mill drug distribution set up. We know where they get the drugs. I've all ready put out the info on that. It will be taken care of when I give the word. It's this other thing that's got me stumped." Buddy paused, obviously trying to organize his thoughts with his thumb nail between his teeth.

David let out an exasperated sigh. "At the risk of repeating myself, what has this got to do with Orville?"

"Wish I knew for certain," Buddy said around his thumb. "The kid knows something. He's scared shitless. What has he told you about heisting the truck?"

Why not, David thought. If he is who he says he is, he could get the information anyway. He gave Buddy a condensed version of Orville's original statement, including changing his story to seeing the truck come into the Park and Ride. Buddy was not surprised to learn the identity of the bearded man. It wasn't a secret. Posters were all over town. David stopped short of telling him about Maggie Lewis. After all, he didn't know the man from Adam, and the thought tickled his funny bone. Having another eye witness would help Orville's case, but he could be as mysterious as the spook. He ended by telling Buddy he was withdrawing from the case.

"No," Buddy said flat out. "That's not possible."

The retort was on David's lips, when Buddy suddenly turned around.

"Oh, shit." Buddy started the car and backed out into the road. David could see another vehicle stopped at the bend of the road. "You got somewhere to go besides your office?" Buddy threw the car in first gear as the pickup truck started toward them.

David had heard of the game of chicken, but never played it.

"Yeeee Hawwww!" Buddy yelled, floorboarded the accelerator, and drove straight at the approaching headlights.

CHAPTER ELEVEN

The pickup truck veered off at the last possible second. Buddy swung the steering wheel sharp left. The big car fishtailed and rocked to the side as it made the turn onto the highway. David swallowed hard when his stomach dropped back down from his throat.

Buddy was laughing wildly, beating his hand against the steering wheel as the vehicle sped back toward town. "Ain't had this much fun in years."

The accent was back and David thought it likely Buddy, or whoever he was, enjoyed his work. Through clenched teeth David told the little man to stop the car.

"Don't think you want to do that, friend. Look behind you."

David had had it. He wrenched open the glove box and grabbed the gun. "I said STOP THE CAR!"

"Whatever you say, friend." Buddy twisted the steering wheel and the big car skidded off the road, braking to a halt appropriately enough back in Shorty's parking lot. "My, my," Buddy nodded his head to the side. "Take a look at your truck."

David held the gun steady as he took a quick look over his shoulder. All the windows of his Durango were smashed and the tires flat. Buddy inched the big car forward, letting it roll into the dark at the side of the building. He killed the lights and the engine as the sound of a pickup truck sped by on the highway.

"You can put the gun down now, friend, ain't loaded anyway." Buddy had the toothpick back in his mouth.

David groaned and threw the gun back in the glove compartment. "How do you know it's me someone is after? Maybe it's you they want."

"Could be," Buddy said nonchalantly, "but I heard them say your name. Right here," he waved a hand, "at Shorty's."

"Why you little son of a...," David exploded. "You set me up." He reached for the car door, and was stopped by a surprisingly strong grip.

"Uh, uh. Take it easy. I didn't let them get you, did I? Just wanted to see what they would do. Looks like they mean business."

Buddy turned the key; the car coughed softly through the muffler like a big marine engine. He let out the clutch and moved slowly toward the front of the building. Music from the jukebox blared as a man came out the door, climbed into a pickup truck and backed out to the road. David suddenly deflated, only now aware he had been holding his breath. He took another look at the Durango and gave in. "Okay," he said, "tell me what to do."

"Damned if I know," Buddy said around his toothpick.

* * * * *

Bobbie turned down the sheets on her bed, made herself comfortable and picked up a book she wanted to read. It was a romance, long time lovers recently re-united after years of separation. She was beginning to feel like that about David. Like they really didn't know each other. She knew he had changed since Desert Storm, but so had she, and for a while it seemed they could pick up where they left off. Making love to him was sheer heaven. She wouldn't change last night for anything in the world. Wonderful as the love making had been, what on earth had gotten into him this morning?

What was this problem he had with her job? Maybe she was making too much of it, but it had been several years since anyone had told her what to do, and it grated that he thought she needed protecting. I've made it this far by myself, and he was proud of me in front of the Secret Service and news media. What's his problem now? Frustrated, she kicked the covers down and turned a page of the book.

There was someone at the door. The knock was soft, and for a moment she thought she read it in the book. No, it was real, the sound coming from the foyer. Bobbie opened the drawer of the bedside table and removed her Policewoman Special 45 Smith and Wesson. She jammed the clip home and released the safety.

Padding softly to the door, she looked through the peephole to see David standing in the hall. Still wary, she turned the bolt lock and opened the door. He was alone, looking disheveled and tired, dressed in the white shirt and casual slacks she had first seen at his office.

She moved aside and he swung on his crutches through the door, bolting it after him. "Sorry," he said, with a sideways grin, "I thought about going to Ellen's house, but this was closer."

"Why?" she asked, moving into the living room. "Sit down and tell me what's wrong." Then she took a closer look at David. Dirt and dried blood ran down the side of his face from a scratch, and the front of his trousers were covered with the rusty stains of more blood. "David! What's the matter? Are you hurt? David! Answer me!" She grabbed his arm to steady him.

"Lil'bit, you can put the gun down now. I don't think we were followed." David sank down on the sofa and laid his crutches on the floor.

Bobbie suddenly felt the weight of the automatic in her hand. She put it on the end table and knelt in front of David. "We?" she said with an obvious question mark.

"Yeah, Buddy is trying to find a place to hide the car. He'll be along in a minute."

"You and Buddy," she said, like it was just sinking in, "you weren't followed."

"No, don't think so." David ran a hand through the hair that was plastered to his forehead with sweat. "Could I have a drink of water?"

"David," she said again, like a mother talking to a child, "are you hurt?" Bobbie's thoughts tumbled over and over in her head. She had never seen David like this. Something was very wrong. There was blood splattered all over him, but he didn't seem to be in pain. She stepped into the kitchen and came back with cold bottled water. She handed it to David, then sat beside him, realizing that he looked pale in the overhead light from the foyer. She got up and switched on a table lamp.

"David, I think you better tell me who Buddy is." She remained standing in front of him.

David finished off the entire bottle of water, then wrapped his palms around the wet surface. Suddenly he looked down at himself, "I'm not hurt, lil'bit, it's not my blood. He looked up at her as a knock came on the door. Three soft taps in a row, then a fourth.

David never saw her move, but the gun was in her hand again as she headed for the door. "Wait," he whispered, "It's Buddy. I know what he looks like."

"A secret knock?" she questioned. "Aren't you being a little childish?" She backed to the wall, then motioned for him to go to the door. He put his eye to the peephole, then unbolted the lock.

A small man slipped quickly inside. "All clear," he said to David, then turned to Bobbie. The gun was staring him right in the face. "Whoa, now lady," he jumped back, "I wear a white hat."

"It's all right, lil'bit." David started to move between them.

"Stay back, David. It's not all right, you look awful and you still haven't told me why you've got blood all over you." Bobbie said through tight lips, never taking her eyes away from Buddy. "Who is this little creep? Both of you had better start explaining." The S&W never wavered.

"Hoo-ee," Buddy turned his back on Bobbie, slapped David on the arm and went to a chair. "You got some little gal there, friend."

David went back to the sofa, his eyes sending Bobbie a message she didn't understand. "Sit down, honey." He didn't ask her to put the gun away.

"Not until you start talking." She deliberately pointed the gun at Buddy.

"Not me," Buddy held his hands in the air, then pointed to David. "He's the one they want dead."

Bobbie looked from one man to the other, and decided she was getting nowhere. She sat on the sofa with David, putting the automatic on the table beside her. "That better, gentlemen? Or would you like me to put on my uniform and take you both down to the jail so Uncle Steve can sort this out?"

David took her hand in his, like he was afraid she would reach for the gun again. "Bobbie, I'm too tired to argue tonight. Buddy called after you and Mrs. Hayes left. I went to meet him at Shorty's out east of town. You know the place." At her nod, he continued, rubbing her fingers with his thumb while he spoke. "Buddy heard men asking where they could find me. They got the information; everybody in the county knows I live above my office. Then he followed two of them to the parking lot and heard them plan to break in and make it look like I was shot during a burglary."

Bobbie heard what he was telling her, but a thought out of context popped into her head as he stroked her fingers. She wondered if he remembered he promised to buy her a ring, and had the absurd feeling that if this was true, he might never have the opportunity. Impossible. What he was saying was impossible. Bobbie's eyebrows dipped and she pulled her hand from his grasp. "David, I don't know anyone who doesn't like you. Who on earth would want you dead? Besides, why would you take the word of a...a stranger?" She made it sound like that was the worst name she could think of to call the weird little man sitting in her living room.

"Buddy's not a stranger. He's Orville's......ah, he wants custody of Orville. Look, we need your help. Two of the men followed us when we left Shorty's. They tried to run us off the road, but we lost them." His shoulders slumped and he reached a hand to her again. "I know, I know, honey, I didn't believe it at first, myself. You should see what they did to my truck. Then we went to my office. They had already been there. They wrecked the place."

David was looking straight at her, and she knew his face well enough to know he wasn't making it up. Bobbie was beginning to feel like she was faced with a giant jig saw puzzle and there were a lot of missing pieces. "Why me?" she asked. "Why not go straight to Steve? And if you didn't bleed, whose blood is it anyway?"

David was sitting forward, holding his head in his hands. He finally looked at her. "Pete Stryker. I...I told him to drop by the office anytime. You know old Pete. The postman. Bobbie, they shot him. I found him in the hall to my office. I tried to help, but it was too late," his voice broke, "he... he died right when I found him. We didn't wait around to see if they were coming back. I called 911 from my cell phone."

Bobbie could hear the shock and sorrow in his voice, and the stricken look on his face tore at her heart. "Oh, David," was all she could think of to say.

"Yep," Buddy spoke up for the first time. "Old man probably came in when they were ripping up the place. The men that were asking questions at Shorty's, didn't know what David looks like."

"Yeah, and you had to go and point me out to the men who stayed behind. Now they all know who I am." David recovered enough to sit up straight and didn't bother to keep a tinge of anger out of his voice. Buddy lapsed into silence.

David leaned back against the sofa. "I'll talk to Steve first thing tomorrow, honey, but we need you to do some work for us tonight. You have a computer here, don't you? Someone knows way too much about what I am doing. The files and printouts from my desk were missing. They smashed both computers and jerked out the phone lines. We need a place to stay, too. I've got a key to Ellen's house, but it's way out on the lake. Kind of isolated out there on the point."

Bobbie looked over at Buddy, but the man had his fingers steepled together in front of his mouth, contemplating a picture on the wall. Apparently he had nothing more to add to the conversation. "All I have here is a laptop. If that will work, tell me what you want me to do."

Buddy came to life then. "Get set up and I'll give you some file addresses and access codes."

Bobby started for the hall, then stopped. "I forgot, Mrs. Hayes is sleeping in that room."

David was on his crutches and had followed her into the hall. "Mrs. Hayes! That's something I have to do tomorrow, Buddy. Can't put it off." The thought of doing something tomorrow helped calm his nerves, until he remembered there might not be a tomorrow. He leaned down to Bobbie, "You go get dressed first, then maybe we can get in and out without waking Mrs. Hayes."

Bobbie looked down and realized she had on absolutely nothing except her long oversized night shirt. A blush pinked her cheeks. She put her hand on David's arm and squeezed, then slipped into her bedroom. He would have given anything at that moment to follow her into the room. A peculiar sense of pride had filled him when he saw her at the door with the big automatic held steady in her hands. She was in control of the situation from that moment on. Obversely, he didn't want her to go to her own door, gun in hand, ever again. He raked his fingers through his hair, feeling a dull headache building. God, if he had brought the trouble to her door, he would never forgive himself. He had enough of senseless killing in the army. He felt the anger and the violence he had so carefully kept buried for the last nine years boiling up in him. When he got to the bottom of this mess, whoever was doing this, for whatever reason, would pay! As he went back to the living room the other bedroom door opened and Mrs. Hayes came out in the hall.

"Mr. Middleton, I thought I heard your voice."

David was again surprised at her beautiful, melodious voice. He turned and dipped his head to the large woman, taking in the ridiculous flowered wrapper that made her look like a papered wall. "Sorry to wake you, Mrs. Hayes. Something important has come up and I needed Bobbie to help."

"Now don't you apologize for a thing, Mr. Middleton. Your sweet girl wouldn't hear of my staying any other place." She bustled down the short hall into the room, then stopped at the sight of Buddy who had moved to the dining table.

"Oh, well, didn't know you had company. Excuse me, I'll just let you be."

"Please stay, Mrs. Hayes. Some equipment Bobbie needed was in that bedroom, anyway. This is my, er, my associate Buddy Adams. Buddy, Mrs. Mamie Hayes. And please call me David." David tried one of his more endearing smiles, hoping he would not look like a serial killer with the blood and dirt splattered all over him.

Buddy didn't look much better. They had plowed through the mess in his office, looking for anything that might give them a clue as to who the assailants were. The small man rose to the occasion. He swept a short bow in the woman's direction. "Charmed, I am sure, my dear Mrs. Hayes. Do you sing, by chance? I am sure I have heard that beautiful voice somewhere," the King's English accent rolling from his tongue.

"Why yes, Mr. Adams. If you watch the Gospel Hour on Nashville television, I appear from time to time with my church choir."

"My favorite show, my dear, my favorite show. Here, let me help you." Buddy pulled out a chair and seated Mrs. Hayes at the table with all the polish and aplomb of a gentleman. David just shook his head over this latest impersonation.

Bobbie came back, dressed in jeans and another tee shirt, carrying the laptop. "I'm so sorry, Mrs. Hayes. If you want to go back to sleep, we will try to keep quiet." Her eyes went to David, then looked at the kitchen clock. The hands were almost straight up on midnight. She set up the computer, then went to plug into the phone line. "Oh, no! I brought the wrong computer back from Paula's. This one doesn't have a modem."

David looked at the ancient, by computer standards, piece of equipment. "It's not much more than a game machine."

"That's what the twins use it for. I took mine so they could use it for a project at school. Looks like I picked up the wrong one." Bobbie looked abashed. "I don't have another. I use Paula's PC or one at work, if I need to. We could go down to the office."

Buddy shook his head in the negative, looking around him. "Who's this Paula?"

"My sister," Bobbie replied, "but her kids have to go to school tomorrow."

"No," Buddy said. "Too many people involved now. Looks like I'll have to go back to Sparta."

"I know," Bobbie interrupted, "Liz Tidwell's got so much computer equipment, her office looks like a space ship. She's out of town, but I know Scottie rents a room over her garage. He house sits when they are gone, so he would have a key."

"Scott Pelham is a deputy, too," David told Buddy, "and good with computers. It just might work."

"He can be trusted?" Buddy's look was on the skeptical side.

"Oh, hell," David threw his hands in the air. "Right now, I don't even know if YOU can be trusted. Maybe Bobbie is right, we should go on down to the Sheriff's office."

"No," Buddy said solemnly, then his demeanor changed. He stood behind Mamie Hayes, hands on her chair. "Why don't you finish your beauty sleep, my dear. We won't disturb you again."

Mrs. Hayes stood, and David brought to mind the picture of a posturing song bird with a plump pigeon as the little man bowed again to the immense woman. Bobbie told her they would return as soon as possible, not to worry, David would make the arrangements for Shemisha tomorrow for sure.

Bobbie came back with her purse and looked for the gun she left on the table. It was gone. She looked accusingly at Buddy, who shrugged and pointed to the kitchen counter. She picked up the gun, checked the loading, as Buddy held out the clip. His prominent teeth gleamed white in a grimace, "Careless of you, love. Don't want an accident, do you, dear." He was still using the British accent.

David moved between them, as Bobbie reloaded the gun and tucked it in her specially designed handbag. "I don't know who you think you are," she said to Buddy, "but if you touch my weapon again I'll break your arm."

David could see her eyes flash, and the dangerous look to her face caught in his chest. Lord, he loved this woman, and he admired the way she handled herself. Still, he knew he would lay his life on the line, before he would allow her to be in danger. His father was always careful to keep guns put away. His mother had shied away from firearms. Now his intended wife handled a pistol as competently as she did a cooking pot. "Let's go, lil'bit," he opened the door.

It was a short drive to the Tidwell farm. The sign leading to the house advertised NEW MOUNTAIN NURSERY, and listed telephone numbers for both retail and wholesale sales. The house itself was surrounded by pastures for cattle and horses, with the nursery sheds and fields visible behind the livestock barn. The Mexican compound was down the road, behind the house used by the family of Carlos Deguiro, the Tidwell's farm manager. Acres and acres of trees, shrubs and flowering plants ran from the road back to the hills by Blue Creek and Center Hill Lake.

Yard lights shed illumination at the house and barn, adding to the bright piece of moon now in its zenith. Shadows from the slat fences gave a checkerboard appearance to the quiet fields. The small apartment above the free standing garage was dark. Stairs ran up the side of the building, ending in a small covered porch at the door. Bobbie checked her watch, twelve-thirty. "I'll go," she said and slipped out of the car before David could stop her.

He and Buddy got out of her Saturn, and David adjusted his crutches. Buddy had produced the small caliber gun from somewhere on his person, and grinned at David. "Ain't she somethin'? Beautiful, too. Man, you got it made."

"You just keep your eyes and your hands off her," David growled as they watched her knock on the door.

Finally a light glowed from the window, and the porch light came on. The door opened, and a tousled headed figure admitted Bobbie. She was back down the stairs in a few moments. "I had to tell Scottie what happened to you, David. He wants to know more and so do I."

"Will he help?" David moved to her.

She nodded, looking anxiously at David. The moonlight added to his pallor and she could see his shoulders slump as he rested against the car. "Don't worry, we'll find out what is going on. You did have insurance on your office?"

"Of course, honey. It's just that I didn't want to involve you in this. Now you are in danger, too. That is, if what Buddy said is true." He gave a rueful look to the small man. "I just couldn't think of anything else."

"David, that's what people in love do, depend on each other. You've been alone too long. Whatever happens, I want to be with you." She moved in front of David and kissed him, ignoring the presence of Buddy.

David responded, feeling the pressure of her breasts on his chest as she leaned into him. He cursed himself for involving her in whatever way this turned out. He dropped his crutches, pulled her closer and deepened the kiss.

"Ahem," Buddy poked them with them with a finger, then held the gun at ready as a figure came down the stairs from the apartment.

Reluctantly David released Bobbie and leaned down to retrieve his sticks. "Thanks, Scott," he said as the deputy came up.

"Anytime, counselor." The man looked pointedly at his watch, scrubbing a hand over his sleepy face. "This couldn't wait till morning?"

"No, this won't wait, Deputy," Buddy said. The gun had disappeared into his clothing again. The soft voiced command was given with clipped authority, as though Buddy was issuing orders to the Army.

Scott looked askance at the slight figure, then produced a key from his pocket. "Well, we had so much computer fun the other day, I thought I might as well join the party." He walked toward the back of the main house, keeping an eye on Buddy.

A large two story farm house, the lower floor was surrounded by covered verandahs. A quartz incandescent lamp atop a tall pole illuminated the backyard. Double French doors were at the corner of the porch. Scott used the key, and opened them. "This is the office. The rear entrance to the main house is farther down. Since the house is my responsibility, this is as far as you get."

Scott reached around the door frame and found a light switch. Overhead fluorescent rods glowed behind glass panels, flooding the large room with light. It was a fully equipped office, almost a suite in itself. A sitting area done in yellow chintz fronted a large desk and a computer work station. Another desk and computer station sat to the side. Various equipment, printers, copiers and fax machines along with a bank of file cabinets ran the length of the wall. Open shelves were on the opposite wall, stocked with plant encyclopedias, seed catalogs and books of all descriptions.

Bobbie went to a shelf and picked up a book. "The Fragrance of Flowers," she read, "how very apropos." The Tidwell farm was one of the larger nurseries in the area. Trees, shrubs and plants of all descriptions were shipped worldwide. Ed and Liz, with occasional help in the office, kept track of all the paperwork for their successful enterprise.

"Let's get to work," David said, as he swung inside.

Scott was sitting at the big work station, and booted the computer. "Liz protects her work with her password, but not the computer. Sometimes she has someone help her with research on new plant varieties." He grinned as the screen came to life. "I trade some computer time for my rent."

"I know," Bobbie put down the book and came to watch. "Aunt Ellen does some work for her, too. That's why I thought about this place."

Buddy moved behind Scott. "Okay," he reached around and tapped in an Internet web site, then hit go to. The loading arrow blinked done, and they were into what looked to all the world like a car dealership web site. The request for a password came up. Buddy typed a short word, so fast no one had time to take their eyes away from the screen. The blue background faded to white and the message on the screen read *Welcome, Agent Zero.* Buddy backed up and Scott turned to look at the little man like he had lost his senses. "Just why the fucking hell did you need a password for this? Who are you anyway?"

Buddy just grinned. "Why, the original, old boy. No need for profanity, you know," the Brit accent making him sound very suave. "Now get to work." He gave Scott a list of file names. "I want to know what any agency knows about the assassination attempt. Then I want to know all there is about the explosion at Oak Ridge." He turned to David. "If your hunch is right, we'll take it from there. This might take a while, if you two want to get some rest."

* * * * *

Ahmed Faziz couldn't sleep. Though the window was open over his bunk, it was stuffy in the dormitory. He found his suit pants, now stained with mud and sweat, and pulled them on. Barefoot and shirtless, he found the door in the dark and let himself outside. He leaned back against one of the work trucks and let the gentle breeze cool his body. He could not continue to remain here. Somehow he had to find why Nadja had been sent after him. He had convinced himself that the failure of the shoot was not the reason. If that were the case, he would have been allowed to return home, to be eliminated at Ibrahim's convenience. He was past his prime, it would happen soon anyway.

Carlos had accosted him with a flyer brought back from town. It was his picture on a wanted poster. Only wanted for questioning, but it had been enough to set Carlos against him. He had owned up to his real identity and managed to convince Carlos that the story he told about his gunshot wound was real. Only the fact that he was a medical doctor who spoke excellent Spanish and would stay on to tend the knife wounds, or other assorted needs the hot blooded Mexicans caused each other, kept Carlos from calling the police. Ahmed knew that sooner or later Carlos would be forced to turn him in. He had to get away before that occurred.

As he watched the big house on the hill, illuminated by the high moon, he saw an automobile turn in the drive. It pulled to the back of the house, but no lights came on. Maybe the owners, returning late from their trip. Or the young deputy who lived over the garage. Ahmed decided it was time to take action. He slipped back inside the door, and reached under the bunk for his shoes and socks.

CHAPTER TWELVE

David didn't realize he had been asleep. Going to sleep was the last thing he should have done. Bobbie was lounged back in the corner of the sofa; he was stretched out with his head in her lap. She had an arm across his chest, and he could hear little feminine snores. He moved slowly, wanting to let her sleep, sat up and looked at his watch.

"What time is it?" Bobbie yawned.

"Three am. Go back to sleep, honey." He looked around the room. The overhead lights were off, but the computer screen glowed and a pile of printouts was stacked on the desk. Neither Scott nor Buddy was in sight.

David straightened his back, held out his arm and Bobbie moved to his side. "This isn't exactly how I thought we would spend the night when we sleep together," she whispered. She curled to him under his arm, and ran her hand down the thigh of his leg.

David brushed aside the curly hair that escaped the pins and kissed her temple. "We'll have more nights, lil'bit. We just have to figure how to get out of this mess."

"Tell me again why you think the attempt on the Vice President and the explosion in Oak Ridge are connected."

Bobbie sounded sleepy and David wanted to tell her to forget everything and go back to sleep. They had talked for a long time, David telling her everything he knew about Jeff Fischer, Karen Fielding, and the experimental vehicle in Oak Ridge. She had asked quite a few questions about Buddy Adams and Orville, too. He confirmed Bobbie's suspicion that Buddy was a law enforcement officer, in fact a government agent of some sort, leaving it there for the moment. She already knew Ahmed Faziz was suspected as the shooter in Carthage, letting Orville off the hook.

"It was something Jeff said when I talked to him at the jail in Knoxville. I just have this hunch that two and two might add up. He was talking about Karen. She was tight lipped about her work, but would feed him tidbits from time to time to keep him coming back. From what he could gather, there was some problem, something wrong with the new motor that powered the car. It was damaging to the environment, possibly detrimental enough to threaten human life. That is the only clue I have, except the Vice President is known for his conservation and environmental concern. It has been his chief program since the election."

Bobbie's eyebrows pulled together in a gesture David had come to know as serious. "It was an international project, wasn't it? That's what I heard on the radio. Surely scientist of that caliber would take safety into consideration. Besides, I once read that around the turn of the century the internal combustion engine was thought to be the work of the Devil, and just as dangerous. Look how far it has come."

"I think we should have listened," David sighed. "Look how many lives are lost on the highways, not to mention smog and the ozone."

Bobbie remembered that David's father had died in a wreck, and tightened her hand on his leg. "I know," she said, "but how many people want to go back to the horse and buggy days?"

David loosened his hold on her. "I don't think Jeff knows much more. Let's hope Buddy can get some information."

"Do you think Jeff killed her?"

"No, even if he can't, or won't account for several missing hours. I know there is more he's not telling me, and it's crucial to his case. There was enough time for him to have gone to Knoxville. The Prosecutor claims to have an eye witness who will testify she saw him at the apartment building near the time of the murder. I've got the same kind of problem with Orville. He won't say where he went after he took the truck. They both act like they are afraid of something."

"Don't worry, you'll sort it out." Bobbie smoothed the frown on his face with her fingers. "Oh, there is something I forgot to tell you. Aunt Ellen might get out of the hospital tomorrow. I guess I mean today; it is morning, isn't it?." She yawned again. "She can't wait to get back to work. By the way, I got your message. I love you, too."

David pulled her back to him while his heart sank. With Ellen back, he would have no reason to keep Bobbie out of her patrol car. Before she could see the expression on his face, he kissed her. He held the kiss until they were both breathless. Finally coming up for air, he buried his face in the curls on the top of her head. Unable to keep his emotions in check, he whispered into her hair, "Oh Lord, Bobbie, what did I ever do to deserve you?"

Bobbie's voice was as emotion filled as his own. "You don't have to do anything David, only let me love you. You kept me away from you for so long, just let me love you. All I ever wanted was you." She turned to put her cheek against his. "I know we won't dance at our wedding. I know you can't carry me across the threshold. I don't need those kind of things, as long as I know you love me."

"Love doesn't begin to say enough." David felt the strain of keeping his feelings hidden begin to diminish. Still, he would never be a whole man again. This was as good a time as any to resolve the problem. "I want to provide for you, protect you, cherish you, like any man would."

"Oh, David," Bobbie responded to the anguish in his voice, "is that what has been the matter? You know you promised not to let your loss interfere with us. You are a better man than any I know. I'm willing to carry my share of the load. We're partners, remember."

"I know that, lil'bit. When I saw you at the door with that gun in your hand, I was proud of you. I know you can handle yourself, I just don't want you to have to prove it. Besides, whether you know it or not, you are the one breaking our agreement." At her gasp, he continued and held her still as she tried to pull away. "You don't have to prove anything to me either. Stop opening doors for me. Don't try to carry things for me. Stop treating me like a cripple. You can't make up for my handicap, any more than I can grow another leg. I want to shoulder my fifty percent of the load, and more. I want to be there for you whenever you need me. I asked for your help, because I really need your help."

David sighed against her cheek. "I know, I know, I came on too strong, and you got your back up, so I didn't explain everything. I don't want you exposed as a deputy. The news media broadcast a lot of information about you. You are too easy to spot in that uniform. The shooter might think you are the one who identified him. And then there's this other. I don't know who is trying to kill me, or why they want me dead, but maybe they are after you too. Maybe whoever was behind the shooting thinks we know something. We were in the building with the Vice President. Maybe they think we know why he was targeted. Look at it this way. If I am right, whoever controls the technology of the new car will be the most powerful person on earth, be it government or corporation. Not to mention the richest. Countries have gone to war over less."

Bobbie sat up straight and wiped a hand over her cheek. She had thought that ignoring the missing leg might be enough to show David it did not matter to her. Until now, she had given no thought to how he might feel about his handicap. She had only tried to help. It didn't bother her to pick up a package, or open a door, but she could see now it made him feel less a man. This was something they could work out. As soon as this mess was over.

"David, now you are scaring me. I hadn't thought about it that way. Still, it's a lot of maybes." She bounced a little on the sofa, moving away from him. "You're right, we have to figure this out." Her voice faded, "I could work without a uniform. Uncle Steve wouldn't let me be in danger, would he?"

"No," David conceded. "Steve wouldn't do that. I don't think he has had time to think that far ahead, but there are some Federal Agencies that might deliberately use you for bait." He propped his head on his hands, knowing that Buddy had set him up. He kept his face down when he spoke to her again. "I don't know, honey, I just don't know what is what anymore. I want to keep you where I can see you, but I don't think that's a good idea right now."

Bobbie pushed up from the sofa and stretched her arms above her head. The premonition she had earlier came back. If this was the last night they would ever have together, she wanted it to be a memorable one. She stood straight and stretched her lithe body. "I suppose splitting up is a good idea, divide and conquer, so to speak," she smiled in a very seductive way, "but not tonight, big man." She advanced on David, swinging her hips like a woman who knows exactly what she wants.

* * * * *

Ahmed stayed by the corner of the barn, watching the two men on the verandah. One of them was smoking, the other pacing back and forth. The automobile he wanted was sitting almost in front of them. He recognized the young deputy from the hospital, even though the light from the backyard lamp was dim under the roof of the wrap around porch. The other, smaller man, was quite a shock. He knew him only by his code name. If fate had not already dealt the final hand, it was coming. With Nadja hunting him and now the man with the reputation and code name of Zero on the scene, what chance did he have? Desperation dampened his armpits.

The younger man threw down the cigarette and both men entered the house through glass paned doors.

Ahmed forced himself to wait. When they did not re-appear, he made his way to the front of the barn. A horse neighed softly, disturbed by his movements, but it was too far to be heard at the house. Had it not been for the presence of Zero, Ahmed would never have approached the house. Transportation was what he wanted. One of the work trucks would have done, but he knew Carlos would immediately turn him in. The car sat by itself in the yard, lit only by the yard light and the now setting moon. It was tempting to just take the vehicle and make a run for it.

Instead, Ahmed made his way silently to the porch. In the shadows of the overhang, he approached a window spilling yellow light through the slits of a venetian blind. It was a large office. A table lamp in the sitting area was lit, spreading a pool of soft light over chairs and a sofa. The men he had seen outside were at a computer station while a third man he did not recognize sat at a desk. A girl was to the rear, with a pot of coffee. The men made gestures as they talked, but he could not hear through the closed glass.

Ahmed knew there was nothing current on him in any computer files. Any information they had would be several years old. No one had closely watched him since he opened the surgery in Niger. His fellah's, the Bedouin tribesmen who looked after him, would know. He had not been in the United State since the late 80's, accepting his speaking engagements in Europe or Africa. And there had been precious few of them in the last several years.

Nor had he been active since Buenos Aires. In fact, that was the one and only time he had ever seen Zero.

He supposed that he was one of a very select few who even knew what the man looked like. Rumors had run through the community in the 80's that Zero had gone free lance, would play one side against the other to accomplish his purpose. It could have been true. Back then Ahmed heard all the rumors, kept his fingers to the pulse of the netherworld they inhabited. He knew, without ever having seen the man, Zero showed up frequently in the world's trouble spots, often the same time as Ahmed. It was only by chance they met in Argentina. What in Allah's scheme of things could be so important as to bring him here? Even more important, which side was the former KGB operative playing now?

As Ahmed watched, the girl brought the coffee pot to the desk. Ah, he recognized, she was the girl who had covered the Vice President. Her picture had been on television often enough. The men stopped what they were doing, and she filled their cups from the pot. Enough, Ahmed told himself. It didn't matter why she was here. It didn't matter why Zero was here. Ahmed was out of it now, he could only try to protect himself.

He faded back from the window and cautiously went to the car. What luck! Would Americans never learn? The keys were in the ignition. He released the brake, made sure the gear was in neutral and gave the car a shove, slowly letting it roll past the house.

* * * * *

Bobbie and David were interrupted by Buddy and Scott before things between them became too intimate. To Bobbie's consternation she blushed as they joshed David, and Scott offered his apartment. David didn't blush, but he did give her an apologetic look.

Buddy had settled down to being Buddy again, and it was plain to see Scott had a bad case of hero worship. Bobbie went to the small kitchenette in the rear of the room to make more coffee. David picked up his crutches and swung over to the pile of papers on the desk.

"Anything of interest, here?" David addressed Buddy.

"You might start with one of your clients," Buddy said, handing him a sizable stack of print lined sheets. David wondered where Buddy had found a new toothpick. He made himself comfortable at the desk, and read.

Allen Jeffrey Charles. Born 1957 in Chicago, Illinois. One older brother, James Edgar Charles. Their father was a well to do banker, ranking high in the financial community. Jeffrey had started life with every advantage. In college he worked for the Chicago Tribune as a copy boy, while his brother was groomed to take over the family business, and their father went into politics.

When Jeff graduated from Northwestern with a degree in journalism, he was hired as a cub reporter. On his way up in his career, he married his boss's daughter and soon was a father. Everything looked rosy for him. Then Desert Storm intervened.

Called up by his National Guard outfit, he held the rank of Second Lieutenant, courtesy of ROTC training and the influence of his father, then a senator. He was sent to Saudi Arabia as a liaison officer at headquarters. It was never discovered how or when he became addicted to heroin.

He was involved in a scheme by some subordinates to raise the money they needed to support their habits. Though it had never been proved that he was more than an unwilling dupe, the men had sold air strike plans to a hard line Muslim sect. That the sect sold the information to Iraq was soon apparent. Hussein was able to avoid locations that were targeted. He was never in any danger from the bombings.

Traitors face the death penalty, but no information surfaced that Jeff had been directly involved in the treason. By the time the Military Court Martial convened, he was in the middle of a nervous breakdown brought on by his situation and withdrawal from the drugs. His military advocate pleaded mental illness. Jeff was sent to a rehabilitation hospital. Nothing about the short lived trial ever appeared in the news. The entire incident, including the alleged conspiracy, was neatly swept under the rug of top rank secrecy.

Three years later Jeff was pronounced able to leave the institution. By then the situation in the Middle East had cooled, and Jeff's father was a powerful senator on the Armed Forces Committee. The top brass did not want to start more investigations, as the sickness that came to be known as the Gulf War Syndrome had emerged. Jeff was labeled with the syndrome, and spent two additional years in the mental facility.

He was a broken man. His wife divorced him and the court awarded her full custody of the children. He was even denied visiting privileges. When he was released, his father and brother no longer acknowledged him as family.

The story David put together came from a combination of clinical reports, top secret military files, court-martial transcripts, and what Jeff told him. Jeff had lied to him about being assigned to the 101st, and his illness. Jeff had lied to Ben Parry, giving his employer a false name and the same story and excuses. What else had he lied about? David rubbed his tired eyes, and said a silent prayer. This had to stop somewhere. He had worked hard to convince himself that Jeff was not capable of murder. Now what was he to believe?

Bobbie brought the coffee pot and filled their cups. David hadn't paid attention to Buddy or Scott while he read the reports, now he felt Buddy's eyes on him. The man put his coffee on the desk and pulled up a chair.

"Sterling character, eh?" Buddy relaxed, leaned back and chewed on his toothpick. "Recognize the family name?"

"Of course, THE name in banking and fabulously wealthy. The brother hardly needed to solicit contributions to finance his Senate campaign. He was a shoo in; highly respected father retiring due to poor health, just in time for his son to fill the Senate seat. Names carry a lot of weight. Jeff didn't mention his family, except for a wife and children. Without his real name I would never have made the connection. Where did you get this information?"

"Fingerprints from the FBI file for the name and social security number didn't match those sent in from the arrest. Turns out the new Jeff Fischer prints belong to the younger brother of Senator Edgar Charles. After that, I knew where to find the information. If you know where to look, even deleted files will show up. The FBI knows about Fischer now, too. The story will have to come out."

Buddy rolled the toothpick to the other side of his mouth. "The name and Social Security number belonged to another veteran of the Gulf War. The sister filed a missing persons report on the real Jeffrey A. Fischer about two years ago. Far as anyone knows, he's never been found." Buddy shifted his position, settling back in his chair. "Anyone suspected, much less accused of treason to the United States of America is never free of suspicion, no matter how powerful his family. If Jeff had tried to approach his former wife, or the Senator, he would have been picked up immediately."

"You mean he has been under surveillance?"

"No, the other way around. The wife and kids re-located with money and help from the rich brother. She has warrants out to keep Jeff away from them. The father was dead; it was in all the newspapers and television. Now, the current Senator Charles has his own bodyguards, plus the Secret Service and Capitol Police, who provide extra security. I know," Buddy waved a hand at David's expression, "Senators don't usually rate that kind of protection, but you can't have a suspected traitor, mentally ill or not, showing up in Washington claiming to be a brother to the man who is being groomed to carry his party to the Presidency. I told you this went right up to the top, didn't I?"

David was flabbergasted, and Bobbie was clinging to the edge of the desk, taking in every word. "Good God, Buddy, you said he's his brother, but how has Jeff survived this long?. I mean, if he is a threat to a man that has a reputation as ruthless as the Senator's...," David trailed off.

Buddy winked at Bobbie, who finally put down the coffee pot and sat on the edge of the desk. "You read too many crime novels. Nothing is ever as pat as they make it sound. The brother was not a risk until he was released from the hospital, then he disappeared. People who try to disappear usually follow a pattern. Oh, some do succeed, but most either end up dead or are fairly easy to find." Buddy grinned at Bobbie and continued. "Sorry, not too many extraterrestrial's out there, you know."

Bobbie grinned and winked back. "Watch out. You're talking to a die hard Trekkie."

David rolled his eyes. "Get on with it," he said to Buddy, "if you have a point to make."

"Fischer, we'll call him, was not trying to evade anyone. His movements were random. He had no home, no family, no friends who would help him, so he could have just drifted. This is a big country. Do you know how many computer searches it would take to track someone who has no place to go? No name, no money, no credit cards and no reason to think anyone was looking for him? The FBI caught up with him, or thought they did, in Denver. A homeless man who matched the younger Charles's description died of a gunshot wound in a drug related bust. The Senator quietly paid for the burial and everybody relaxed. Until now, no one even wondered what had happened to him."

"Why wasn't that information included in the reports I read?" David picked up a pencil and rolled it between his fingers.

Buddy answered with a question. "Why won't the Kennedy assassination ever be solved? Why won't you ever know the truth about Vietnam or the Gulf War? Or closer to home, Waco, Oklahoma, Ruby Ridge. Do you think the government will ever admit they target dissidents? Or that mistakes are made?"

David had a quizzical look on his face. "Do you mean to tell me the attempt on the Vice President was...?"

"Nope." Buddy finally threw the toothpick in a trash can and held out his coffee cup for a refill. "I only said it could happen."

David looked at the doodles he was drawing on the paper in front of him. This was getting nowhere fast. "Forget Fischer for a moment. Tell me about Orville."

Buddy sighed, "I wish to hell I knew what to do about Orville."

David gave him a disgusted look. "There is about three hours missing from the day Orville took the truck. I think he went to whoever runs the militant group. He won't tell me. Says he swore an oath to protect the group. Maybe you can get him to open up. He thinks you are his kin. Custody won't be granted, now that the state has taken him as a ward unless they send him to a foster home. That's not likely any time soon, not with the guns connected to the assassination attempt."

"Can't do it," Buddy looked up. "I've got to make contact and get my end of the Sparta gig closed. You'll have to have another go at him, friend." He reached over and caught Bobbie's hand. "Sugar, why don't you just go and see that youngun. He should melt right nice under that smile of yours."

"Bobbie stays out of this," David growled.

"Wait, David." She pulled her hand away from Buddy. "I'll give it a try. I've learned a little teen jargon from my niece. Maybe I can convince him I know what he is saying."

"That's my girl," Buddy said.

David sat back and bit his tongue to keep from arguing. The scowl on his face said enough.

* * * * *

Ahmed started the car when it drifted to a stop at the bottom of the hill. He drove slowly into the town and passed the brightly lighted Sheriff's Office. He looked at the car clock. 4:00AM. Everything looked quiet. No movement around the square. Ahmed began to question himself. Where had the posters with his picture come from? Why was he wanted for questioning? How was he connected with anything? Who had turned him in? Posters, both with the beard and without were circulated.

There had to be a traitor. Possibly someone with whom he had worked, who now had changed affiliations, as the photos could only have come from the CIA or Interpol. The pictures were not recent, but close enough that he would have to change his appearance again. Who, though, who would know him well enough to tie the bearded tourist or the prominent Dr. Faziz, to the former suspected terrorist? For that matter, how had Ibrahim Hassim escaped from Israel? Was it with the help of the Americans? Ahmed knew there was an organization behind Ibrahim. Money had flowed freely in Nashville, and while incomplete and incompetent, a package was waiting for him at the boy's apartment. A package that in years past would have given him the information he needed to study. Before, he would have been given weeks to make his plans, arrange for his own equipment and size up the mark, the surroundings and the situation.

So, the thought came to him, the former Palestinian was the only one who could have pulled in Nadja and Ahmed at the same time, not to forget Zero. The only one who knew enough about the old days.

Ahmed drove slowly out of the downtown area, remembering the five miles of isolated road from the highway to the campground on Center Hill

Lake. Several cabins had been built in the area. He needed a place to hole up until he could make some plans. He was beginning to see a pattern.

CHAPTER THIRTEEN

A grinning Scott opened the back door of the patrol car to let David and Bobbie out at her apartment. Bobbie's mouth was set in a grim line. To think that someone was watching them and close enough to steal her car. Embarrassed by the fact that she had made it easy by leaving her keys in the ignition, she dared any of the men to say anything. Buddy joined them and Scott went to park the car. The door of her apartment was standing open, with the entrance blocked by Mamie Hayes.

The immense woman moved aside and they entered to the tantalizing smell of bacon, eggs and biscuits. "I hope you don't mind," Mamie looked at Bobbie, "I helped myself to your kitchen. I already ate, but I made plenty, just in case you came back. I'll just whip up some fresh eggs. Be ready in a minute."

"Wonderful," Bobbie responded, "I'm famished. I could hug your neck."

Both David and Buddy were quick to agree. The men went to wash up, then seated themselves at the table, while Bobbie set plates piled high with scrambled eggs, crisp bacon and feather light biscuits in front of them. Mamie followed with a big bowl of grits.

A knock on the door sounded. David rose from the table, but Bobbie motioned for him to remain. Buddy never looked up from the biscuit he was buttering. She returned almost immediately with Scott.

Scott looked enviously at the hot food, but shook his head when told to sit down. "Call came over the radio. The Sheriff's about to tear his hair out. All deputies have been called in. They have been to your building, David. You better go tell them what happened. They know Bobbie is with you."

David looked at Mamie. "Well, yes," she told him, "the Sheriff called here and I told them she left with you. That was probably about six o'clock this morning. Oh, dear, did I do wrong?"

Buddy stood up. "Mamie, my dear," the Brit accent was back, "you can do no wrong. Only angels can cook this good. Bobbie, David, you better go with Scott. I've got to get back to Sparta." He grabbed a napkin and wrapped it abound a couple of bacon and egg filled biscuits.

"Wait!" David was standing, too. "Just what am I supposed to tell them? Who am I supposed to tell them you are? Do I tell them why I was with you last night?"

Buddy shrugged, "Tell them anything you please." He nodded toward Scott. "There are two deputies to vouch for you. Me? I'm just a used car salesman who knows how to use a computer." He winked at Bobbie and was out the door.

David plopped back down in the chair. Where had his calm, sane, boring life gone?

Bobbie came to stand behind David. "Scottie, use my phone and call Uncle Steve. Tell him we're all right, that we've been up all night. We'll be down to the office after I clean up, and tell him about my car. Uh, right now, do you think you could leave Buddy out of it? I can't explain now, but don't tell Steve anything about last night. David and I will talk to Steve later."

Scott grinned at her in return. "I'll call," he said, reaching for the phone. "I'll tell him we'll be down right after breakfast." He sat at the table and looked up at Mamie Hayes. "Mam, we haven't been introduced. I'm Scott Pelham, and I'm sure Buddy's right. You are an angel straight out of heaven. I haven't smelled food this good, since I moved out of my mama's house."

Mamie put a loaded plate in front of him. "Go on with you, Mr. Pelham. Do all you policemen sweet talk old ladies?"

Bobbie messaged David's shoulders with her hands. "David, come with me. That scratch on your forehead needs cleaning." She went to the back, leaving David to follow.

David swung on his crutches after her. "Lil'bit, I already washed it, and used the salve from your cabinet."

Bobbie entered her bedroom and motioned David to follow her in. She closed the door. "David, we need to talk. What are you going to tell Uncle Steve?"

David sank down on the side of the bed. Had it been less than a week since the most exciting thing in his life was going to the gym in the mornings? What would he tell Steve? He would have to explain the wreckage in his office and apartment, then more than that, how old Pete Stryker died. How would he explain Buddy Adams when he could no more prove anything than the man in the moon? This was a mess that smelled like catfish in a bucket, and bound to get worse. The one thing he knew he had to do, he needed to get to Knoxville and talk to Jeff Fischer. Or Charles, or whoever the hell he was. Right now he wasn't sure about anything. Except the woman standing in front of him. He loved her.

Bobbie kicked off her shoes, then went to the closet and opened the door. She took out a cotton housecoat, pulled off her tee shirt and jeans and turned to David wearing only her pants and bra.

David was leaning back, propped on his arms, slitted eyes watching the gorgeous woman standing before him. "If you want me to turn around or close my eyes, you're out of luck," he said with one of his Hollywood smiles. She told him she loved him. He believed her. More than that, her love made him feel like a whole man again. With her beside him, anything was possible. They could tackle this problem and come out winners.

Instead of slipping into the wrapper, Bobbie stretched up on her toes in a limbering exercise. Whether she planned it or not, David experienced the effect of seeing her near-nude body in broad daylight. Tired as he was, he could feel the bulge in his trousers rubbing the zipper. He held out an arm, "Bobbie, come here."

"Umm," she sighed, as she continued the stretching routine. "I'm going to shower, David. Then it's your turn."

"It's my turn right now, woman." David caught her around the waist and pulled her down to the bed. He tossed her across him to the middle of the bed, then pinned her down with his one leg.

Bobbie giggled softly and raised her hips for him to peel down the underwear. "Well, I guess it's okay, big man. When it's your turn, it's fast," she teased.

David showed her just how fast he could undress.

* * * * *

Steve had not been easy to placate. After he knew Bobbie and David had been safely away from David's office, he accepted David's explanation that David was out with a client and then went to Bobbie's apartment. David winced at the lie, but said he didn't know until this morning that his building had been ransacked. He did remember inviting Pete Stryker to come by, so the old man could have surprised the burglars.

Not so easy to explain was why Bobbie's car was stolen out at the Tidwell farm.

"What were you doing out there at three in the morning?" Steve rubbed his hand over his face. Getting called out in the middle of the night was beginning to be a way of life, and neither the Sheriff nor his long suffering wife liked it.

"I needed a computer to help David," Bobbie told him. "I left mine at Paula's and the Tidwell's farm is a lot closer."

"That's about the poorest, lame brain excuse I've heard in a long time," Steve scoffed. "Why didn't you two just hit the sack at Bobbie's apartment?"

Bobbie drew herself up. "Mrs. Hayes is staying with me. Besides, nothing happened at the Tidwell's. Scott let us in and helped with the computer. Ask him if you don't believe me," she sniffed, like thoroughly insulted.

David had to bury a smile. She really was something to behold. "Bobbie is helping me while Ellen is in the hospital," he explained.

"Yeah?" Steve huffed, then turned away. He turned back with his hands on his hips. "Why didn't you go to your office, David, if you needed a computer? You might have stopped an old man from getting killed. When you two decide to tell me the truth, let me know. Scott!" he yelled, and slammed down the hall to his office door.

Scott rolled his eyes, and followed his boss inside the door.

* * * * *

Ahmed bolted upright from the bed when a bright ray of sunlight caught the edge of the dresser mirror. Still caught in the dream of the hot sun shimmering on the sands of the Sahara, he was drenched with sweat. Using a corner of the sheet to wipe his face, he calmed his breathing and looked around.

Last night, he had patiently sat in the car long enough to make sure there was no traffic in the vicinity. A security street light at the corner of the next house had shed scant light in the yard, but that, and what was left of the setting moon, had enabled him to check for other vehicles. Nothing in the carport or driveway of either house. Finally deciding it was worth the risk, he used his pocket knife on the rear door of the cabin. When he jimmied open the door he had not turned on a light. A small flashlight from the key ring of the automobile had guided him through the house. After a brief check to make sure the house was unoccupied, he had fallen on the bed fully dressed.

How long had he slept? A look at his watch clocked the time at 9:36 am. Not bad, he thought, but he had better do a through reconnaissance of the area this morning.

Nothing turned up. It was a peaceful little bit of lakeshore. The sky was a crystal blue, the humidity low and a rusty thermometer nailed to the wall registered the temperature at barely seventy. A beautiful early fall day. The lake, with its green tinted water was mirror calm. From the looks of the road, most cabins were weekend, or recreational places. The one he had chosen sat perched on the high side of the gravel road. The front of the structure was a covered deck only a few feet from the street. From this vantage point, he could see the buoys that marked the channel from the cove into the main lake.

Below the road, nothing but brush and trees ended in the rocky cliff-like edge of the lake. Buckeye trees were already shedding leaves. Hickory, poplar and oak would wait for cooler weather. Across the cove, he could see the campground. Deserted now, the double iron bar gates were locked across the access road. Ahmed took a deep breath and time to think of the young black girl. He could wish the gates had been locked the day he brought her here. Too late now, but surely not enough people had seen him to think he was anything other than a tourist who had taken a wrong turn, as he had tried to tell the park attendant.

The day use area below the campground gates was open. A small loading dock projected into the clear, shallow water. A couple of pickup trucks, with empty boat trailers attached, sat waiting in the parking area. No one was in sight.

The interior of the cabin definitely suggested occasional use. The furnishings were second hand at best, and little of them, but the pantry held a good supply of canned and dry goods. The refrigerator freezer was amply stocked with meat and what looked like trout or some type of fish from the lake. He found opened coffee in a canister, and plugged in the drip coffee maker. A tin of stale oatmeal cookies and canned orange juice made a satisfactory breakfast.

* * * * *

Bobbie filled out the paperwork to request a leave of absence. Not only was she angry with her uncle, the sheriff, she had decided that David's theory of splitting up was baloney. He needed her. She would be careful to let him play the gentleman, holding doors for her and so on, if that was what he wanted, but one look at his office had convinced her they were in serious trouble. When the wrecker brought his Durango in, she knew it. After a morning with the insurance adjuster, they were going to Knoxville. She wanted to be there when David accosted Jeff with his true identity.

While David worked with the adjuster, she went to the third floor storage area to look for some clothes for David. The vandalism on this level was as thorough as the office and second story apartment. The whole building had been methodically searched and ransacked. Stored boxes of legal papers and records were strewn across the floor, and the storage closet door off the hinges. The smell of mothballs from the closet tickled her nose. Wool suits and winter jackets, put away until cold weather, were slashed to pieces, same as the clothes in the apartment closets. About to give up, she found a black plastic garbage bag full of David's cast off clothing destined for the Salvation Army's charity store. She picked out a pair of cotton khaki slacks and a white knit golf shirt They could always stop in Knoxville and buy him some clothes. He had showered at her apartment, so at least this would give him something clean to wear.

On her way down the stairs she heard someone come in the front door. Bobbie hurried and met the sheriff as he kicked debris out of the hallway on his way to David's office.

"There you are." Steve's mouth was rigid, and Bobbie knew he was still angry. "Ellen has been trying to call. She was upset when she couldn't reach either you or David and called me." He looked at her yellow short sleeved sweater and navy slacks. "Why aren't you working?"

"I'm taking my leave time," she said, still a bit angry herself. "Somebody wrecked David's home, and you act like we are the ones who have done something wrong."

"I take everything that happens in my county serious," Steve snarled. "I have assigned Scott to this investigation and to help David, IF, and that's a big if, I can keep the city police out of it. You…, I've got something else for you to do."

"I told you, I'm on leave," Bobbie huffed. "I'm going to Knoxville with David." Bobbie was having a hard time holding on to anger against a man she had always loved and respected.

"No, you're not." Steve's voice had softened. "I tore up your leave papers. Until you tell me what's going on, I want you where I can keep an eye on you. Besides, somebody has to go get Ellen. They are ready to release her from the hospital. That's why she called."

"Oh, Uncle Steve," Bobbie nibbled at her lip, then smiled. "You really are worried about me."

Steve only shrugged, but a grin crossed his face. "Lil'bit, just go get Ellen. That's an order." He brushed past her and continued on to David's office. Bobbie followed him into the room, torn between her loyalty to David, and her duty to her aunt.

David's office was the worse hit. His beloved wooden pedestal chair was a pile of splinters, and the roll top desk caved in. David and the insurance man were sitting on the torn, slashed cushions of the sofa, the only piece of furniture still upright. Book cases were overturned, their contents scattered through the room. Glass, from smashed diploma frames crunched under her feet. There were even holes in the beautifully restored wainscoting and walls. Someone had taken an ax and set out to do as much damage as possible. It made her sick to her stomach to even think what might have happened if David had been here.

As it turned out, David thought it a good idea for her to go after Ellen. He even solved the problem of transportation. He produced a car key from his pocket and handed it to Bobbie. "Ellen's Park Avenue is in the shed next to where I keep my truck. It's been here since you went to Carthage with Liz Tidwell. Didn't see any need to move it until Ellen needed it. I'll pick up a rental car from my insurance company. That way I can go on to Knoxville."

Bobbie wasn't happy about the arrangements, but it did take care of the immediate problems. She was tempted to argue, but promised herself David wouldn't get rid of her so easy after this. Making a date to meet him for supper, she left, telling Steve he might as well sign her leave papers. She would take the time, even if she had to quit.

Backing the car from the shed, she drove quickly to her apartment. Ellen would need something to wear. She picked up a cotton skirt and blouse, and a pair of her soft house shoes. On impulse, she asked Mrs. Hayes if she wanted to ride along. Mamie was delighted, welcoming the diversion from daytime television.

Ellen was happy to see them. Bobbie went to the desk to make sure her aunt's insurance was filed, only to be told there would be no charge. All bills for services would go to the office of the Vice President. Besides, publicity for the hospital more than made up for any extras that might pop up. The nurses and orderlies made a ceremony of wheeling their celebrity patient to the door. At Bobbie's suggestion, Ellen donated the many plants and flowers she had received to the hospital for other patients. If they had to take the plants, Bobbie didn't know how they would get home with all the gifts and presents that had poured in for Ellen.

Intending to take Ellen to her apartment, Bobbie passed the turn to Ellen's house as they approached Smithville.

"Bobby, you missed my turn." Ellen was sitting in the front seat while Bobby drove. Mamie Hayes crowded in the back with the many boxes and packages. The trunk was filled with a wheelchair and walker.

"Aunt Ellen, you're not thinking of going home, are you?" You couldn't possible manage in your house, what with all the stairs. Anyway, it's way out on the point by the campground and I don't think you will be driving anytime soon. You better come to my place, or maybe Uncle Steve's."

"No thank you, dear. All I could do in the hospital was dream of getting into my own bed. Of course I want to go home. Don't worry, I'm pretty good on that walker. I do think I can manage, but then there is the car." Ellen's voice sounded disappointed. "The doctor did say not to drive for another week."

Mamie spoke up. "Bobbie, maybe I could stay with Mrs. Taggart. Before I retired, I was an aide at Meharry Hospital in Nashville."

Bobbie pounced on the suggestion. It would let her get back to David without having to worry about either woman. "Aunt Ellen, that's perfect. Mrs. Hayes needs to stay in town for another day or two, and I know for a fact she's a good cook. Looks like you've got your own private nurse."

Ellen turned enough to look at the back seat passenger. "If I will not be an inconvenience to you, I would be happy to pay you for your services."

"No indeed, Mrs. Taggart. I owe your sweet niece a lot of favors. I will be happy to help for as long as need be." Mamie beamed at the idea of being needed.

"In that case," Ellen said with a beautiful smile, "please call me Ellen."

Bobbie swung the car in a u-turn.

****

Ahmed set out to explore the area on foot. The sun was pleasant on his shoulders, and lazy bees buzzed among late blooming black-eyed susans growing wild along the gravel road. Used to the unchanging seasons of a latitude near the Great Sahara Desert, he had forgotten how pleasant an early fall day could be. I cannot relax my guard, he reminded himself, though he knew now that he would never go home. He would never see his mother, even one last time; never again work in the little infirmary he had built with the labor of his own hands. For years he had lived life with the knowledge that one day the time would come when he would pay for his crimes. He could not go back to Africa. In fact, he had no place to go. Only the billfold in his pocket held any indication of who he was. His luggage, the new sunglasses, his former life, was all abandoned when he jumped out of Nadja's car. He had no money. He had not worked at the farm long enough to get his pay. Even the credit card in his pocket was useless. It would be traced to the Smithville hospital, but the trail would end there. He patted the still sore arm and looked at the steep, rocky drop to the dark lake water below the road. This is not the time to get maudlin, he thought, but at the same time could not bring his mind to accept where he was.

A long, long time ago he had loved a woman, but when she died with his baby inside her, something in him died too. That was when he began accepting assignments at Ibrahim's urging, taking out his grief and rage on an unsuspecting world. Then, he had not cared if he lived or died.

Now he knew no wife would be waiting for him, no one to wonder what had become of him. When the grief of his loss abated, and the life he led wore thin, he had thought of taking another wife. Just as well he had not. Instead, he had tried to make amends by serving the cause of medicine. The African boy he had sent to school in England was adopted in name only, not legally. The child was young enough to only remember the kindly doctor who had taken him in when his mother died. A trust had been set up to support the boy until his majority. Mentally he shook himself, none of this mattered now. Arrangements were made for his mother's care as long as she lived. The balance of his bank accounts would go to the Djado surgery and research into the AIDS virus. The monies would transfer in thirty days. He had set it up that way. In thirty days, unless he made an appointed contact three days from now, Dr. Ahmed Faziz would cease to exist. All he had to do now was survive that long.

Striding along, Ahmed's reverie had taken him around the bend in the road, probably a half-mile or so from the cabin he had chosen. The roadway under his feet had changed from gravel to blacktop. In the daylight he saw a house he had missed when driving in. It was on the lake side of the road, clinging precariously to the cliff that dropped into the water. This was no cabin. This was stone, glass and huge wooden timbers, set so close to the edge of the water the house was actually hanging over the lake. There was little front yard or grass, just room enough to park a couple of cars on the concrete driveway.

There was no car there now. Ahmed did not hesitate. Whoever owned this house might have left money and clothes. Who knew if it was a weekend hide-a-way, or a permanent residence, it was certainly more prosperous than the poor cabins. The drapes were open and there was no sign of movement inside. He rounded the house to go to the back, and barely stopped in time when he found himself looking at a seventy to eighty foot drop to the lake. Evidently, this point of land bordered the old channel of the Caney Fork River. Eons ago the water had cut through the limestone mountains, leaving sheer cliffs and deep water pools. Ahmed had read as much about the area as he could get his hands on while with the Mexicans. Important when you have to know where to run or hide.

He went back around the front and contemplated the double door main entry. He continued to the other side of the house where a small concrete porch sheltered a back entrance. As he went to the door a gray cat purred against his legs. He reached down to scratch its ears. The cat went to the door before him, sitting expectantly, waiting to get in. "What's the matter, *gato,* no one home to let you in?" He slipped the small knife from his pocket. In a matter of seconds, the door was open.

****

David wasn't any happier about the drive to Knoxville than he had been the first time he was summoned by Jeff's phone call. First, he really wished Bobbie was with him, but he was in enough trouble without countermanding the order the sheriff gave her to go after Ellen. Then there was the car. The only vehicle available in Smithville was an older Metro. After driving a big SUV, the tiny car scared the bejesus out of him. Big trucks blew it all over the roadway, and forget about passing anything. If he lasted the day in what felt like to him, a cardboard box with wheels, it would be a miracle. To make it worse, the shirt and pants Bobbie had picked out for him were too small. They had gone in the give-away bag when he started to bulk up from the gym workouts. Now the waistband of the slacks cut into his stomach, and there was a good two inches from the cuff to the top of his shoe. The shirt stretched a little better, but his shoulders could feel the material strain, and the tail barely tucked into the trousers. By the time he got to Knoxville, he was in as bad a mood as he had ever had. Jeff had better come clean. David had enough mystery to last a lifetime.

The usual paperwork and wait finally got David into a private meeting room where the conversation would be confidential. Jeff ambled into the room, like he had all the time in the world. When he saw David, he grinned, "Well, hello counselor. Got my bail set yet?"

The scowl on David's face should have warned Jeff that things had gone bad. David didn't try to stand, he just motioned for Jeff to sit down. For a moment he didn't say anything, looking at Jeff with almost a sneer. He held out a yellow legal pad with two names written on it. Fischer? Charles? Then he spoke, "Well, which is it?"

Jeff slumped farther down in the chair. "It's Charles," he said without any preliminaries.

David pulled back the pad. "You know I have a legitimate reason to terminate my services. Tell me why I should not do that."

Jeff brought his head up. "Because I didn't kill her."

David sat on his side of the table and stared at Jeff, waiting for an explanation.

Jeff squirmed around in his chair. "Look, David, I did lie to you about a lot of things, and you don't know the half of it. But not about this. You've got to believe me. I never left Smithville that night. I made a phone call sometime towards morning from the market, at the outside pay phone. There will be a record of the call in Houston. I didn't think it was important enough to mention.

David's face did not soften. "Why don't you start all over at the beginning.

Jeff sat for a moment, then put his head down and started to cry.

"Oh, forget it!" David gathered up his papers, stuffed them into his briefcase.

"Please don't go." Jeff was blowing his nose on a paper towel. "Just don't go. I'll tell you everything,-- everything I know."

David let out his breath and returned to the chair. "Why don't you start with Saudi Arabia."

Jeff nodded, blowing his nose again. "I couldn't stand that place. I'm not strong, not strong at all like you. I started using hash to get through the day, then another officer gave me horse, so I could sleep at night. I'm,..., sorry, so very sorry." He blinked and ran a hand over his eyes.

David didn't think he could stand it if Jeff started crying again. Seeing a grown man broken to the point of tears was a sight he didn't want to live with. Even a sorry loser like Jeff. The substances Jeff had named were street slang in the Middle East for hemp and heroin. David himself could testify to the easy availability of the drugs.

Jeff didn't cry again. After clearing his throat, he started talking. He admitted being suckered into the scheme to raise money for the drugs that had swiftly hooked him. When he realized what his confederates were doing, he finally found the courage to turn himself and the conspirators in, but no one would listen to him. The word of a junior officer telling tales on his superior officer was not tolerated. Then things had gone from bad to worse.

Except for the try to right things, which David only half believed, most of what Jeff was saying was a repeat of the reports David had read. Jeff brought it up to date with being released from the hospital. He tried to contact his brother, but never made it past the security officers. He couldn't find his ex-wife, his father was dead, and his brother could not be bothered. He was turned away from the family home by servants he did not recognize. Broken and homeless, he hopped a freight train.

After wandering the country for two years, he sold an article from his experiences as a homeless man to a national magazine. He found himself in East Tennessee, working as a day laborer for the TVA at a nuclear plant, when he began to take an interest in the technology that the National Laboratory produced. Using a Social Security card and name from a man who had died of exposure one extremely cold winter in the cardboard shack they shared in Kansas City, he found a soft touch in Ben Parry. He applied for a job and was hired as a reporter. Ben knew his background only as far as Jeff told him, but was swayed by the excellent writing in the national magazine.

After getting established in Knoxville, he had tried again to see his brother, the senator, to find where his former wife and children were. This time, he made contact.

CHAPTER FOURTEEN

Senator Edgar Charles had not been happy to see his brother. In fact, it was quite a shock to know Jeffery was alive. He had been led to believe the man buried in Denver was his brother. That should have ended it. He had not thought of the younger Charles in quite some time. Now, his brother was not only alive, but standing in front of him.

The setting was not at all acceptable; the entrance to the Marriott Hotel on Michigan Ave. in downtown Chicago. Senator Charles had just capped off a luncheon speech, by accepting the endorsement of the Chicago Tribune for his re-election bid. The press was snapping pictures, the TV cameras rolling, and the nominal crowd, provided by the newspaper, eager to shake hands with him.

Of course it would be hard to recognize the shabby, thin man with a balding head, as the same cocky, handsome young man in uniform they had photographed some eight years ago as he left to serve his country. The Senator took that route. He reached in his pocket, pulled out a fifty dollar bill and made a big show to the press of helping a destitute panhandler, then brushed on past to the waiting limousine. The bodyguards pushed the crowd back and the limo pulled from the curb.

It was enough. Jeffrey, his younger brother was alive, not only alive, but in Chicago where he could contact any number of people who could vouch for him. Charles could not afford to wait. He stopped the car around the corner, and re-entered the hotel by a service door. At the desk, he booked himself into a room, then held out a twenty dollar bill to a bell hop and asked him to give the room number to the shabby man still standing by the outside door.

Jeff had almost thrown the money on the sidewalk, but times were tough for him and the fifty was enough money to get him on the bus back to Tennessee. He didn't know whether he was angry or amused. The look on his brother's face when he realized who Jeff was, had been priceless.

The meeting in the hotel room was brief. The Senator first offered a good deal of money to have Jeff simply disappear again. When Jeff refused and requested his share of the estate left by their father, Edgar laughed in his face. The will was changed when Jeff was hospitalized, making the elder brother his trustee. Now that their father was dead, and Jeff legally dead and buried in Denver, the trust had passed to Jeff's children and Edgar was still the trustee. Jeff had tried blackmail, threatening to go to the newspapers and national magazines. The brother countered with hospitalization on a permanent basis for his unstable younger brother.

141

Jeff knew when he was beaten; the rich, powerful senator could easily sweep him under the rug again and no one would ever be the wiser. According to all reports, he was already officially dead. He went back to Knoxville, his interest in technology, and a few weeks later met Karen Fielding.

He was concentrating on trying to get on with the new life he was making for himself, when early one morning a plain suited man with a Government badge led him to a Suburban truck parked by his apartment door. It was his turn to be surprised when he entered the vehicle with its blacked out windows. His brother sat calmly on the back seat. This time he was offered a deal he could not refuse. Keep an eye on Karen Fielding and the work she did at Oak Ridge. Report to his brother through a contact in Houston on a regular basis, and when the project at the National Laboratory was completed and Karen left the country to return to Israel, the senator would turn the trust fund that belonged to Jeff over to him. He would even tell him where his wife and children had relocated. In other words, he would give Jeff back his former life, if that was what Jeff wanted.

Jeff jumped at the chance. He did not even question the sincerity of his brother's word. After all, they were brothers, and the older had always looked after the younger. Jeff had faithfully kept his end of the bargain, making regular reports on the required schedule.

David sat quiet through the recitation. He didn't know why, but somehow he couldn't quite believe what Jeff was telling him. For one thing, even if the facts were verified by the reports he had read, and the ruthless reputation of Senator Charles preceded him, what did Charles have to do with the Oak Ridge project? Was there a reason that made Karen Fielding more important than the other physicists and researchers working at Oak Ridge, or was it only an effort by Charles to keep track of his brother? Even more important, did the assassination attempt mean the Vice President was somehow mixed up in this?

Jeff had finished, mouth slack, not looking at David. He just sat there, rubbing one hand against the other, staring at the yellow pad with the names boldly scrawled across the middle. Fischer, Charles. David shuffled some of his paperwork around, giving himself time to think.

"You know more about Karen Fielding than you have told me," David stated. He had to reach over with a pencil and prod Jeff to get him to look up.

Jeff straitened with a shrug. "I,…I told you all that I could think of.

"I read the Knoxville paper. You know a lot more about her work than what you told me."

Jeff did look up then, with a sheepish grin. "That newspaper article was a fake. It's fiction, I made it up. Karen didn't tell me any of the technical terms I used. I could guess at some of the new car's technology. For a while I had a source at Arnold Engineering, and I knew that part of what Oak Ridge developed was tested at their facilities. From what Karen did tell me, it wasn't hard to put a few things together." Jeff looked back down at his hands. When he raised his head again he looked squarely at David. There was no smile on his face. "I used her. The story alone could get me back to the big time newspapers. Then there was the deal with my brother. My part of the estate came to a little over thirty million dollars. Even if the courts only named me trustee for my children, the salary would be substantial. Thirty million dollars is a lot of money to control." Jeff nodded slowly, his eyes leaving David and his voice taking on a distant quality. "But more than that, I could be Alan Jeffrey Charles again." He sat up straight and pinned David with a steady gaze. "I didn't love Karen. I did use her David, but I didn't kill her."

David winced. People killed for a lot less than thirty million dollars, but something ticked on the edge of David's mind. That didn't make sense. Why would Jeff kill the only person who could help him get the money, find his children and take back his name and rightful place in society? David still had ambiguous feelings about Jeff. On one hand, he didn't like the man at all, then on the other, he was beginning to sympathize with him. David ran a finger under his too tight collar and felt the material of the shirt stretch over his shoulders. He was feeling really miserable. Maybe he wasn't cut out to be a lawyer after all. Or, maybe he should have specialized in corporate law and have only facts and figures to deal with. People were too complicated. How do you tell the truth from the lies? In the long run, it didn't matter. He was sworn to do the best he could for his client, and unless he cut himself loose from this case, that was exactly what he would do.

David shifted uneasily in his chair. "You want to know something?" He looked back at Jeff with an unwavering gaze of his own. "I could walk away from here and never loose a minutes sleep over you. But I won't. Don't ask me why, but so help me, I'm in for the game." He tapped the legal pad with the names scrawled across the middle. "You know all this will come out at the trial. It's going to be nasty."

Jeff sagged against the table. David pulled the yellow legal pad to him and picked up his pencil. "Okay? So let's get to work."

* * * * *

Ellen heaved a great sigh of relief as she settled herself in the wheelchair. She motioned with her hand to the side of the house. "Let's go in the back. It will be easier with only one step up and goes right into the kitchen. Onward, troops, it's great to be home!" Mamie pushed the chair toward the walk going around from the driveway, white teeth gleaming in her dark, perspiring face. The happy mood of celebration was catching.

Bobbie was certain the black woman had not forgotten her reason for being in this county, but for the time being she knew Mamie wanted to be useful. She started unloading the boxes of gifts, stacking them at the front double doors. She leaned the sturdy metal walker against the side of the entrance porch, then followed the two women to the kitchen entrance.

Inside the house Ahmed had momentarily frozen when he realized a car had pulled into the driveway. He had just finished filling the cat's dish from a can of cat food he found in the refrigerator. The gray cat was happily munching his dinner, purring so loud Ahmed almost didn't hear the sounds at the front of the house. Quickly he found the door to the front hall and peered through the stained glass insets of the double doors. Women! Three of them. It was hard to see through the colored glass, but he recognized the girl in the yellow sweater from the TV news programs. What was she doing here? Then she lifted the wheelchair from the trunk of the automobile. He did not recognize the woman who was helped to the chair, or the stout, African American woman with them. Softly he padded to the staircase and climbed to the exposed balcony. He heard the back door open, and from the voices he knew at least two of the women were entering the house. There might be a window on the balcony level in one of the rooms that opened to the rear, but that could draw attention from outside the house, and he thought of the sheer drop to the lake he had seen from the yard. Where was the girl? He tried to look through the transom windows above the double doors, but could only see the road above the house. He had to take the chance. He slipped back down the stairs, and down two more steps into the sunken living room. Cautiously he peeked out the window with the open drapes. No one. The car sat alone on the driveway. He went to the double doors, needing to quietly as possible exit the house.

It didn't quite work out as he planned. Instead of running lightly to the road, he knocked over a stack of items left at the door. He stumbled over several boxes and grabbing at any handhold brought down a walker with a loud metallic racket. It was enough to swing open the door.

"Oh, dear," the girl said from the doorway. "Are you hurt?"

Ahmed swore softly in Spanish, sat up, then climbed to his feet. "No, Señorita. I am so sorry, I didn't mean to break your things." He laid on the Mexican accent, giving a little bow of apology.

The girl surveyed him up and down as he brushed his clothing. "Is there something I can do for you?"

Ahmed wished for a hat in his hands, so he could appear more humble, but his poor clothes would have to do. There had been a flannel shirt that was way too big for him at the cabin, and he had put it on over his stained tee shirt. He had shaved this morning, taking off the mustache with a disposable razor and had used a toothbrush he found at the cabin. "I am looking for work, *señorita*. Do you own this place?"

The huge black woman loomed behind the girl. "What's this? Everything all right, Bobbie?"

The girl nodded without turning around. "Mamie, would you please ask Aunt Ellen if Tommy from down the road still mows her yard," she said. There wasn't a lot of yard to cut, but it was obvious the lawn needed care. She turned to Ahmed. "If you will wait at the side door, I'll see if my aunt needs help." She picked up several of the boxes that Ahmed had scattered.

"*Por favor, señorita,* allow me." Ahmed gathered several of the packages in his arms, and without waiting for an invitation, strode past Bobbie into the house.

Bobbie picked up another box and entered behind him. He paused in the hallway until Bobbie indicated the door to the rear. Ahmed had rushed from the kitchen before, and from the hall never noticed the room. It was a combination dining and family room with a floor to ceiling glass wall that afforded a magnificent view of the lake. Now, sitting in the wheelchair in front of the view was the most beautiful woman he had ever seen. Pausing for a moment to take in the vision in front of him, he suddenly realized the girl was placing the boxes on the table. He placed his packages along side, and stood, still wishing he had a hat to crumple in his hands. Then his brain kicked in. The girl resembled the woman. The woman in the wheelchair must be the one who had gone down from the rifle in Carthage. He swore to himself again, this time in three different languages.

The black woman was addressing him. "I said, do you speak English?" Like a lot of people her voice was loud. Why do people think volume makes foreigners understand, Ahmed wondered as he turned to her.

"*Si, señora*, very well." Again, he stood and waited. The gray cat, finished with its dinner came in and purred against Ahmed's ankles.

Bobbie took over. "My friend asked for your name." She took a stance to the side, obviously suspicious of the man who had entered uninvited.

Ahmed tried to move away from the cat. "Miguel. Miguel Rios. I would be happy to work off the cost of whatever I broke at your door."

"I doubt anything is broken," Ellen spoke up. "Besides, the kitchen door was open when we got here, and Shadow," she indicated the cat, "had fresh food in his dish, so I guess Tommy has been here. Sorry, but there is nothing else that needs attention right now. Are you staying in the area?"

"*Si, Señora*, a friend has loaned me the use of his cabin down the road. I will go," using his hands in the Mexican manner, he indicated the hall to the front doors. "Perhaps later I can repay you if I have caused damage." Ahmed ducked his head, and backed to the hall. He had to get out of the house before these women pinned him down for more information. With the best smile he could muster, he turned and made for the front doors.

Bobbie followed him to the door. She watched until he turned down the road toward the campground. What was it that was nagging at her? Somehow the man seemed familiar. She picked up the bent walker and went back to her aunt and Mamie.

* * * * *

David spent over three hours with Jeff, writing a volume of notes along with the tape recorder running. Phone numbers, addresses, remembered reports to Houston, and anything else he could wring out of Jeff. When he left, he stopped in the parking lot and dialed the number from Josh Petry's card. In the mood David was in he didn't expect Petry to answer the phone himself, but minor miracles still occur and David made arrangements to meet the lawyer at a restaurant for dinner. The only thing good he could say about the little car he was driving was the gas mileage. Without having to stop for gas, he drove across town to a shop that catered to the handicapped. He found a brown loafer style shoe in his size, then looked for a black dress oxford. He left with his purchase, knowing the match for the shoes would go to a guy who needed only a left shoe. The next stop was the mall, where he bought off the rack slacks and shirts, with a worsted wool sport coat, changing in the dressing room. When he asked the clerk to throw away the old clothes, she smiled shyly, told him to bend down and snipped off a tag he had not seen sticking out the collar of the shirt.

Feeling like he could breath again, despite the crease of fold lines in his clothes, he picked up his cell phone to call Bobbie. No answer at her apartment. He left a message that he would be late getting back to Smithville, then on a hunch called Ellen's house.

Mamie Hayes answered the phone with a professional "Taggart residence. May I ask who is calling?"

David, who was good at recognizing voices, grinned into the phone. The ID window on the phone would name the caller, but the professional voice sounded confident and strong asking for the information. Just what Ellen needed. "Mrs. Hayes, this is David Middleton. Is Bobbie there?"

"Oh, Mr. Middleton. No, she just left here to go meet you. Would you like to speak to Mrs. Taggart?"

"Yes, if it will not disturb her." David grinned again, remembering Ellen's penchant for using formal names. Ellen and Mamie would make a great team. And of course, that left Bobbie free to be with him. His smile got even wider.

Ellen came on the phone in a gush. "Oh, David, it's wonderful to be home. I'm doing just fine, can even walk some. I can't wait to get back to work."

"Don't you hurry," David said. "Take some time and be sure there are no complications with your leg. Besides, it will take a while to get the office back in shape."

"I know," Ellen's voice held sympathy and concern. "Bobbie told me what happened. That poor Mr. Stryker. That's, that's...,"

David interrupted, "I'll tell you all about it soon. I promise. Right now I'm still in Knoxville and I need to reach Bobbie. I'm tied up here for this evening on the Fischer case and won't make it back in time to meet her for supper. Mrs. Hayes said she just left your house. Was she going to her apartment?"

"I'm not sure, David, but if she calls here, I'll give her your message. The same as last time?"

David laughed out loud. "Aunt Ellen, you are something else. It's the same. I love her, and I love you, too." David pushed the call 'end' button on his phone, still laughing.

Life was funny, wasn't it? Life and death were all mixed up. Good and evil, truth and lies, you just had to take what came, when it came. Like love, it had been there all the time. David knew Bobbie had never given up on him. All he ever needed to do was reach out to her, to let her know he cared for her, too. When he finally found the courage, and she had not rejected the maimed, disfigured, and yes, the handicapped man he was, that was when he began to live again. David did a quick mental inventory of all that had happened in the last few days. Threats and tragedy were nothing new to him. He had been to hell and back. Bobbie was right, and dear God, he loved her for it. He had tried to hide from the world, to push life aside. But the choice was not his. God had given him brains as well as legs, and if he had to lose a part of himself..., well, he had the best of that deal. When the facts came out, the Fischer, he was still calling Jeff by the name Fischer, the trial would be mega news. I CAN do it, he thought, building his confidence. I think I can, I think I can, I KNOW I can, like the little train, he hummed. David was still humming as he pulled the small car into a narrow parking space left open by larger vehicles close to the entrance of the restaurant. Josh Petry was waiting for him at the door, but already on the list for a table. The two men shook hands as the hostess led the way inside.

Petry was fairly bursting at the seams. "I kept trying to call your office today. I kept getting a message that your phones are no longer in service. What's the problem? Can't pay your bill?"

David thought Josh didn't know how close to the truth he had come, but he appreciated the fact that the voice held a hint of humor. "Uh, no, not exactly," he answered while searching for a piece of paper. The only paper napkin was under his water glass. He extracted the soggy material and wrote his mobile phone number on it, then thinking again, he added Ellen's number. He stopped short of listing Bobbie's phone. "Someone with a grudge against me tore up my office and apartment last night. I haven't had time to do more than file a claim with my insurance agent. Has something come up?"

Petry took the soggy napkin and spread it out on the table cloth. "Sorry to hear somebody's got it in for you." The waiter brought their salads, and Petry paused until the man moved away. "Do you know who your client is?" he said, quietly stirring his iced tea.

David silently blessed Buddy Adams for breaking that information to him, but thought he would play it cool until he knew where Petry was leading. "Of course. He's a reporter for the Knoxville newspaper, the former lover of the victim, the alleged killer, arrested and currently being held in jail while awaiting arraignment for the crime."

Petry held up his hand. "This is serious, David, don't kid around. Big trouble. The fingerprints were identified, but nobody named Fischer owns them."

David felt the urge to brag, but Petry was treating him with courtesy. The prosecutor could have withheld the information until the pre-trial discovery summaries were ready for David. "You didn't let me finish, Josh. My client is also the previously presumed dead brother of Senator Edgar Charles. His name is Alan Jeffery Charles. The social security number and name Fischer belonged to a homeless man who died of exposure in Kansas City."

Petry was nonplused. "So, what are you going to do?"

"If you mean am I going to drop the case, the answer is no." David forked lettuce into his mouth.

Petry leaned back from the table and a look close to admiration curved a smile on his face. "I should have known a scrawny football player that never worried about the big linebackers wouldn't let any of the Washington top guns scare him off. You know, I was all set to handle this case, now the DA himself wants it." Petry worked on his salad, chewing with concentrated effort. He kept quiet, eating silently for a moment, then said, "I envy you, David. You've got the chance of a lifetime."

"If I can pull it off, you mean." David pushed the salad dish aside as the waiter put mouthwatering manicotti, swimming in marinara in front of him. He loved this restaurant and Italian food. Maybe he could take Bobbie to Rome for their honeymoon. IF he could pay his phone bill by then. IF he could pull off the trial. Both men ate in silence for a moment.

David reached for the bread basket. "I've got to do this, Josh. You're right, it's my chance in more ways than one. But I need help. My few hours of court appearances consist of domestic cases, some petty theft, an occasional assault and one case of cow rustling."

Petry looked bland for a moment, then exploded with laughter. "Cow what? Oh, that's rich. If I weren't married and about to become a daddy, dammed if I wouldn't go to work for you. Hey, I never got to play football on the team, but I can still run pretty good interference." He wiped his eyes and mouth with the napkin, then sobered again. "You've got to tell me all about the cow sometime, but why did you call me today?"

David scraped the last of the ricotta cheese from his plate. "I was going to feel you out about my client, to see if you knew his real name, then ask for your help in getting a reasonable bail. Now, I think I've changed my mind. I really don't know why my office was trashed or who wants to kill me. Maybe it's connected, maybe not. Maybe the safest place for Jeff right now is in jail. I've got another client, too, that's possibly...," David hesitated. He would leave Orville out of it for now, at least until he could get hold of Buddy Adams again.

"Wait," Petry held up the spoon from his coffee cup. "You said 'kill you'? Somebody attempted to murder you? And you are sitting here calmly eating spumone?"

David looked at the melting ice cream, and suddenly it resembled the blood soaking into the oak floor of the hall when he found Pete Stryker. He threw down the spoon. "A man was killed. The Sheriff thinks the intruder thought it was me." The enthusiasm of a few minutes ago evaporated. David put his hand to his head. Even the productive session with Jeff paled as he thought of the tangled web he had around him. He was sure Josh Petry could see right through the bravado he was putting on. No, he thought, I won't quit. I never quit on the football field until I was brought down, then I got up again, and again, and again. I just need some time to figure this out.

David realized the waiter had handed the bill to Petry. "Give me the tab, Josh, I invited you."

Petry handed the waiter a credit card and waved him away. "Pay your phone bill, counselor. I might need to call you. You do plan to be at the hearing tomorrow?"

"I'll be there. And, Josh, thanks."

"Hey, call it payback. You were what kept me in college. You called me friend back then." Petry held the door open for David as they walked out into the setting sun.

* * * * *

149

Ahmed sat on the deck of the cabin and watched the sun's reflection on the rippled surface of the lake. Lost in thought, he began to notice the bright image was sinking into the shadows. The air was cooler and beginning to feel damp. A pickup truck backed a trailer onto the ramp for a waiting boat. Neither of the men with the truck looked up at the houses above the access area.

Lassitude had settled on Ahmed after he walked away from the house and the women. He knew he should get away while he could, but where to go? There were still ideas nipping at his mind that he needed to think through. Nadja never worked alone, and money was the only incentive she needed to kill. Causes and ideologies meant nothing to her. Ibrahim Hassim thought he was helping the Palestinian cause, though he could be as cold blooded as the Russian. How was Zero involved? Had the man really been a double agent between Moscow and Washington? Zero had to be at least twenty years younger than Ahmed. He had come into the game late, only a few years before the fall of the Berlin wall. During that time every operative in Europe had known they were in danger of being exposed. There was still plenty for them to do, what with trying to stay ahead of each other's governments, but the game was over, with agents dropping out like flies. Somehow, he and Zero had survived, to meet in South America a year later. But what had the diminutive agent done since then?

Ahmed's mind came back to the present as the Park Ranger, driving his white government truck turned into the boat ramp area. He melted further back in the shadows of the covered deck. Earlier, he had seen the girl from the house drive slowly past on the gravel road. The girl from Carthage. He had read her easily when he entered the house with the packages. She didn't buy his story. She was suspicious and would cause trouble. Then again, maybe she was his answer. He would have to think about it.

CHAPTER FIFTEEN

Bobbie parked the car before the café on the square, waiting for David to join her. When she left Ellen's she went straight to the Sheriff's office without stopping at her apartment. Sure enough, Steve had torn up her request for leave time. I'll have to report to work in the morning, she thought, with a little regret. She knew David expected to spend the night at her apartment, the only place he had to go unless he rented a motel room. A smile quirked her mouth. Maybe that wasn't such a bad idea. She knew a place out on the lake where they had mirrors on the ceiling, and…, well, she hadn't stayed there of course, just seen it when she and another deputy were sent to put down a disturbance. She sat in the car as dusk settled over the courthouse. Parked on the opposite side of the courthouse from David's building, she couldn't see the shattered glass and boarded up door. She shuttered just thinking about it. What if it had been David in the hall instead of Pete Stryker? I've only now broken through his reserve, she told herself, and the very thought of losing him left her desolate.

Speaking of David, where was he? It was past time for him to meet her. She hoped he hadn't run into trouble in Knoxville. Dear Lord, the man needed a keeper. Someone wanted him dead, and he went traipsing around the country by himself. HE thought SHE needed protecting. Getting out of the car Bobbie entered the café and ordered a roast beef sandwich, then on second thought made it two to go, in case David hadn't eaten. Paying the tab, she asked the cashier if David might have called and left her a message. No, but if he did, the girl replied with a smirk, she would be glad to tell him Bobbie asked.

I'll bet you would, Bobbie thought as she thanked her with a polite nod. She knew the girl had eyes for David and flirted with him every chance she got. Not only that, there were a few more women in town who would gladly trade places with Bobbie. David didn't realize what a striking man he was, even with only one leg. He stood straight and tall, making no apology for his handicap and all he ever had to do was smile to melt women. Bobbie allowed herself a moment to indulge in jealousy. If the troubles that plagued them now kept them from the preacher, it was really the commitment that mattered. She had waited long enough. Tonight, and every night from now on they would sleep in the same bed. Not that she didn't want to marry David, she did with all of her heart, but I'll take him any way I can get him, she thought. The sooner, the better.

Putting the Styrofoam boxes of food in the car on the floor of the front passenger seat, she started the engine and drove to her apartment. I forgot to ask Steve about my car, she thought as she parked the larger vehicle close to

151

her entrance. She had opened the car door when suddenly Bobbie felt like a dash of ice water hit her in the face. Something wasn't right. She glanced around the parking area, where most of the apartment residents were already home from work and parked in their usual spots. A couple of strange cars, but nothing out of the ordinary. She still had that prickly feeling, like eyes were on her. More than a little spooked, she tucked her hand in the side pocket of the handbag and released the safety on her Policewoman Special. Keeping her hand on the gun in the bag, she pushed the car door with her left hand and edged from the vehicle. This time she took a good look around. No one in sight. Daylight faded fast this time of year and the short sunset was gone. Only a couple of street lights farther down the building illuminated the area, but the light at the entrance door was only a few yards away. Wanting to seem natural she made herself walk to the door when what she really wanted to do was sprint to the safety of her own apartment. Still no one. Maybe I'm just edgy, she thought, with all that's been going on and seeing David's apartment, but she breathed a sigh of relief when no one was in the hall and she opened her own door.

No! Bobbie stopped, then silently closed the door. Someone was in the apartment. Light spilled out of the small kitchen into the dining area and dim living room. Bobbie inched closer to the dining area, now holding the automatic at ready by her shoulder. The refrigerator door was open and a man had his head stuck in the space. Bobbie leveled the gun. "Stop!" Her voice meant business. "Turn around and put your hands up!"

The man did stop, but didn't turn around. "Jesus, girl, don't you keep any food here?" He continued to move bottles of pickles, catsup, and a tub of margarine.

Exasperated, Bobbie lowered the gun. "I left roast beef sandwiches in the car, Buddy, but I'm not about to go back after them."

Buddy Adams stood up straight, his usual grin revealing his prominent teeth. "Hey, sugar, I knew you wouldn't starve an old friend. Where's your car?"

"Wait, there's someone out there. I didn't see them, but I could feel them watching. After what happened at David's I'm not taking any chances. Besides, what do you think you're doing here? Just how did you get in?"

Buddy displayed his toothy grin again, "Easy. This morning I helped myself to that extra key you keep hanging on the hook under your sink. Figured you might need some help. That hard-head you're in love with thinks he can do it all by himself. Where is he, by the way?"

"David went to Knoxville to talk to Jeff Fischer. He should have been back to meet me in town at the café. Let me go check my answering machine." Bobbie turned back to the living room with Buddy right behind her.

The message light was blinking. Bobbie pressed play and listened to Ellen's call, then Steve, then finally David telling her he was detained in Knoxville and would miss their supper date, but meet her later at her apartment.

"Oh shit," Buddy mouthed and sprinted for the door. Bobbie grabbed her .45 and followed on the run. At the outside door he stopped and let her catch up. The small caliber gun appeared in his hand from somewhere. "Give me your car keys. Stay here and back me up. Which car is it?"

"The blue Park Avenue two spaces over." Bobbie handed him the keys. "The sandwiches are on the front passenger side floor." She watched Buddy go out the door and saunter toward the car like he was out for an evening stroll.

He deliberately went to the wrong car, looked over the parking lot then called loudly, "Hey, babe, where'd you park our car?"

Bobbie didn't know if she was supposed to answer or not, but called back, "The next car, dummy!" Maybe Buddy wanted to let the watchers know he wasn't alone. He's good, she thought, wonder if he really is who he says he is?

Buddy retrieved the food, then stood trying to balance the boxes in his arms. After a few minutes of juggling while he surveyed the parked vehicles again, he turned back to the building door. "Meals on wheels, little lady," he yelled and pushed Bobbie ahead of him to her door.

"Did you see anyone?" Bobby turned the bolt on the door, then added the chain.

Buddy went to the table and put the food down. "Yeah, it's the Feebees."

"Who? Feebees? Oh, you mean the FBI. How do you know who they are? Why would they be here?"

Buddy shrugged as he took a sandwich from a box. He did have the grace to look a little apologetic. "Don't mind, do you?" He took a big bite, then said through the meat, "Two men in suits and ties, sitting in the white car down almost to the light pole. You couldn't see them past that pickup truck. That's their style, sit and wait, now that the public can sue if they rough up somebody. Probably waiting for David. If it was you they wanted, they would have stopped you when you got out of the car." He reached for a French fry.

Bobbie went to her kitchen, put a pot of coffee to drip, then opened the other sandwich box. Buddy continued to eat without adding more to the conversation. Bobbie twisted her napkin and arranged the food twice, never taking a bite.

"Relax, girl. Your man can handle it. He's a lawyer, remember." Buddy went to fetch the coffee and cups.

"He's a lawyer somebody is trying to kill." Bobbie shivered as she accepted coffee. "You're the expert. Aren't you going to do something about them."

Buddy grinned. "What you want me to do? Go introduce myself? They got as much right to be here as I have and I'm not about to blow my cover. Besides, I'll bet you they just want to talk. That's David's department, right?"

Bobbie finally began to eat, "We just sit and wait, too?"

"Best idea I've heard in a long time." Buddy picked up the other half of his sandwich.

* * * * *

David drove the little Metro into the parking area and settled for a spot marked VISITOR. He extracted himself from the small vehicle and righted himself with his crutches Sliding the strap to his stuffed briefcase over his shoulder, he started across to Bobbie's building. He saw a man get out of a white car on that side of the complex, but thought nothing of it until the man turned in his direction.

"Mr. Middleton? David Middleton?"

For some reason David did not stop walking. "Yes. What is it I can do for you?"

The man kept pace with David. He flipped open a billfold. "FBI. We'd like a word with you. Do you have an apartment here?"

David stopped out in the driveway, "I gave a statement to the agent with the Vice President, then again at the Sheriff's office in Smithville. I don't have anything to add to it." David didn't know why, something was pushing him to be rude. "If you don't mind, this briefcase is heavy and I've had a long day."

"Sir," the agent was the soul of politeness, "let me help you. Could we go inside and talk?" Before David could object, the briefcase was pulled off his shoulder. He had to let go of a crutch, upsetting his balance.

David hopped sideways to keep from falling. The agent jumped, then realized David was not trying to escape. "Sorry, sir. I didn't mean to startle you. We only want to talk to you about your client, Alan Jeffery Charles." The man stooped to pick up David's crutch and handed it to him.

David grimaced as he balanced himself between the crutches, "What is there to discuss? I know who he is, and who his brother is. That doesn't change the fact that he deserves counsel. I have agreed to represent him."

"Of course, of course." The agent motioned David to follow him to the sidewalk. "However, I must warn you there is more involved. There may not be a trial."

David was taken by surprise. He stopped dead still at the curb. "On what grounds? Surely a man who has never been convicted of anything, much less being a traitor, is assured a fair hearing."

"It could be the charges will be dropped. After all most of them are circumstantial at best. Do we have to stand out here to discuss this? If you invite us in, we won't take much of your time." The agent moved in the direction of the entrance.

"As far as I can see, we have nothing to discuss, so if you will excuse me, I need to get to work on this case." David stubbornly refused to move.

The agent turned back to David. "Mr. Middleton, like they always say, you can make this easy or hard. It's your choice. If we cannot discuss this here, you will have to come with us."

David didn't like the way the conversation was going. "Do you have a warrant for my arrest?"

"No sir, not at this time, but I can get one if you prefer."

"And what would the charges be?" David was thoroughly puzzled. He tried to keep his voice calm and on the same plane so the agent would not know David was thinking of Bobbie. For all he knew, this could be a set up. He didn't want them to pick her up, too.

"Sir, this is a matter of national security. I'm asking for your cooperation." Another agent joined the first on the sidewalk.

"Fine," David said. "Let's go down to the sheriff's office and get this straightened out."

The men made no comment, just turned with David between them and headed toward the white car. A rear door was opened and Agent number one joined David in the back. The other man got behind the wheel and switched on the headlights. David caught a glimpse of Buddy Adams as the headlights swept the building entrance door when they backed out of the parking space. Somehow, he wasn't surprised.

Out on the highway they passed the turn to the square and the sheriff's office.. David pointed it out to the driver, who ignored him and continued on past the outskirts of the town to the road with the sign pointing to the airport. David was more than apprehensive. The small field was used mostly by Tennessee Wildlife Resource for aerial reconnaissance helicopters. A couple of charter planes were based there and several would be pilots who built ultra-lights flew off and on. It did have a jet length runway for daytime use. Even so, David was surprised to see a small Lear on the tarmac.

The car pulled up to the aircraft, to be met by another suit and tie carrying a rifle over his shoulder. Now David was beginning to be just plain scared. A knot formed in this stomach. The agent in the seat with him prodded him to exit the vehicle and followed with David's briefcase. To make matters worse, lightning crackled to the west as thunder clouds rolled overhead, obscuring what stars had shed a little light on the scene.

At the aircraft David had to stop and hook his crutches on his wrists as he used his hands to pull himself up the door steps into the plane. Adjusting the crutches again, he moved to where a distinguished looking man sat on a leather arm chair in the lounge area. A table in front of him held snacks, liquor bottles, glasses and a copy of the Knoxville Chronicle. David had no problem recognizing his host.

The man rose. "Mr. Middleton. Please forgive this intrusion to your evening. I would have come to you, if you had agreed to discuss this matter at your apartment. Please be seated. It is very important that we talk." He did not extend his hand, eyeing David's crutches.

David still had that gut feeling of danger, but sat in a matching chair opposite the table. Talking was one of the things he did the best. "One of your men said it concerned national security, Senator Charles. Surely you don't think your brother is still involved in treason."

The Senator remained standing. "Would you care for something to drink? No? Okay, let's get to the brass tacks. Jeff always was a whiner. Always took the easy way. I was surprised he survived two years on the streets. But to answer your question, yes, perhaps unwittingly as before he could be involved again. Also, before you ask, I'll tell you I don't believe he is capable of cold blooded murder, but there is another side to him that can be devious, to say the least."

The Senator poured himself a whiskey, cut it with water, then sat in the chair. He pointed to the newspaper, "What did he tell you?"

David shook his head, "Sorry, privileged information. Attorney, client, you know, but to set your mind at ease, he did tell me of your agreement with him. We talked for a long time. He filled in some blanks, most of it pretty much what is in the newspaper." David folded his hands, wondering what was coming next. "Except for the fact, which I am sure you already know, the new engine developed in Oak Ridge is worth mega-millions to whoever puts it on the market first. Is that what you consider a threat to the nation?"

Charles sipped his drink, then reached for a handful of peanuts. "What you say is true. The technology is worth all of that and more, much more. However, who has the vehicle first on the market is not the threat to national security. Jeff didn't tell you anything about that?"

The fact that Charles asked the question puzzled David. He almost said no, then decided to play it cagey. "I spent three hours with Jeff today. He told me a lot of things. None of which I can reveal to you. Your man also said there might not be a trial. With the evidence the prosecutors have, arraignment is a shoo in. Not even you can stop it."

Charles let out a sigh. "Maybe so, but you don't even know the half of it. The point I want you to get is that it would be to your best interest to withdraw from the case. I know about the destruction to your office and the dead postman. You don't begin to know what you are up against. You would be wise to stay as far from my brother as you can. More happened in Saudi Arabia than what is in any of the reports I am sure you have already seen." Charles paused when he saw the look in David's eyes. "No, it wasn't my men who ransacked your place. I don't have to resort to violence of that sort."

No, David thought, he doesn't, not when he has the FBI to run errands for him. He hooked his crutches on his wrists and stood up. "Much as I have enjoyed this visit, I must be going. I have a lot of work to do tonight. Oh, there was one thing Jeff apparently didn't know. It didn't seem important or make any difference to him, he just wanted to get his life back, but why did you single out Karen Fielding? Why was Jeff to keep track of her?"

The Senator stood facing David. A finger brushed the neat mustache on his lip, hesitating like he was trying to decide whether to answer. He lowered his hand, then spoke. "Because she was the one involved in treason. Don't believe everything my brother tells you." He reached to the table then handed David a business card. "If you learn more, or have need of me do not hesitate to call." He turned his back on David and went through a door to the rear of the cabin.

Buddy Adams relaxed when he saw David descend from the Lear. The old muscle car responded to the key when the government sedan left the airport. Buddy waited a few more moments in the dark to the side of a hangar. The Lear was buttoning up, preparing for takeoff. The airport night watchman pulled the chocks, and the running lights came on as thunder sounded from the west. Buddy shivered, remembering a few fast liftoffs he had made from uncontrolled airports. As the plane turned to taxi to the runway, Buddy could read the tail number on the otherwise unidentified aircraft. Private, he thought, or maybe military from the stock used by OSI. He tucked the number away in his memory. A phone call would give him the information he wanted.

* * * * *

Bobbie opened the door for David, then burst into tears. David set his briefcase on the floor and pulled her into his arms. "Honey, what's wrong?"

Her words were muffled as she sobbed against his shoulder. "I, umph,I jus, I jus luv you so much."

"Is that any reason to cry? Hey now, lil'bit, hush and blow your nose so I can kiss you." David edged back to the wall for balance, so he could unhook a crutch and tilt her face to him. Tears ran down her cheeks and nose. She just burrowed her face back into him and sobbed harder.

"Come on, honey, let's sit down and you can tell me what is bothering you." David hopped with one crutch and an arm around Bobbie toward the sofa.

Bobbie grabbed a couple of tissue from a box on the end table and blew her nose. "David, where have you been?"

He sank to the sofa, pulling her with him. His heart was doing double time. He couldn't stand to see her cry. "I left you a phone message, honey. Didn't you get it?"

Bobbie was getting control of herself. "I heard the message, David, then I saw those men put you into the car. If it hadn't been for Buddy, I would have panicked." Tears were threatening at her lashes again. "You must think I'm a ninny." A sob caught in her throat. "I can't lose you, David. I won't lose you. Promise, promise me we won't separate again."

David sat holding her to him. He wanted with all that he was worth to tell her what she wanted to hear, but it was not possible. He followed her backbone with a finger. "What's this, kitten? Two days ago you were spitting mad because I wanted you where I could see you." He raised her chin with the finger and tried a smile. "Bobbie, you know that's not good right now. I've got work to do and so have you. We'll stick together as much as we can, but I can't make that promise." Then it was his turn to be emotional. "God, don't you know I won't let anything happen to you. It works both ways, sweetheart. I don't want to lose you, either."

Bobbie's voice was small. "David, you're squeezing me."

He laughed then, but loosened his grip. "You're hugging me just as hard. Fine pair we make. A little bit of trouble and we go to pieces. Speaking of Buddy, I saw him at the door when I went with the FBI. What was he doing here?"

"He took my extra key this morning. He was here when I gave up on you to meet me for supper and came home. I didn't get your message until then. Buddy said he came just in case you needed help. I don't know how he knew they were FBI, but he followed you when you drove off with those men. Didn't you see him?"

"No, but guess where I went? To the airport." Bobbie looked as if she might break into tears again, so David hastened to add, "Not to catch a plane, but I did get on one."

Bobbie snuffed. "David, make sense. You went to the airport, got on a plane, but didn't go anywhere?"

David was enjoying her confused look, but decided he had teased enough. He claimed the kiss he had wanted earlier. "Oh, baby, you make a man want to spend the day in bed," he breathed into her mouth.

"I'll settle for the night," she breathed back, "if you will tell me the rest of what happened at the airport."

David released her and went to retrieve his briefcase. He set it on the dining table and pulled out a chair. "I had a talk with Senator Edgar Charles, or rather, he had a talk with me."

Bobbie gathered up the Styrofoam boxes from her and Buddy's supper. "So? Keep talking, I'm listening."

"Do you have anything cold to drink?" David knew he was stalling. How much should he tell her? He had no idea what national security had to do with the Oak Ridge project, but apparently that was why he was in danger. It wasn't hard to figure out that Charles thought Jeff might have told him more than he did. Jeff had not mentioned Karen's involvement with anyone else, so where did the treason come in? Come to think of it, David knew he had missed an opportunity to get some of his own questions answered. All of this was just getting him in deeper and deeper.

Bobbie handed David a canned cola. He popped the top and took a swig before he looked at her. She raised an eyebrow like a question mark as he took another drink. She was in control now that the tears had passed. David knew she was scared. He was scared too, but he knew that she would be there for him when push came to shove, same as he would do for her. She was his mate and partner. She needed to know everything he knew.

"The Senator advised me to drop his brother's case. Said there might be treason involved, but didn't explain why it was a danger to national security. Something to do with Oak Ridge and Jeff's girl friend, Karen Fielding. I didn't play it too smart, lil'bit. I clamed up, claimed client attorney privileges, when I should have gone on the attack."

Suddenly David shoved the briefcase away from him. Anger colored his face. "Of all the rotten…"

Bobbie was at his side in a flash. "What is it, David?"

"Those SOB's took my notes from this afternoon." He held the yellow legal pad with CHARLES, FISCHER, scrawled on the first page. Several sheets behind it were missing. "And my recorder!"

"Can you remember what you need, David, or will you have to go to Knoxville again tomorrow?" Bobbie peered into the paperwork littering the table.

"I wasn't planning on going anywhere tomorrow, but Petry told me Jeff's arraignment was moved up and is scheduled for 10:00am. I have to be in Knoxville for that. Shouldn't take more than an hour. I need to see about Orville, and check with Judge Jenkins for Mrs. Hayes. I need to find someone who can retrieve at least part of the files from my computers, if possible, and I have to have a place to work. It's a full day. By the way, it was a stroke of genius to put Ellen and Mamie together."

Bobbie grinned. "Well, thanks, but they kind of settled it themselves. You know how stubborn Aunt Ellen can be. She wanted to stay in her own house and Mamie retired as a nurses aide so it worked out fine. There was something, though. An older man, a Mexican, knocked on the door as soon as we got there. Said he was looking for work and staying in a nearby cabin." Bobbie jumped up. "I think I will call and make sure they are all right." She reached for the phone.

Ellen and Mamie were glad to hear from Bobbie and know David was back from Knoxville. No, they didn't need her to bring the car back tonight. Everything was fine out on the lake, not to worry, but didn't David want to come out and use the spare bedroom? No, Bobbie told Ellen, he had work spread out all over her dining table and they would make do with the bedrooms here. Bobbie heard Ellen's giggle as she hung up. Uncle Steve, now Aunt Ellen knew she and David hadn't waited for a preacher. Bobbie sighed, that's what comes from living in a small town close to your relatives.

David was immersed in what notes he had left, so Bobbie went to put on her pajamas. She added a chenille robe and fuzzy slippers in case Buddy decided to come back, then curled up on the sofa with a book.

* * * * *

Ahmed Faziz relinquished his rocker on the deck. It was full dark now and he had been idle long enough. A through search of the cabin turned up five one dollar bills tucked away inside an empty pet food can in the refrigerator. He had helped himself to fish from the freezer and canned goods for a meal, but had run out of coffee. There was small bait shop and grocery store on the corner of the main highway. Surely he could get there and back without notice. The day use access area was deserted now, but left open for night fishermen. No light showed from any of the other cabins. He would get the car from the shed and have coffee for tomorrow, and maybe get a little news on the radio or at the store. Tomorrow would have to be his last day here. Keeping on the move was the best way to survive. He thought of the beautiful woman in the large house. He would like to stay. It was pleasant here in this part of the world, so unlike the land of his voluntary exile. He sighed. He would pay the price for his sins. There would be no home for him.

He drove the car to the boat ramp in the access area and splashed mud on the sides and wheels, then made sure dirt covered the license plate and back bumper. Many of the cars he saw in the Mexican compound looked like they were never washed. No one would notice him. He drove to the little grocery store.

CHAPTER SIXTEEN

The store was poorly stocked. Half empty shelves, concerned more with fishing bait than food, lined a narrow aisle. Ahmed settled for a jar of instant coffee. Item in hand, he started to the check out when headlights flashed through the front window. He back peddled to the far side of the small market where vending machines were located. A bell called attention to the door as it opened for a huge man in the uniform of a Deputy Sheriff.

"Hey, Jim Ed. How's it going tonight." The clerk reached behind him for a pot of perked coffee and poured it in a paper cup.

The Deputy took the cup. "All's quiet on the western front," he said as he lounged against the counter. "What's biting out at the lake?"

"Walleye, mostly. Some crappie and bass. Hey, did you know the big fall fishing tournament starts tomorrow?"

"Yeah," the big man responded. "Means I'll be working around the clock keeping those knuckle heads from killing each other. Anybody coming in that I know?"

"Tommy Marsh and that bunch. You know, the ones that own those cabins by the day use. They'll fish all day, then get drunk as skunks. Mean bunch of SOB'S. Glad all I have to do is sell 'em bait."

The deputy made the appropriate disgusted face, then tossed the paper cup in a waste basket. "See you later." He saluted with two fingers and went out the door.

Ahmed brought his jar of coffee to the counter. "Many people tomorrow? Good business for you? Many strangers stop to ask about the fishing?"

"Yeah," the clerk rang up his total. "I sell more bait than anyone else around. You want a sack?"

Ahmed picked up the coffee. "No, is good. Maybe I stop tomorrow for some worms." He ducked his head goodnight and headed for the door.

Another car swung into the parking lot. Ahmed turned back. "You got *azucar*? I forget, sugar?." He quickly went between the shelves, as a stocky man with a bushy brown beard came into the store. Ahmed froze in place, as he recognized the used car lot manager, the one who sold him the green Pontiac.

The man pulled out a rolled up poster, one from town with Ahmed's pictures. "You seen this man?"

The store clerk didn't like the tone of voice, or the abrupt manner of the inquiry. He pointed to the pictures. "A Deputy Sheriff was just in here. If I see that man, I'll tell him."

The stocky man re-rolled the poster. A nasty grin spread over his face. "Can he make that information worth your while?"

The clerk did an about face. "Doesn't say there's a reward. You want it bad enough to pay for it?"

"What's it matter to you, as long as I pay. Say fifty bucks if you tell me, not the deputy."

"Sure," the clerk said. "Make it a hundred, and I'll even keep my mouth shut to that Mex over there."

Bushy beard turned to see Ahmed crouched behind the canned goods. "Hey you! Hey you, greaser! Yeah, I'm talking to you. Can't you hear. Get your butt over here."

Ahmed pulled his oversized shirt collar higher and moved to the end of the shelf. "What you want, *señor*? I got to go. *Mi amigos* wait in the car." He laid the accent on, thick and heavy.

"You seen this man?" Bushy beard held the poster up.

"No, *señor*, I see no one." Ahmed ducked his head, mumbling a few Spanish words under his breath, while cowering back by the shelves.

"Hah, don't have a green card, huh?" The man turned back to the clerk and slapped down a business card. "You see this man, call me. Fifty for the call. If I get my hands on him, a hundred it is." He sauntered out of the store.

Ahmed fumbled around with his purchases until the car pulled out on the road. He paid for the sugar and quickly went to the car, feeling the cool night air dry his sweat drenched shirt.

He swore again. He had to get out of this area. Now. There wouldn't be time to make plans. He needed money, a credit card, something that would get him on a bus, train, or plane. He had already made a through search of the cabin. A visit to the other cabins on the road might be in order. The only other possibility he could think of was the large house with the beautiful woman.

By the time this passed through his mind he was turning on the road to the cabin. Allah, help him. Lights blazed from several of the cabins above the lake. Two pickup trucks with boats in tow, were parked beside the house he had used.

Seething with the frustrated feelings that increased with every turn of recent events, he backed the car around to the day use area. A dash light flashed in his eyes and his attention went to the red symbol of a gasoline pump. Now what? Then he realized the automobile was warning him it was almost out of gas. That did it. He might as well call the Sheriff himself. Becoming increasingly angry by the minute, he drove back up the hill toward the main highway.

Sustained by the anger, thoughts from years past filled his mind. He hadn't survived these many years by giving up. He swung the car around in a wide spot in the road. Dr. Ahmed Faziz might cease to exist, but Miguel Rios was alive and well, for the moment anyway. He turned on the lakeside road again, doused the lights and pulled the car to a stop in front of the big glass, rock and timber house. It was still early evening, so surprisingly the front of the house was dark. Then he remembered the family living areas were to the rear. A shed like building loomed on the opposite side of the road. Making sure no other traffic was coming, he left the car in the road and tried the door of the shed. It opened easily. One side of the interior was occupied by a riding lawn mower, but there was plenty of room for the small car. Checking the house again, he pulled the car into the space, closed the door, then settled in the back seat for a nap.

* * * * *

Bobbie put the book aside and stretched. "David, it's past eleven. I've got to go to work tomorrow. Are you coming to bed?"

"You go on, honey. Give me a few more minutes, then I'll be in."

She watched for a moment while he scribbled on the yellow pad. "David?"

"Yeah?" he answered without looking up. When she didn't respond, he raised his head. Bobbie was standing in the hallway, one hand reached out to brace herself against the wall. She had on a two sizes too big wrap around robe, older than he was, with oversized fuzzy slippers. Her curly hair was tousled and loose over her shoulders, making her look like a child. "Yeah," he said again, "what's the matter, honey?"

"Come to bed, David. Please."

"Need somebody to tuck you in?"

"Not somebody. You. I need you, David."

David felt himself beginning to be aroused. It had happened so many times before. Before he told her he loved her. Before he asked her to marry him. All he ever had to do was look at her. Now he knew she would not reject him, even crippled and missing a part of himself. He let the sensation blaze through him, while he put the papers in order and back in the briefcase. The pencil followed. David savored the notion of making slow, sensual love to Bobbie. When he looked up again she was twisting the ends of the robe's belt.

He couldn't resist teasing her. "Bobbie, come here," he beckoned with his seductive Hollywood leading man smile. Her walk to him was as sexy as if she wore nothing instead of the old robe. "Here," he told her. "Put your hand here." He guided her hand to the bulge at his crotch. "The only tucking I'm going to do is with this," he chuckled in a deep, husky voice.

163

Bobbie rubbed her fingers over the fabric covering him, then pinched him, hard. "Why did you make me ask?" she smiled sweetly, then sped down the hall to the bedroom. David was close behind her.

* * * * *

Ahmed woke up right on schedule. He had set his internal timer for two hours. This acquired ability was an asset in his former profession and served as well when he was the only doctor for miles around. He sat up and worked a kink out of his leg from where it had lain on the car seat. He felt rested, another asset from his ability to nap. He checked his glow in the dark watch. 11:00pm. Not very late by most standards. A peek out the door showed no changes in the house across the street. Nothing on the road, either. He would wait another hour, then see if he could gain entrance to the house. Surely someone prosperous enough to own such a place would have cash on hand, or at least a credit card.

Slipping from the garage, Ahmed decided to check on the cabins again. He really didn't want to disturb the beautiful lady or her large friend, and it occurred to him that someone else, possibly the woman deputy, might very well be in the house, too. Trotting down the road, he reached the cabins and approached a mobile home with a built on room and porch. He could see through the window, four men sitting around a table, cards held in their hands. Poker chips and beer cans were piled by each man. Not good. Ahmed looked for another cabin. He saw a dark outline down the road and headed for it. He was nearly to the walkway when a dog started growling and barking loud enough to wake the dead. The large animal was chained to the front porch. He quickly stepped into the nearest bush as the door opened and a shoe hit the dog. "Shut up, Bozo. Ain't nobody around here," a man yelled and slammed the door.

Ahmed admitted defeat. It was the big house, or nothing. He turned back the way he came. From the road, he could see that the back of the large house was dark. He checked his watch again. Almost midnight. He was heading for the kitchen door that had yielded to his knife earlier this afternoon, when a loud meow echoed, followed by the cat rubbing against his legs. He tripped and stumbled into a metal garbage can. Reacting quickly he grabbed the lid and righted the can before it crashed onto the concrete of the porch. Heaven help, he swore silently as he scooped up the cat and petted the soft fur. Even the animals would trap him.

"No, *gato*, you cannot come inside this time," he softly told the purring feline. "You go catch a mouse." He put the cat down, "Go. Go," he shooed the animal away from him. Something in the yard caught the attention of the cat, and Ahmed breathed a sigh of relief as it pounced into the grass. Again, the blade of his small knife opened the door to the house. Moving silently, he closed the door with only a soft click and felt his way into the kitchen. Diffused light from appliance digital clocks gave him a view of the room. The tiny flashlight attached to the car keys was growing dim by the time he checked the well stocked cabinets and drawers. He found nothing that would help his cause.

He moved into the hall, remembering a desk in the family room. Nothing again, unless postage stamps could be converted into cash. It was a risk to go to the bedrooms, but there was nothing else to do. To wait until morning could involve danger, if someone recognized him from the posters, and he was sure the store clerk was not the only one who was promised a reward. He had to chance it.

Taking the dark hall to the front of the house, he stopped short. Heavy breathing, the sound coming closer. Suddenly, a very large soft bulk started screaming like all the banshees of hell. He tried to back out of the arms that circled him, stumbled and fell with the screaming demon on top, weighing him down.

Wall sconces came to life as light blazed into his eyes. The large black woman lay across his chest, screaming her head off. He didn't say a word. He couldn't breathe.

* * * * *

"Don't get that," David growled, as the bedside telephone rang. Bobbie kissed his ear, then reached for the phone. David groaned. What on earth, now? He had better marry her fast. It would take a life time of no interruptions to give him all the time he needed to make love to her. He rolled away from her inviting body so she could reach for the bloody thing.

"Calm down, Aunt Ellen. Yes, David is here. You WHAT?"

David grabbed the telephone from Bobbie's hand. "Ellen, what is it? Wait, slow down. Now say that again. Mamie fell on the Mexican man who was in the house this afternoon, and you think he's dead? She thinks she killed him? Wait, don't say any more. Hang up and call 911. We'll be there as quick as we can."

David shoved his way to the edge of the bed and reached for his clothes. Bobbie was already in her jeans and checking the cartridge clip of her gun. David jerked on his pants, tucked the empty leg up in the belt and grabbed his shirt and shoe. "Come on, you drive, I'll dress in the car." Bobbie pulled a tee shirt over her head and led the way from the apartment, David swinging on his crutches right behind her.

David had only thought Buddy Adams was good with a car. Bobbie drove the big Buick like a professional. Ten minutes from her apartment, and no blue lights behind them, they parked at Ellen's house.

"Wait, David. I'll go first." Bobbie had her automatic by her shoulder.

"I'm not going to argue this time, honey, but don't plan on leaving me behind you again. Hand me the keys. I'll open the door for you." David moved to the double front doors and inserted the key from the ring. He pushed the door open, and Bobbie slid by him into the house.

The hall blazed with light. Ellen, aided by the bent walker was waiting by the family room door. She motioned them to come back. "Oh, dear, I didn't know what to do, but everything is all right now. He's not dead, just had the wind knocked out of him. Mamie is with him now. Oh, dear," Ellen said again, "I hope you weren't sleeping." Then she saw the grimace on David's face. "Oh, dear," she said one more time.

"Ellen," David broke in, "did you call 911?"

"No. Now, David, don't look at me like that. It was the cat. Shadow must have pushed the back door open before we went to bed. Sometimes he does that, then it doesn't latch good."

"Ellen," David said patiently, "what has the cat got to do with a man breaking into your house?"

"Well, he didn't exactly break in. You can ask him yourself. He's in the family room. Mamie is watching him. We can call the police now, if you think we should."

David let out a loud groan, and Bobbie brought the gun up to her shoulder again. "A man you don't know came into your house uninvited, and you didn't call the police?"

"Honestly, Bobbie, you and David act like I've lost my mind. Of course I know him. You do too. He was here and introduced himself this afternoon," Ellen huffed.

"That does it," Bobby pushed by Ellen and entered the family room. The intruder, or should she call him a guest, sat relaxed in an easy chair with a purring Shadow on his lap. Other than looking a little worse for wear, he appeared to have recovered his breath. Mamie sat opposite the chair on the sofa, griping a baseball bat in her hands.

"Ah, *señorita,* so sorry to trouble you," Ahmed started to explain, then something clicked for Bobbie. She brought the gun in front of her, two handed, pointed straight at him.

"Mamie, you just captured the man who may have killed your granddaughter."

David came into the room to see the man slowly put the cat on the floor, then extend his hands over his head. "No, Deputy, I didn't kill her. I tried to help, but she was too far gone by the time I found her." His English was excellent and clear. There was no trace of a Spanish accent to his voice.

"What's going on?" David was standing beside Bobbie, ready if she should need help, but the man in front of them remained seated.

"This is the man from the posters, David. The same one Maggie saw in the campground when she found that dress."

David took a closer look at the clean shaven man. She was right. "Dr. Ahmed Faziz," he said and reached for the telephone on the desk.

"Please wait." Ahmed lowered his hands, then quickly put them in the air again. Bobbie was holding the gun steady, aimed at the middle of his chest. "Please, let me say something first, then you can call the police. I will turn myself in, but hear me out. You, all of you are in danger. I have information that can help."

David had the telephone in his hand, then replaced it when the tone alerted him to the open line. "You've got exactly two minutes and a lot of explaining to do."

Ellen had joined Mamie on the sofa, and both women looked like they were in shock. Mamie's grip on the baseball bat was so tight the wood groaned. Ellen's lips made a straight line, and both of them had their eyes riveted on the man in the chair.

Ahmed gave as much of a bow as he could while seated. "I am indeed Dr. Ahmed Faziz. At least I will be for a few more days. A medical doctor, yes, but then I will be Miguel Rios, or perhaps another name. There have been a dozen or more names over the years. You see, I was a professional assassin, retired until little over a week ago. Then I was tricked, one last assignment, Ibrahim said."

"Get to the point," David growled, picking up the phone again.

"Please," Ahmed smiled sadly, "it is important you know this." He turned to the women on the sofa. "My dear lady, the girl was your child? Your granddaughter?" Mamie nodded, unshed tears shining in her eyes. "I do not know who killed her. The man raped her, cut her, then drove off in a pickup truck before I could get to her. I tried. Please forgive me for failing. I took her to the hospital, but she died on the way. I am new to this country, but knew the police would detain me so I drove to an isolated place. I did not know it was a campground. I left the dress, and would have left the girl, too, if the woman who ran the park had not found me. I should have done better for her, but at the time that was not possible. I am glad she was found and you can give her a decent burial."

Ahmed's eyes went to Ellen. "Ah, beautiful lady, I would never hurt you on purpose. The shot was intended to hit another target. I did not know at the time the rifle scope was defective. I was deliberately aiming at the security men, at the telfar vests I knew would turn away a bullet fired from a hunting rifle at that distance. You moved too quickly. I am sorry, but that does not excuse me."

"Apologies don't cut it," David interrupted. "Tell me why I shouldn't call the sheriff now. You're out of time."

"May I lower my hands?" Ahmed did so without a response from Bobbie, but she continued to hold her weapon at ready. "You are a marked man," he turned to David. "They think you know more than you do. They killed the wrong man, but now they know who you are. You, and all those you love," he indicated the women with a sweep of his hand, "are in danger."

David had already suspected as much, but he needed proof. "Just why the hell should I believe you? You could be exactly what you are wanted for, an assassin and cold blooded killer. You better come up with something better than that."

Ahmed shrugged. "I know who is behind it. I now know who pulled me out of retirement, certain I would no longer have the heart to kill needlessly. I put it together when I saw you with a man I know only as Zero."

David drew a mental blank until he remembered the computer screen when Buddy Adams tapped into the government computer files. WELCOME, AGENT ZERO. What the hell was going on? Couldn't anyone be trusted? "Don't try to tell me you work for the government, too," he frowned.

Bobbie had lowered the gun and leaned on the desk beside David. "David," she touched his arm, "Buddy Adams," she whispered.

"I made the connection, lil'bit," he found the chair beside the desk and sat down. Bobbie perched on the desk, gun in hand. "You didn't answer my question," he told Ahmed.

Ahmed let out his breath. Americans were not known to be reasonable. They acted first and thought later. While his relaxed posture was a pose, his muscles were tense, ready to spring if there was an opening. But then, why? If what he suspected was true, maybe he could make a deal with the authorities.

"David, call Steve." Ellen had an arm on Mamie's shoulder as tears streamed down the woman's face from her silent crying. "This man has just admitted shooting at the Vice President, and he knows what happened to Mamie's granddaughter."

"Yes, Ellen, I'm going to call Steve. You take Mamie and go to the living room and watch for him." David saw them down the hall, then turned back to Ahmed. "I am going to call the sheriff and Agent Zero if I can reach him. If you know him, you know he works for the government. He will be very interested in what you have to say."

Ahmed nodded with a resigned sigh. "The sheriff will complicate matters, but I will be happy to talk to Zero alone. If he is working for YOUR government, I will tell him everything I know. Then I will turn myself in."

David was standing stiff as a rod. "What do you mean, MY government?"

Ahmed sniffed. These backwoods, small town people were as innocent as children. "Zero and I have worked together in the past. I, too, have worked for the American government in certain instances. You see…, oh, there is no time to explain. Let's just say Zero and I share the same occupation. If his loyalty does lie with the United States now, he will know what to do."

"No!" Bobbie picked up the telephone, "I'm calling 911 and getting help out here quick."

David grabbed the phone from her hand. "Bobbie, let me try your apartment. Buddy might have gone back there. I haven't told you everything Senator Charles told me. I've got questions and I need some answers!"

"David!" Bobbie struggled for the phone, then gave in. "Okay, but then I am calling Steve, the FBI or somebody."

Before he could dial the number they heard the front door open. Bobbie was in the hall in a nano-second, gun pointed straight ahead. "David," she looked back over her shoulder. "You don't have to call. Buddy's here." She returned to the family room while Buddy put on his charming act for Ellen and Mamie.

Both women were talking at the same time. Buddy was beginning to make sense of what they were saying when he saw Bobbie in the hall with the gun. He ushered the women back to their seats in the living room and came on the run.

Ahmed rose from the chair as Buddy rushed into the room. Buddy skidded to a halt beside Bobbie. "Hang on to your piece," he said out the side of his mouth, then addressed Ahmed. "Well, well, if it ain't my old friend from Buenos Aries. Thought you would be pushing up daisies by now." The down to earth, southern version of Buddy was back.

"Hello Zero. I can't say it's a pleasure." Neither man offered to shake hands.

Bobbie had moved to David's side. Buddy turned to them, "Sugar, looks like you caught the man they're all looking for. What you goin' to do with him?"

David spoke up. It was obvious the men knew each other. "This man says he wants to talk to you alone, then he will turn himself in. I'll give you ten minutes, then I'm calling the Sheriff. By the way, how did you know we were here?"

"Easy," Buddy grinned. "I been tailing you for sometime. How was your meeting with the right Honorable Senator Charles? I waited awhile outside the apartment, when you got back, so you and honeybunch could have some time to, ...well, you know what I mean. Had some phone calls I needed to make, anyway. When you hightailed it out of there, I went in and checked the answering machine. Tsk, tsk," he wagged a finger at Bobbie. You forgot to turn it off. It recorded the call from here. Took me a few minutes to find the address." He pointed to Ahmed. "Did you search him?"

Bobbie shook her head and David groaned. He felt like it was amateur night and knew they were in over their heads. "Like I said, you got ten minutes," he told the men and pushed Bobbie ahead of him out of the room.

CHAPTER SEVENTEEN

"No offense, old man, but you better let me see what's in your pockets." Buddy motioned for Ahmed to spread himself against the wall.

Ahmed, knowing it was useless to argue, assumed the position. Buddy ran his hands over Ahmed's clothes and fished the pen knife and car keys out of a pocket. Ahmed turned around to face his adversary, or could it be friend?

Buddy handed him back his knife. "Come in handy, don't they? Whose car do these fit?" He jangled the keys, then it dawned, "Never mind. I can guess. Want to tell me why you're here, and who you're working for?"

Ahmed moved to sit in the chair. "Why am I here? That, I would like to know myself. I came to the United States to take part in a seminar on Aids. Do you know the name Ibrahim Hassim?" Buddy let out a low whistle, but kept silent as Ahmed continued. "I was given no choice but to follow orders. The answer to who, is only a guess. Only the U. S. could force Israel to fake the execution and release Hassim."

Buddy got up and walked the length of the room. "They have your child, don't they?"

Ahmed cleared his throat and stood again to stare out the dark window. When he spoke his voice was strong, but tinged with worry. "No. I have checked. He is still at his London school. Threats have been made. I have no doubt they would be carried out." Ahmed faced Buddy. "You are very well informed. Before this goes farther, I must know your loyalties."

A ghost of a smile flickered at his mouth, then solemn for once, Buddy answered. "The same they've always been. Sure, I play the double agent at times. Seems you and I share a talent. We can be whoever, whenever, as necessary. I've used more than a dozen names, lived as many lives. It's lonesome, but then you know that. I've bounced around all over this planet, but the U. S. of A. is the greatest nation yet. I'm still doing what I can to see it stays that way. Maybe one day I can have a son, too."

Ahmed nodded. "I thought I was out of it and made a home in Niger. Now I can never return. By failing to make a contact, I have put into motion safeguards for my son and mother. In two days, Dr. Ahmed Faziz will cease to exist. There is a sanction on me. Whoever I become is still a marked man unless...," Ahmed stopped and stared at Buddy.

Buddy shook his head and spread his hands. "Not me. I heard about the sanction from my contacts, but I think there is a better way to handle this. You did attempt to assassinate the Vice President. There's going to be hell to pay for that. Let me think for a minute."

Ahmed sank back in the chair, while Buddy walked the room. Finally Buddy sat down, too. "There just might be a way, but first I've got to know more. Give me something…, anything… to go on."

Ahmed needed to make a decision. Would he trust this man he had only known as agent Zero, or take the chance he could disappear? He was tired, tired of running, tired of hiding, why not get it over? Whichever way Zero leaned now, it did not matter. He sat forward, the better to look Buddy in the eye. "I faked the assassination attempt. It needed to look good, but I knew that make of rifle was not accurate at an extreme distance. If it were not for the defective scope, no one would have been hurt. Then I saw a face through the rifle scope that I recognized. One I never expected to see again. A face you and I both know. We knew him as…" Ahmed looked up to see David and Bobbie push past each other in their hurry to enter the room.

Buddy looked at his watch, as sirens and flashing lights screamed down the road. "Thanks a lot, kids. This way, Faziz. My car is down the road." Without waiting to say goodbye, the two men made for the kitchen door.

* * * * *

"I don't know what you're talking about!" A tearful Ellen stood in front of her brother, the irate Sheriff.

"I pulled in every man I could find in the county to get out here when you called. Don't tell me I don't know your voice."

David put his arm around Ellen. "Take it easy, Steve. If everyone will calm down, we'll straighten this out."

Bobbie came to support her aunt while Ellen limped to a chair. "I didn't call," she insisted. "David said he would call after he talked to those men."

Steve rubbed a hand over his face, then answered a page on his radio. "All of you," he threatened, "stay put!" and slammed the door as he left the house.

The assemblage in the living room looked at each other. "Okay," David glared at Bobbie, "who did call?" No one said a word.

"Well, it wasn't me," Bobbie glared back. If looks could strangle, David was in trouble. "I was with you the whole time, if you happen to remember!"

"Okay, okay," David said again, calming his voice. "This isn't going to work if we keep arguing. "Whoever called did us a favor, except the timing was wrong."

Steve came back, this time fingers making the hair on his head stand up straight. "They got away. I can't believe it. I left a man to watch that old car parked down the road. Two men came out of the bushes and jumped him before he could stop them. He managed to get to his car and chased them out to the highway. They must have afterburners in that old wreck to leave a police car in the dust. Shit!" Steve collapsed on the sofa beside Ellen. "Okay, so I apologize. There was somebody here, but you only said one man on the phone. Where'd the other come from? Will somebody PLEASE tell me what's going on?"

David looked at Bobbie. "Lil'bit, I think it's time we filled Steve in on what we know."

An hour later, with Steve the only law enforcement besides Bobbie in the house, it was David who was mopping his face. "Give us just a little more time, Steve. I need to see if I can catch up with Buddy to see what he found out. Oh," David threw his hands in the air and released a few words not normally in his vocabulary, "I just remembered I need to be in Knoxville for Jeff's arraignment hearing. Bobbie, you try to contact Buddy. Go see Orville and get his address and phone number. Ellen, you have a computer here, don't you? Write this down. They were web sites on my computer when those men smashed it. Print them out. I had started checking them when Buddy called that night."

Ellen, glad to have something to do, held pencil at ready. "What am I looking for?"

"Any and everything to do with the Oak Ridge project."

Steve suddenly interrupted. "Hey, hotshot lawyer, I haven't agreed to more time. I should call in the FBI right now. You know harboring a known suspect is against the law."

David swung around and levered himself from the chair. Steve was standing while Bobbie sat wringing her hands, torn between David and her oath to enforce the law. Steve reached for the phone. "Wait, Steve. Is there anyone else here? How can you harbor someone who is not here? We saw a suspect; he got away. We have not been aiding and abetting a known criminal. No offence has been committed that I can see."

"I ought to haul all of you in just to keep you out of trouble. Getting in the way of an investigation is an offence. You know that. Locking you up would be for your own good. For God's sake, man, somebody tried to kill you. Next it could be Ellen, or Bobbie. Anyone close to you is in danger. No," Steve shook his head, "you can't talk your way out of this one." He started to dial.

David's fist shot out and caught Steve on the chin with a right upper-cut. Astonishment crossed Steve's face then he went down like a pole axed ox.

"David!" both Bobbie and Ellen screamed and Bobbie knelt by the downed Sheriff.

The phone rang, stretching taunt nerves even farther. David grabbed it up from the floor before Bobbie could reach for it. "Yeah, Scott, the Sheriff is here. No, he can't come to the phone right now. Just give me the message." David, grinning as wide as his mouth could, listened to Scott.

"Sure, I'll tell him. Yeah, everything is cool here." He put the telephone back in the charger.

Steve was sitting up, holding a wet kitchen tea towel to his chin, while Mamie went to make an ice pack. "Jesus, David, you didn't have to hit me. Deputy Foster," he pointed to Bobbie, "put that man under arrest."

"Scott called," David was still grinning. "Message for you. Two men just broke Orville Wright out of jail."

* * * * *

"Jeeze, Buddy, I didn't think you were ever going to come get me." Orville bounced sideways as Buddy swung the muscle car around a curve.

"Stow it kid. What we did is illegal. It's against the law, and you could do extra jail time for the break. I think I can square it, but first you have to come up with some answers." Buddy looked at the other front seat passenger for help.

"My name is Miguel Rios. I was the bearded man you saw leave the truck at the Park and Ride before you took it. I stole it too, only to use for a short while. The registration form in the glove compartment had the name Jack Taylor. Your cousin here," Ahmed pointed at Buddy, "says you know the man who owns the truck."

"Maybe I do, maybe I don't. Hey Buddy, where'd you pick up this Mex?" Orville sneered.

"Cut the crap, kid. First, I'm not your cousin. I wanted to get into that white supremacist chapter you're tangled up with, so I could go to the hunting lodge. The Mex here is with me. That's all you need to know. Unless you want to tell me who's the top man in the organization so I can talk to him, I'll take you right back to that jail."

Orville was silent, then a sound suspiciously like a sob came from his throat. "I might a knowed it was too good to be true. Nobody ever gives a shit about me. You can kiss my ass before I'll tell you anything."

Buddy laughed, not a pleasant sound. "I just might do that, laddie boy. Break you in a little for prison. Lot of that goes on when punks like you get sent up. If you're smart, you'll talk."

Silence from the back seat, as the headlights sliced through a thin mist. Buddy slowed the car and turned into a gravel road. A cabin loomed in the distance.

Buddy closed the door and stomped his feet on a rag rug after parking the car in the shed. "What'd you do with Orville?"

"In there," Ahmed looked up from the chair where he sat and motioned to a door. He handed Buddy a key. "I made sure the window was nailed shut."

174

"He won't go anywhere." Buddy pitched the key on a sideboard. "He's scared and I don't blame him. That Nazi gang would hang him up by his balls."

"Then why did you take him from the jail?"

"I got word he was to be picked up by the FBI. We need what he knows. I've been putting some things together. The Neo Nazi's, the assassination, and the bombing at Oak Ridge are all tied together. Maybe murder in Knoxville, too. You're right, all of it points to Washington. When you told me who it was with the Vice President, it threw me, but it still looks that way. That how you see it?" Buddy handed Ahmed a beer and sat down at the oak plank table. When Ahmed just looked at the can, Buddy grinned. "Sorry, I forgot you Muslims don't drink alcohol."

Ahmed popped the top. "Now that I am Mexican, I guess I will learn to like Tequila." He took a swallow of the beer, making a wry face. "Tell me, how did you arrange for the jail to be almost empty?"

Buddy laughed again, this time with pleasure. "I knew where to find you from an answering machine tape in Bobbie's apartment. Her aunt called for help. I swiped the machine, deleted a few names and words, and *voilá*, the Sheriff's sister called him for help."

Ahmed managed a laugh himself. It was beginning to feel like old times. Still he couldn't afford to trust the man before him. They had come to the same conclusion about the source of the troubles by different routes. If they put their heads together, a solution might be found. But not before he heard what the boy would say and the name he knew. And talk, he knew the boy would. Zero was not one to toy around.

A knock sounded from inside the bedroom door. Buddy went over and unlocked the door. Orville, with the blanket from the bed wrapped around his shoulders, came into the main room. "It's cold in here," the boy complained. "Jeeze, Buddy, why'd you lock me in? I ain't got any place to go." He looked around the sparsely furnished cabin. "Got anything to eat?"

Buddy went to a cabinet and handed Orville a box of crackers and a jar of peanut butter. "Go back in the bedroom. Miguel and I have more to discuss."

Orville started toward the bedroom door. The blanket kept slipping from his shoulders with his hands full. He put the food on the table to retrieve his wrap. Clutching the blanket around his shoulders, he stood staring at Ahmed for a moment. "You don't look like the man who parked the truck."

Ahmed smiled at the youth. "I shaved the beard," he said. "Sit down and eat your snack here. We can talk."

Orville pulled out a chair and sat. He opened the crackers and offered them to Ahmed, ignoring Buddy.

Buddy caught Ahmed's eye and winked. "Got to go to the loo," he said and disappeared through the door to the small bathroom.

Orville put peanut butter on a cracker and munched. Ahmed reached, took the jar and did the same. Silence followed while they ate more crackers. "Can I have a beer?" Orville asked. Ahmed shrugged, found a glass and poured it full from his can. They ate more peanut butter and crackers. Finally Orville asked, "Can Buddy hear us?"

"I don't know," Ahmed said truthfully. "Does it make a difference?"

"I guess not," Orville snuffed, "I'm just mad at him. He lied to me. He's not mama's kin. That one-legged lawyer fella don't want to help me neither. He's too busy to bother with me. Guess I got nobody now." Orville shoved the peanut butter jar away from him, anger obvious in the movement. "If you left the truck at the Park and Ride, that rifle and gun must belong to you. Did you really shoot at the Vice President?"

Ahmed nodded, "Yes, I did."

Orville looked impressed. "Did you mean to kill him?"

Shaking his head, Ahmed simply said, "No."

The boy took a swallow of the beer. Water could be heard running in the bathroom. He took a quick look in that direction, then leaned toward Ahmed. "Jack Taylor owns that truck, but he ain't got nuthin' to do with anything. He's a teacher at my high school. My shop teacher heads up our Chapter. His name is Myron Smith, but it's his wife who really runs things. I met her once before, then saw her at the jail. She said she would help me if I keep quiet, but I ain't seen her again. I need to get to the lodge. They got to take me in, don't they? Help me get there an' I won't tell on you, if you don't tell on me."

Ahmed was tempted to chuckle, but kept a straight face. Buddy already knew all there was to know about Ahmed, and apparently from the posters circulating, many other people did, too. "It's a deal," he told Orville. "Don't tell anyone I shaved, or what my name is, okay?" The boy nodded as Buddy came back into the room.

"Nap time, Orville," Buddy thumbed toward the bedroom door. "It'll be getting light soon. I need to make some plans." Orville tossed off the rest of the beer, glared at Buddy, then did as he was told.

"I heard," Buddy quietly told Ahmed. "Not what I wanted to hear. I already know Myron Smith and his wife. Orville still knows more."

Ahmed nodded in silent agreement. Buddy went to a door Ahmed had thought another bedroom. This one had the window boarded up completely and was filled with the latest computer and communication equipment. An impressive array of rifles and handguns resided in a glass front cabinet. Ahmed nodded again to himself in satisfaction. Now he knew for sure Zero was an American agent. Only the Americans could afford those toys. Trust was a long way away for either man, but as he relaxed the body aches he had tried to keep at bay seemed to lessen. Buddy went into the room, but did not close the door. Is the man so arrogant he believes I am no danger, or has he decided I can be useful? What does it matter, Ahmed thought. For the moment, it was agreeable to let Zero take charge. He leaned his head back and cleared his mind for sleep.

* * * * *

Technically, David was under arrest. Bobbie, driving her aunt's Buick with David in the passenger seat, headed back to town. "I should put you in a cell and let you rot," she hissed through clenched teeth. David's tight lipped silence told her he was as angry as she.

"Okay," David finally uttered. "I'm sorry I hit your boss. Was I supposed to let him pull his gun and lock us all up? Bring in the FBI so we could hand over the only two men who know enough to help us?"

She glanced his way to see an amused half grin appear on his face. "David, you just..., you only..." she huffed. "oh, just forget it."

"Honey, I don't want to argue. Fighting each other won't solve our problems. Steve was right about one thing. We could all be in danger. Senator Charles told me more by what he didn't say than the warnings he gave me."

Bobbie swung the car around the turn to the courthouse square and the sheriff's office. Suddenly David yelled "Stop!" Startled, she slammed on the brakes so hard the seatbelts caught their forward motion. "Bobbie, I need to go to my office. Please, honey, I just thought of something. I'll go to jail meek as a lamb after that. I promise."

"Da-a-a-vid," Bobbie drew out his name, "all right, but you try something and I'll shoot you, I swear I will. I've got handcuffs, too." She pulled the car in front of his boarded up door, then remembered it was nailed shut and turned the corner to pull in the alley.

"Handcuffs, hummn?" David purred deep in his throat. "I can think of a few things we could do with them. Shame they tore up the bed." David was trying to think of what he could say to put Bobbie at ease. He knew that without the resisting arrest charge, the Sheriff had no probable cause to detain him. Steve knew that too, so this was only an effort to protect both David and Bobbie. The Sheriff himself had elected to stay with Ellen and Mamie, until he could leave a deputy on guard. This effort was appreciated on Bobbie's behalf, but some risks had to be taken if they were ever going to get out of this mess. David was willing to be the risk-taker, but if he could get those handcuffs it would be Bobbie who was in protective custody.

David reached for the flashlight Ellen kept in the glove box. The utility company would not restore the electricity until repairs were made to his inside wiring. "Give me fifteen minutes, honey." He opened the car door.

"Not on your life, Mister. You're my prisoner, remember. I'm going with you." Bobbie slammed the door on her side. "This had better be good, or I'll lose my job over you."

David ground his lips together. It would come to a showdown over her job one day, but not now. He knew she was as worried and tired as he was. Too little sleep, too many nights in a row. "Trust me, Bobbie. I know what I'm doing." He put all the confidence he could manage into his voice, but knew he was lying through his teeth. A lawyer has to develop a good, reliable memory, and bits and pieces of information kept floating around in his mind. If he could get them to gel, maybe he could make sense of what had happened. "Well, if you're coming, come on."

The backdoor didn't need a key. It had been forced open, the wood frame splintered. David turned the flashlight into the dark room. Nothing looked disturbed from the previous morning, trash and debris all over the floor. "Watch where you step," he warned Bobbie, then fell forward as his crutch caught in some of the rubbish. He ended up stretched out on the floor, his head wedged between two overturned bookcases. The flashlight went out when it hit the floor.

"David," Bobbie was feeling her way into the room. "What happened? David, answer me! Are you all right?" She stumbled into him and fell sprawled across his body. She sat up and reached to his shoulders, then up to his head. "David?" He didn't answer. She shook him. He still didn't answer. Bobbie fought back panic.

Light! We've got to have light! On her hands and knees she crawled toward the door, realizing glass from broken picture frames was cutting her hands and knees. She shoved the door open and enough light from the street let her move outside. Quickly she backed the big Buick and turned the headlights into the building. The car was lower than the door, but on bright some of the illumination helped.

Shadows jumped out at her as she made her way through the junk scattered across the office. Reaching David, she pulled on his leg until she had him clear of the bookcase. She knelt then, and lifted his head only to realize with horror there was blood at his temple and in his hair. "Dear God," Bobbie prayed and rolled David enough to reach his pockets. His face looked ashen in the dim light. No cell phone! They left her apartment so fast, he hadn't picked it up. She cut her hand again searching for her handbag, pulled out the Smith & Wesson and did the only thing she could think of.

* * * * *

In Knoxville the sleepy jailer muttered curse words as the FBI agent handed him a release form to sign. With an audible snort he signed, then went to get the prisoner. End of housing a celebrity killer, the man snorted again. Now the Feds would get all the news media attention. The jailer had tallied up a tidy sum taking bribes from the reporters who wanted to see and speak with the accused. He roused the sleeping prisoner and told him to get dressed.

Jeff Fischer Charles shook the sleep from his mind and started to dress. Then what the guard had said sunk in. He yelled for the guard. The large hall clock on the wall set the time at 2:00 AM. He yelled again, still with no response. Fearful now, Jeff finished dressing except for his shoes and got back on the bunk, pulling the cover up to his neck. The jailer was back, opened the cell door and dragged Jeff out of the bunk. "What you trying to do, shit-head? The man's waiting." The guard manhandled him out of the cell.

"What's going on?" Jeff hopped on one foot, wishing he had put on his shoes. "Am I being transferred? Somebody tell me something. I've got to call my lawyer and tell him. I got to go to court tomorrow."

Smoothly the agent took Jeff's arm and snapped on handcuffs. "Come with me, Mr. Charles. Everything has been taken care of. You can call your lawyer in the morning."

Jeff tried to relax and walked out of the building with the agent holding his arm. A panel van waited at the door, and the sliding door opened as they approached. The agent pushed Jeff in and followed, closing the door as the vehicle picked up speed. Jeff couldn't see the driver through the screen separating the passenger seats from the front. He glanced around, but could see no one else in the van. It seemed only a few blocks from the jail when the driver pulled into a side street and killed the lights. A door rose slowly in the building wall ahead of them. The van entered the shadowed ramp to a parking garage.

Once the outside door closed the van lights came on and it pulled across to an access door. The agent with Jeff exited, allowing Jeff to slide unaided, still handcuffed, from the van. "Where are we?" Jeff looked around, but saw nothing to tell him what building this garage serviced. Before he could ask more, the agent latched onto his arm and pulled him into a freight elevator.

Instead of going up, the cage descended and when the door opened Jeff could see from the steam pipes and lines running across the room, it was the service maintenance floor of a large building, again nothing to identify the location. The agent led him to a narrow metal door, unlocked the handcuffs and pushed him in. The door slammed shut and a key turned in the lock.

Judy Lucas

Before Jeff could survey his new quarters the lights when out, leaving only a wall of terrifying darkness in front of Jeff's eyes.

CHAPTER EIGHTEEN

The Sheriff's Deputy on night patrol was approaching the parking lot after what seemed an interminable night of trying to keep peace between the card players and beer drinkers who had invaded his county for the big fishing tournament. He was looking forward to some supper and sleep. After doing his paperwork and turning it in, he'd make one more pass around the courthouse square, then he could go home.

Before he could exit the patrol car the unmistakable sound of gunfire echoed through the still air. He raised his head from the clipboard and doused the overhead light. There it was again, the sharp, quick report of a handgun fired in the near distance. He stepped from the vehicle, sure the shooter was far away enough to have another target. Then again, another shot fired. Three measured shots. The international signal for help. He got back in the car and drove in the directions of the sounds. At first he didn't see anything, then turning the corner from the square, he saw light in the alley behind the boarded up law office of David Middleton. Quickly swinging the patrol car into the narrow space, he saw the automobile turned to throw light into an open door. Unsnapping the covered holster on his hip and picking up a night stick, he stood with his patrol car door for protection. "You!" he yelled. "Put the gun down and come out with your hands in the air!"

A distinctly feminine voice yelled back. "Jim Ed, we need help. Call for an ambulance. It's David."

Instantly recognizing the voice of the only female deputy on the force, he reached for the radio mike and passed the message. With a large emergency flash, he went to the door. "Bobbie, where are you?"

"Shine the light over here." Bobbie was on her knees beside a supine David.

"Is he hurt?" Jim Ed swung the light beam around the room, checking for any hidden danger before he moved to David. He put a finger to the pulse at the neck, finding it strong and steady. "What happened?" They could hear the ambulance screaming in the pre-dawn silence.

"He went in before me. Told me to be careful of the mess on the floor, then he fell. I was coming up the stairs. I couldn't see, but I think he hit his head on that bookcase. The side of his head is bloody. I rolled him over, but haven't moved him more than I had to."

Jim Ed put a hand on Bobbie's shoulder to stop her shiver. "EMS is here now. Let's get out of the way." He guided her to the side through the broken remains of David's desk and chair.

"I couldn't believe my ears when I heard the shots," Jim Ed said to Bobbie. "What you been doing, girl, reading Westerns?"

Bobbie was still shivering in her thin sweater, more from tension than cold. Jim Ed put his jacket over her shoulders and she clutched it around her. "Yeah, I guess. Anyway, that was all I could think of. I didn't want to leave David in case he came to. Thanks for coming, Jim Ed."

"Don't worry, girl. That man of yours has got the hardest head in these parts. Take more than a fall to hurt him. Need to have him checked out, though. How long has he been out?"

"I don't know, maybe fifteen minutes or a little longer. You were here almost as soon as I fired the third shot and it took EMS another five after you called it in." Bobbie looked over to where the medics were working with David.

"Pshaw, that's nothin'. When I was boxing I been down that long. No concussion, neither. Don't you worry your pretty head over that no-count lawyer. They got to be hard headed for that line of work."

Bobbie reached over and touched the big man's hand, knowing they both cared for David. A low moan came from the subject of their conversation. The emergency personnel finished fitting a neck brace, then let David sit up. He raised a hand to the bandage applied to his temple and winced. One of the medics motioned for Bobbie to come over.

Bobbie squatted by David. "David, are you okay? No, no, don't move. I think you should go to the hospital and let them check you out."

David grimaced as he tried to turn his head in the neck collar, but the rueful smile on his lips was reassuring. "I know what they mean when they say you see stars." He tried to get his leg under him to push up, then thumped back down again, hard. "Maybe it won't hurt to have it looked at. Sorry, honey, I don't mean to be so much trouble."

Bobbie leaned over and kissed his cheek. "There, that's for not dying on me, but I should lock you up for scaring the wits out of me. You came in here for something. Tell me what, and I'll get it for you."

David looked puzzled. "I wondered how we got here. The last I remember, we were in Ellen's car on the way to jail. I said I wanted something?"

Bobbie glanced at Jim Ed's pressed lips and saw the medics nod to each other. Concussion, they were thinking. She smiled brightly at David. "You get along to the hospital now. We'll figure it out later."

* * * * *

The mist clung to the underbrush and lower branches of the trees creating cobweb-like pockets. The incline became steeper as the road twisted upwards along a rock outcrop overlooking a sheer drop to the wooded hillside. The rising sun had yet to penetrate the heavy canopy of leaves. The old muscle car rounded another curve and came to a halt before a barred gate in the barbwire fence. Buddy Adams reached out the window and opened the access door of a wooden box nailed to a fence post. The telephone he picked up was answered immediately. He turned to face a pine tree beside the road where he knew a camera was located.

"Buddy Adams, Ray. How about letting us in."

"Who you got with you, Buddy?"

"Orville Wright and Miguel Rios."

"Tell them to step out of the car so's I can see 'em."

Buddy motioned for Orville and Ahmed Faziz, now known as Miguel Rios, to exit the vehicle. Orville knew to face the tree, and poked Ahmed to turn around. After a minute the man on the phone told Buddy to come in, but stop at HQ and sign in. Rios would have to be cleared. The gate buzzer sounded as they got back in the car.

A quarter of a mile farther into the hillside, a white clapboard two story farmhouse sat beside a battered red-painted barn. While not in disrepair, it was obvious the buildings had occupied their sites for many years. Smoke from a chimney and chickens scratching in the dirt yard were the only signs of life. Buddy pulled the car up under the shade of an apple tree and killed the engine. "Orville, I want you to stay with me. You got that? You so much as open your mouth and I'll see to it you do hard jail time." He put a hand on Ahmed's shoulder. "Okay, Miguel, you ready to play a little one two?"

"*Si*," Ahmed answered. Every leftover, has-been agent from the cold war knew the code for a 'good guy, bad guy' routine. The men got out of the car, keeping Orville between them.

"Clean your feet." A middle-aged woman in a print dress with a white apron met them at the door with a broom in her hands. "I got enough to do without cleaning this floor again. How you doing, boy?" she looked at Orville, who only ducked his head. "Coffee's on the stove," the told the men. "Myron's out in the barn. Be back in a minute." She gave a quizzical look at Ahmed, then went back to sweeping the floor.

Buddy helped himself to the coffee, pouring three mugs and setting them on the large table in the middle of the over-sized kitchen. Just then the back door opened and a burly man with a bristly brown beard stepped in. He stopped in his tracks, staring at Ahmed.

"You know my friend?" Buddy asked, slowly stirring sugar into his coffee. "Miguel, this is Myron Smith, our Chapter Leader for this region. Myron, Miguel Rios."

Ahmed, stunned by the appearance of the used car lot manager kept his wits about him and answered, "*Jhola, Señor*. It is a pleasure."

Myron continued to study the now clean shaven, short haired Ahmed. "I could swear I know you from somewhere. How long you and Buddy been friends?"

"We go way back," Buddy interrupted. "Look here, Myron. We broke Orville out of that two bit jail. I heard the FBI was going to pick him up to stand Federal charges for having those guns. What were you going to do? Sit by and let them have him?"

"What the hell is it to you? You sure fucked up our plans. Jenny, here had it fixed, so's our top man would get him. Now, you little shit, take the kid and this Mex over to cabin three and stay there. If the kid talked, no telling who will come around looking for him."

"I didn't tell nuthin' to nobody, I swear it. Not even the fella who was supposed to be my lawyer, an' he asked a bunch of times. I thought you was supposed to help me," Orville spoke up. "I don' want to go to jail," he ended on a wail. "Jus' give me enough money to go find my Pa. He'll know what to do."

Myron backhanded the boy. "Shut up. Ain't you caused enough trouble, taking that truck? Now we got more trouble with your so-called cousin bringing this man along." Orville stumbled back, grabbing his chair for balance, a look of complete disbelief on his face.

"Wait just a minute," Buddy snarled at boss man. "We didn't come here to get holed up. You going to help the kid, or what?"

Tempers were on a short fuse that was sizzling. Ahmed took the initiative. "Please, *amigo*," he addressed Buddy. "We do as the man says. Maybe we can find somewhere else to get money and gasoline." He glanced over his shoulder, at the woman holding the broom. Her round cheeks were flushed and her rose bud mouth pursed.

"You're not going anywhere," she brandished the broom handle like a weapon. "Myron, meet Dr. Ahmed Faziz. Looks a little different than his pictures, but I'd bet my best Aunt Fanny quilt that's who he is. Well, well, Dr. Faziz, how did you get tangled up with these two clowns?"

Myron stepped around Buddy and extended his hand. "We met before at the car lot, not that I would recognize you now. I been looking all over for you. I got orders to get you out of the country." The man was looking Ahmed up and down, obviously confused over the change in appearance.

Ahmed caught sight of Buddy palming a small revolver as he shook Myron's offered hand. "Yes, the green Bonneville. A very good automobile. Shame I couldn't keep it."

"Myron," the woman interrupted, "don't be a bigger fool than you already are. Hide them in the coal chute until our visitor has gone. You know, VISITOR, the one we're expecting this afternoon."

"Oh, yeah," Myron agreed, "I forgot about that. You know the way, Buddy. You did us a bigger favor than you know, but you're not out of the woods yet. I still want to know why you broke the kid out of jail, and how you know Faziz. Now, get, before I let Jenny take this broom to your hide."

Orville had been standing wide-eyed, taking in the conversation. "You said you'd help me when I talked to you at the jail. You said you were some kind of cop and could help if I wouldn't tell I knew you before. I ain't seen you since. Don't nobody mean what they say?"

"Save it, kid. I had it arranged for the man who will be here this afternoon to pick you up and take you with him when he leaves town. Your kin, over there, screwed it up. Don't think the man will want you, with a jail break charge keeping all the county deputies on the look out for you. Get along now and I'll have Ray bring you some breakfast from the mess hall." Jennifer Smith, agent for the Tennessee Bureau of Investigation, domestic terrorist expert, and wife of a Neo Nazi Chapter leader, smiled her homey, favorite aunt smile at Orville.

Reluctantly, he joined Buddy and Ahmed, and the three headed out the back door.

* * * * *

Jeff Fischer woke to the gentle sounds of music on the clock radio. Last night when the lights went out, he had slumped to the floor in panic. He had never gotten over being afraid of the dark, even in the years he had been on the streets. At first he feared he might have made a mistake and the men who removed him from the jail really were FBI. He didn't question it when they came for him; for his plan to work it had to look good.

As he crouched beside the door in the dark, just as suddenly as they had gone off the lights came on and he found himself in a luxurious apartment. Relief cooled the adrenaline in his blood. He threw back his head and laughed out loud. It felt good, really good, to finally let go and be himself.

He knew no one would hear him. The walls were concrete and the door solid steel. Fresh air filtered in from vents in the very high ceiling. He explored, finding a stocked refrigerator and fresh sheets on the bed. Mixing himself a Bourbon and Coke, he relaxed, lighting a cigarette from a pack of Camels. He didn't know when he had felt so good. It was coming together, just as he planned. He stripped out of the orange jail coveralls to sit in a lounge chair wearing only his shorts, sipping his drink and smoking. Finally he stretched out on the bed and went to sleep.

The clock radio showed 9:00 am. Somebody must have set the alarm for it to have come on. Jeff shoved off the bed and padded over to the full bathroom. Commode and vanity sink, whirlpool tub and separate shower, plenty of mirrors, too, with big fluffy towels. He peeled off his underwear and stepped into the shower, finding shaving equipment, soap and body wash on the ledge. Feeling like a new man when he finished, he wrapped a towel around his middle

He opened the bath door, then dropped the towel in surprise. A gorgeous blonde in a skin tight dress was sitting in a chair, legs crossed at the knee. She was staring at him. He didn't bother to pick up the towel from the floor. "How did you get in here? I didn't hear the door open." He returned the blonde's stare with narrowed eyes.

The blonde laughed, a melodious sound. "Now I know why Karen was so keen for you."

Jeff leaned against the door jam, arms crossed over his chest, not bothering to hide himself from the woman. "Don't you ever sneak up on me again," his voice held a hint of danger, then softened, "but I'm glad you came." He gestured around him. "Thanks for fixing up this place."

The blonde shrugged, pushing long hair behind her ear. "If you will look in that wardrobe," she pointed behind her, "you will find clean underwear and clothes your size, I think."

Jeff walked across the room to the closet. The clothes she described were there. He glanced at her watching him. The only items missing from the attire were shoes. Properly clothed in slacks and golf shirt, even wearing socks, he turned to the blonde. "You will have to get me some shoes. Not now, later. Are the other plans in place?"

The woman laughed softly again. "Of course. You worry too much." She rose gracefully and went to the mini-kitchen to take prepared food from the oven. "Come, eat," she said, "you will need your strength later."

Jeff went to the bar where she had placed the food. She uncovered coffee in a Styrofoam cup and set it before him. "I don't want to eat alone," he told her. "Come eat something, or have some coffee with me."

"I'm not hungry," she answered, but settled on a bar stool opposite him. "I don't care for coffee like you Americans." She paused to light a cigarette, then handed it to him.

Gratefully, he drew smoke into his lungs. "How did you know what brand I smoke?"

"Karen told me a lot about you," was the answer.

"I didn't kill her, you know. That wasn't part of my plan." He sat on the stool and picked up a plastic fork. "Want some?" he offered again. She shook her head, then tucked hair behind her ear. Jeff dug into the scrambled eggs and hash brown potatoes.

When he finished, she disposed of the paper plates, then approached him as he sat on the stool, smoking another cigarette. She hiked her mini-skirt up her hips and put her long legs on either side of his knees. She put her mouth to his and tasted the tobacco on his lips, sharing the smoke in his mouth. He found an ash tray on the bar by touch and left the cigarette to smolder. Pushing her slightly away, he unzipped his fly, then pulled her down on him. "I've missed you, Nadja. What took you so long to get this place set up?"

* * * * *

Bobbie accompanied David to the hospital where they did a scan of his head and neck, then wanted to keep him for observation. David stubbornly refused, even when Bobbie urged him to stay.

"I never saw anybody so pig headed," she complained as David swung on his crutches beside her, heading out to the parking lot. "I talked to Steve. He dropped the charges against you, but said to tell you he puts you in my custody until further notice."

David grinned, his face lighting up best it could over the collar brace the Emergency doctor insisted he keep wearing. "Best sentence I could ever get. Want to make it permanent?"

Bobbie smiled back at him. "The sooner, the better. I can't let you out of my sight without you getting in trouble. You do know I love you, don't you?"

"If you know I love you the most," David teased.

"No, you don't," Bobbie countered.

"Do so."

"Don't."

"Do."

"Okay, you win," They both laughed at their childish nonsense, relieving the tension of the last few hours. "Come on, you can buy me breakfast." She got in the driver's side of the car. David settled in the passenger seat. "The scan did show cranium blood," she told him. "You can't drive for a while. You have to stay awake all day, and I have to watch for signs that your pupils are dilating and get you back to the hospital fast if that happens. You might even get your memory of last night back in a few days. David," Bobbie turned serious, "I love you very much. I couldn't stand for anything else to happen to you. Please don't give me any trouble today."

"Not today, honey, not ever if I can help it." David checked his watch. "Let's get something to eat, then I have to call Knoxville and check on Jeff. The hearing is set for 10:00 am."

"Here we go again," Bobbie moaned and started the car.

Over breakfast at the café, David suddenly sat up bolt straight. "I need to go to my office, Bobbie."

"What is it, David? Did you remember what you wanted last night?" Bobbie raised up higher to look in his eyes. They looked okay to her and she heaved a sigh of relief.

"No, I still can't remember, but I never go to court without two legs. Let me go get my prosthetic leg so we won't have to double back from your place."

Bobbie laughed. "Vanity, thy name is man," she misquoted. "Only if you let me go in first, this time."

In the daylight it wasn't hard to navigate through David's trash strewn office. Together, David and Bobbie climbed the stairs to the living quarters. This floor was only a little better than the office. Bobbie could have cried when she saw the shattered crystal goblets and broken china. David went to the bedroom and let out a massive groan. The leg lay on the closet floor in pieces. David, in a rare fit of temper, threw one of his crutches at the remains, and dropped to the slashed mattress on what used to be a bed.

"David?" Bobbie came into the room and looked in the closet at the shattered prosthesis. When he didn't answer, she knelt before him and raised his face to her with a hand. His pupils were pinpoints from the bright light flooding in the window. "Come on, David, you do fine on crutches. Besides, you have another leg, don't you?"

David's face was stony, all emotion seemed drained from him. "Yes," he said calmly, too calmly. "The other one is at the VA hospital. I left it there for some work on the brace." David grabbed Bobbie by the arms, gripping so hard she winced. "Sorry," he said, turning his face and shoving her away. "My head is killing me." He held a hand in front of his eyes to block out the bright light.

Bobbie moved across the bed from him, then sat down. "David, you're scaring me. What's wrong? Talk to me. David--?"

"That lying son of a bitch. Damn him! I should let him go to death row."

Bobbie was trying to see David's eyes, but he slung away from her and threw the other crutch across the torn bed so hard it clattered off the opposite wall. "Are you talking about Jeff? Talk to me, David, I don't understand." Bobbie crawled across the bed, pain reminding her of the cuts and abrasions on her hands and knees from the night's traumatic experience. She winced again, and suddenly David seemed to see her.

"Sorry, honey," he said in a more normal tone, "something I've been trying to put together just matched. Jeff Fischer couldn't have sat on my back stoop to smoke the night Karen Fielding was killed. Jim Ed would have seen him and Jim Ed hasn't said a word about that night. The downtown merchants and I pay the Sheriff's Department for an extra swing through the alley. Even if you hadn't fired your gun, Jim Ed would have seen the Buick when he made his last rounds."

"What has that got to do with your leg?" Bobbie asked, puzzled by the vehemence of David's outburst.

"I saw the leg, lying there on the floor. It could have been my real leg, my own leg in the desert sand. I remember seeing pieces of it before I passed out. Somehow, it pulled me back to Kuwait. I'm beginning to make sense of what the Senator told me. He told me I didn't want any part of Jeff. Now I know why."

Bobbie's face reflected her concern. She picked at a corner of the ragged mattress with a nervous finger, staying back from David. "I've never seen you this angry. What are you going to do?"

"Get the truth out of that bastard. That's what I should have done to start with. Oh, hell, lil'bit, I've been had. Why didn't I think of the night patrol in the alley before now? He hooked me good and I swallowed it all, bait, line and sinker. I knew the second conference with him he had lied about himself the night he stayed here. Boy, am I dumb!"

Bobbie stayed on her edge of the bed, but reached a hand toward David's arm. "So much has been happening, it's a wonder you can think at all. Don't be so hard on yourself." She got up from the bed and stood hands on hips, looking down at David. "I'm going home to get cleaned up. You want to come or not?"

David looked up, then literally threw himself on the floor, crawling on hands and his one knee to the closet. When he grabbed the crutch he had thrown there, he hauled himself up to stand by holding to the door frame. Bobbie came toward him, arms outstretched if he needed her help. "Don't touch me!" David shouted, agony and anger in his voice.

Stunned, Bobbie stepped back. David hopped with the aid of the crutch to the other side of the bed and retrieved the mate to his support. When he balanced himself he looked at Bobbie, his voice sarcastic and clipped when he said, "Well, aren't we leaving? Or maybe you don't want to go to court with a cripple? Never know, it might be fun. You can watch the one-legged lawyer stumble his way around the courtroom and make a fool of himself. No jury today to play on for sympathy, but it might be a woman judge and maybe she'll feel a little maternal instinct for the poor handicapped excuse for a man who shows up claiming to be an attorney. Ever try to hold evidence documents when you need to walk with your hands? Ever..."

Bobbie's hand went to her mouth to stifle her emotional shock. Then she straightened and faced David. "Stop it, David. Just..., just stop right now! You're acting like a two year old," she choked out. "There is nothing, I said nothing, wrong with you except that bump on your head. You do more on crutches than most men do on two legs, so quit feeling sorry for yourself. I'm leaving. You can go with me or stay for all I care." With that she turned her back and left the room.

David threw both crutches on the bed and flopped down beside them, ready to give in to the rage that filled him, then he heard Bobbie start down the stairs. He realized she had waited at the head of the stairs for him. Reluctantly he admitted he was acting like a child. He quickly picked up the sticks and made it to the stairwell before she was out of sight down the hall. "Wait, lil'bit. I'm sorry I blew up. Wait please, honey, I said I'm sorry." He went down the stairs at a reckless pace.

Bobbie was standing in the hall waiting for him. She didn't say anything, just turned toward the back. David reached her before she got to the outside door. He released a crutch and slipped his arm around her waist. "I'm sorry, Bobbie. It's not you. I just get so frustrated sometimes. You don't know what it's like." David could feel the adrenaline pumping in his blood. He didn't know what he would do if she walked out on him. He always tried so hard to keep his emotions in check, had kept the rage bottled so tight that no one in town, not even Ellen, knew the dark side of him. Now Bobbie knew a little of what he was capable when the black rage took hold and what he could be like. If she turned away he could not blame her. He didn't deserve her loyalty and love.

Bobbie's heart was pounding, sending her a message she could not ignore. She pushed aside her anger and fears, and rested her hand on the arm that circled her, then leaned back into David's chest feeling his tall body, muscles solid with tension, behind her. She could hear his rapid breath; his heart was pounding as hard as hers. Slowly she turned to him and raised her arms to his shoulders and on tiptoe, to reach over the neck brace, kissed him with every bit of strength she possessed.

David returned her kiss, pulling her closer, feeling her fit to him like a soft leather glove. She broke the kiss, and would have moved back, but he would not allow it. He reached to the Velcro strap that held the neck collar and threw the brace on the floor. "Don't move, please lil'bit. I need you. I need you more now than you know." He buried his face in her soft, curly hair, and simply held on to her. For a moment they were in their own place and time with nothing around them except the love they shared.

When they broke apart Bobbie was startled to see tears clouding David's eyes as he gazed down at her.. Her own eyes, too, felt damp from the effects of the emotion packed episode in the bedroom. She made herself smile and reached up to catch a teardrop starting to roll down his cheek. "You're right, David. I don't know how you feel about yourself, but I know one thing for certain. I loved you when you had two legs and I love you now. That's not going to change. You can rant and rave all you want and I'll still be here. Throw me out and I'll pick myself up and walk right back in. I'm here to stay, mister. You better get used to it."

David's stellar smile shone in his wet face. "You are something, lil'bit. You're a miracle, my miracle." He ran a hand over his face, then quickly kissed Bobbie again. "Let's get going. We'll be late for court."

CHAPTER NINETEEN

The coal chute was exactly that, a shaft in the side of a cliff where coal was dug out of the mountain. The vein had played out years ago and the surrounding layer of prehistoric forest that eons of years had decomposed and compressed into coal was not large enough to commercially mine. Orville, Buddy and Ahmed shivered in the chill air that seemed to come from the very center of the rock that enclosed them. Buddy was studying the walls of the tunnel, side-stepping as he encountered rivulets of water seeping from cracks in the stone.

Ahmed was at the gate that barred the entrance and only exit to the shaft. Heavy wood timbers, reinforced with steel hardware would make using that manner of escape very difficult. He tested the dirt floor under the gate to find solid rock an inch down. Squeezing over the top or through the spaces was not feasible, even for someone as thin as Orville

"Buddy, it's cold in here," Orville whined, as though Buddy could conjure up a fire on command.

"Yeah, kid, you're right, it's cold in here and that gives me an idea." Buddy's sigh was audible as he disappeared down the dim tunnel away from the light at the entrance.

Orville turned to Ahmed. "Where's he going?"

Ahmed pulled off the flannel shirt he had worn away from the fishing cabin. He handed it to the boy, who held it like it would bite. "Go ahead, put it on. I don't think you have anything on under those prison overalls. It's not dirty, just old." Ahmed couldn't suppress a shiver when a gust of air hit his dirt stained tee shirt.

"Here, you need this," Orville tried to hand back the shirt. "What's Buddy doing?"

Ahmed shook his head and stepped back out of the draft. "You put the shirt on. I've got more meat on my bones to keep me warm. I expect Buddy is looking for a way out of here. Do you know where this tunnel goes?"

Orville shrugged his thin shoulders into the shirt. "Just back into the hill for a ways. They built a room at the end, call it the vault. I think they keep some kind of records in there. Don't have any other way out that I know of."

A short man with the barrel chest and massive shoulders of a seasoned coal miner appeared at the entrance gate carrying a towel draped tray. Orville eagerly went to meet him. "Hey, Ray. Why you got us locked in? It's cold. Can't we come eat at the mess hall?"

The short man managed to unlock the gate and hold the tray at the same time. He passed the tray to Orville who was doing his best to inch forward out the gate. Ahmed tried to judge what it would take to disable the man's considerable bulk, but even if Orville weren't in the way Ray would be hard to take down. Besides Buddy was still missing. He went forward and took the tray of food from Orville. "*Gracias*," he thanked the man called Ray. He motioned with his head to back in the chute, away from the entrance. "Come, *Chico*, let's eat before it becomes cold." He found a spot out of the draft of air, and sat cross legged with the warm tray on his lap. Orville followed him, looking over his shoulder at Ray retreating around the corner of the shaft entrance.

The tray held plenty of food for the three of them. Thick country sliced bacon strips, fat sausage links, eggs fried in grease that was beginning to congeal in the cold air, and grits that were turning to concrete as they cooled. A basket contained big slabs of bread toasted on one side only. Everything was highly salt and peppered. Orville tore into his food like he hadn't eaten in a month. "Good, huh?" Orville said through a mouthful of the grits.

Ahmed was hungry, too. The peanut butter and crackers during the night had only taken the edge off, but the food held little interest for him. He handed the tray to Orville. "Eat all you want. I'm going to see what Buddy is doing." He shivered again as he moved into the draft at the center of the passageway. As he walked away from the entrance the light dimmed, and the fresh air draft increased. Pausing a moment to let his eyes adjust, he rubbed his arms for warmth and quickened his pace until forced to slow again as the darkness closed in. Unable to see more than a few feet in front of him he traced his fingers along the wall of the passage in lieu of the light. He expected to stumble but the floor was smooth and clear of debris. The passage narrowed and the ceiling lowered until he had to bend his head, then suddenly the shaft turned in a sharp curve and a square of daylight illuminated the side wall and floor. Looking overhead Ahmed could see what appeared to be branches of a tree and blue sky about fifty feet above his head. Exactly what he expected to find, a vertical air shaft, and knew that was what Buddy had been looking for, but there was still no sign of Agent Zero. Ahmed could touch the opening with his hands, where there was no purchase or grip to use for climbing. The edge of the square was smooth as a polished gravestone. The blast of air howling down the narrow shaft left little doubt this was the only vent, so how had the small man reached the opening and then climbed out? There had to be another way to the surface.

Ahmed entered the far side of the shaft and when his eyes adjusted again to the dim light moved in that direction. Another twenty-five yards and the entire passageway was blocked by a massive steel door with hinges embedded in the solid rock. It really was a vault, he thought, remembering Orville's words. A better, stronger vault than any bank could build. He wished for brighter light so he could look at the locking mechanism, but could not believe someone would have gone to the trouble of installing a vault door unless the locks were adequate. Probably more than adequate. He refrained from touching the door, in case infra-red sensors were activated. Unless Buddy had the combination to the vault, the only place he could have gone was up the air vent.

Ahmed returned to that location and began studying the opening when a voice behind him sent him spinning around, - -to see nothing. "Zero, where are you?"

"Up here." It was eerie the way Buddy's voice seemed to echo from the walls. "Sorry, didn't mean to startle you. Ever do any rock climbing?"

Ahmed shaded his eyes with his hand and finally located Buddy peering over the edge of the air vent. "Some," he answered.

"Good. Go get Orville and let's get out of here."

"Leave the boy. He doesn't look strong enough to make the climb with no experience. The woman will make sure he is not mistreated."

Buddy's chuckle seemed to surround Ahmed, tweaking already tense nerves. "We need him. Guess who their important visitor is? I went to the shaft entrance to see if I could get you out that way, but the Head Man brought a small army with him."

"You mean the man I saw with the Vice President? He's here?"

"The one and the same. In the old days we called him El Boca. Appears The Mouth is still giving orders, only this time I don't think Uncle Sam knows what he's saying. We need Orville to give us the name he goes by now. I could do a computer search, but that would take time. Besides, the climb is easier than it looks. Ever done the chimney on the Zugspitze?"

"Yes," Ahmed remembered those days with pleasure. "It was where I vacationed when I could."

"Me, too," Buddy said, "good training grounds. Feel the wall to your left, the one in the shadows."

Ahmed moved in the direction Buddy indicated and ran his finger tips over the surface of the black coal wall until he found a niche with an embedded steel ring. Using the opposite hand he moved a little higher and found another niche. He looked up at Buddy and made the OK sign with his fingers.

"The cuts run all the way up, hand, toe, hand, toe. If you need to rest you can always wedge in like a straight chimney climb. The walls are pretty smooth. This vent takes in air and doubles as an escape route."

"You really think Orville knows the name we need?" Ahmed queried.

"I'd bet my best Aunt Fanny quilt on it."

Ahmed let a laugh rumble in his chest. Suddenly his spirits, as well as his eyes were looking up. "Don't go away," he told Buddy and purposely strode toward the entrance of the shaft.

* * * * *

Bobbie opened the door to her apartment and let out a sigh of relief, "Do we have time for a nap? Oh, sorry David. I'm not supposed to let you sleep until tonight."

David gently moved his head side to side. "Got any aspirin, honey? The top of my head is coming off. I should have taken the prescription the doctor wanted to give me. Wish I could stretch out on the bed for a few minutes, but I'd be out like a light. We need to be getting ready to go. Knoxville time is an hour ahead of us, remember. Did you check your answering machine?"

"Not yet," Bobbie wearily made her way to the end table with the phone. "David, it's not here. It's gone. Oh," the word came out like a frustrated groan, "I know where it is. Buddy said he heard the taped conversation. He took my phone! Why, that bastard. Wait until I get my hands on that little rat!"

David grinned at her choice of words, in spite of the pain in his head. "You go on into the shower. I'll call Ellen and see if anyone has contacted her. I gave her number to Josh Petry. Don't be too long. Traffic can be heavy in town." David continued on into the bedroom and picked up the phone on the night stand.

Mamie answered the telephone in her formal manner, to David's amusement. He told her he would see the judge this afternoon for sure and asked if she had a place picked out for the burial. Yes, Mamie told him. She had purchased cemetery lots at Mt. Olivet in Nashville. Her son was buried there and three adjacent plots were in her name. David expressed his sympathy and apologized for the delay in making arrangements. Mamie politely thanked him for his help, and with no other comments transferred him to Ellen. Though Mamie's voice was calm as ever, David could tell she found making the arrangements for her granddaughter's funeral difficult.

Ellen came on the telephone with a list of people who were trying to contact David. Chief among them was the electrician who wanted to know if David needed extra outlets put in when he made the repairs to the office. David mentally sorted through the list, asking Ellen to take care of the bulk of them. She could handle the office repairs as well as he could from her home phone. He kept the call from Josh Petry for himself. He was about to hang up when Ellen said she had other information. The computer search had turned up something rather strange. A memo sent by the House Representative for this district, had inadvertently been posted to his web-site, then disappeared almost immediately. Ellen had caught it during the few minutes it was active. What it had contained was relative to the following information. A Washington newspaper had printed a small blurb on an incident at the House of Representatives. Seems the Vice President had tried to stop the funding of the vehicle research at Oak Ridge. The Way and Means Committee refused, and referred to his objection as scare tactics to promote his environmental agenda, but the Vice President had allegedly become angry, showing a temper no one thought he possessed. He as much as said that the members of Congress had better start listening instead of arguing, because much more than the environment was at issue in Oak Ridge. After the piece was printed the VP's office had sent notice to the newspaper that nothing else was to be reported about the incident if they wanted to avoid Federal prosecution. Ellen told David that from that date on, nothing else had shown up about the Oak Ridge project on any files or websites she accessed. Not even after the assassination attempt and the explosion at Oak Ridge, which logic would assume might be associated with the incident.

David listened to Ellen recount her investigation, realizing it tallied with what Senator Charles had told him. Something about the experimental vehicle was very wrong and way out of line with a product that was designed to be mass produced and take over the transportation industry. Another of the items Jeff Fischer had better tell the truth about to him. David kept a cool head this time when he thought of Fischer/Charles, whatever or whoever he turned out to be.

David thanked Ellen and asked if she needed her car. Yes, she said, sometime today, no hurry. He told her Bobbie was fine, she was going to Knoxville with him and they would return the car this afternoon.

When he hung up the phone, he could hear Bobbie splashing in the shower. The bathroom was steamy when he opened the door, so he could only see an outline of her behind the transparent shower curtain. She was humming to herself in an alto voice with her back to him. He shucked his clothes, wishing he could just step into the tub with her. She saw him, moved so he could reach the safety bar on the back wall as he sat on the edge of the tub and swung his one leg inside. Pulling up with the bar, he reached for a sponge and soaped her back. She hunched her shoulders and said "a little more to the right, please." He complied, but then that was all the washing they accomplished for the next twenty minutes.

The streets of Knoxville were as crowded and busy as usual. The notoriety of David's client had placed the hearing at the end of the docket, but time was running out. David's frequent glances at his watch confirmed they would be late. He picked up his phone, thankful he had found it safely tucked away with his briefcase on Bobbie's table. Dialing Petry's mobile number, he left a voice mail message, then dialed the courthouse. He left a message for the bailiff that he was on the way and might be late.

Bobbie dropped David off at the entrance, then looked for a parking place. She found a row of spaces marked for attorneys only, and parked quickly, anxious to find David before he got to Jeff Fischer. After this morning, she was afraid that David's temper might get out of control again. As she made her way toward the courthouse, a uniformed motorcycle patrol officer stopped her. "Miss, may I see your parking permit?"

"What?" In her hurry Bobbie had missed what he said to her. "Your car doesn't have a parking permit on the windshield. Those spaces are for lawyers here for court today," the officer reminded her.

Bobbie smiled graciously. "Yes," she acknowledged, "I just dropped David Middleton at the front door. He's an attorney with a case here today. I'll just go get a permit and bring it back." She started up the walk, but the officer stopped her with a hand on her arm. "Sorry, you'll have to move the car until you display the proper document."

"Oh, fiddle," Bobby told him and shrugged his hand from her arm. A passing man apparently thought she needed his help and stepped between her and the patrolman. "May I be of assistance?" he offered.

"No," Bobbie told him, "I have to re-park my car, that's all." Annoyed that she would miss speaking to David before the hearing began, she turned back to the Buick when the policeman got on his motorcycle. Surprisingly the gentleman who had offered help, turned and walked with her. "I really am fine," she told him. "The officer was only doing his job. I'm from out of town and didn't know a permit was required to park here. I appreciate your concern, but there really wasn't anything to it but a misunderstanding."

The tall, thin man with a narrow face matched her pace as she quickened her steps. At the curb in front of the Buick he reached and took hold of her elbow. "I think you will find my automobile more comfortable."

Bobbie's heart rate picked up as she found she could not pull away from his grip. She looked up to see a black sedan with darkened windows pull in behind, blocking her aunt's car. The chauffeur came around to open a rear door and Bobbie was propelled forward between the cars parked at the curb. Using her police training, she braced her arms on either side of her on the cars and kicked backwards at the kneecap of the thin man. He howled with pain and grabbed his leg, but before she could run past the sedan blocking her exit, the chauffeur clipped her neatly on the chin. Stunned, she fell back to trip on the man she had kicked. She fell hard and felt her hand bag beneath her hip. Rolling to the side, she shoved her hand in the specially designed pocket of the bag. No weapon! No gun! Nothing! She cursed under her breath for leaving her Policewoman Special at the apartment. Yanking the bag off her shoulder, she tried to stand and swung the bag at the car's driver. He easily took the purse from her and caught her head in an open handed slap. She went down again, made it back to her knees, but her ears

197

were ringing from the blow. Trying to stand, she tipped sideways into the fender of the automobile as her damaged equilibrium threw her balance off. The narrow faced man yelled something in a language she didn't understand and the chauffeur bodily picked her up and threw her into the backseat of the black car. While she was trying to shake the fuzzy images in front of her eyes into shapes she could recognize, the men got in the front of the automobile and a dark shield rose up to close off the back. Frantic, she grabbed the door handle, then shoved with all her might. The door didn't budge. The car was moving now, out of the parking lot into the street. Bobbie was too angry for tears, but groggy from the blows to her head, and being thrown in the car. Taking a deep breath, she tried again to clear her vision to see where they were taking her. The windows were too dark. She twisted in the seat, then with all her strength aimed her feet at the window. It cracked as the hard, square heels of her shoes hit the glass. Bracing to kick again, she was thrown to the floor as the vehicle came to a jolting stop. A door was jerked open, then the thin man was there with a shinny chromed automatic in his hand. Bobbie let out a scream that should have been heard for miles around, only to have the gun shoved in her mouth. The man got in and closed the door.

"Please do not make me shoot you," he said in English. "You are far too young and beautiful to die today."

* * * * *

"Keep climbing, *Chico,*" Ahmed encouraged, "don't look down."

Orville went up another notch. "I can't do this! I told you I'm scared of heights," he wailed.

At the top of the air vent, Buddy motioned for Ahmed to start up behind Orville. "What's the matter, kid? Want two old men to beat you to the top? Miguel is behind you now, he won't let you fall. Just keep climbing. Nothing to worry about."

Ahmed had reached a level directly below Orville and wedged, feet braced on the vertical wall, knees bent and shoulders against the opposite wall, effectively holding himself in place and blocking any descent. "Go, *Chico,* I am here," he told the frightened boy. Orville, no longer able to see the bottom of the shaft, scampered up the notched ladder as Buddy reached to grab his shirt and pull him from the vent.

Ahmed groaned with the stretch it took him to again reach the notches carved in the fairly smooth sides of the narrow opening. Muscles protesting, he still made the climb look easy. Buddy was at the top to help him over the lip, then the two men lifted a screened cover and replaced it over the opening.

Orville was clinging limply to a small tree like they might decide to throw him back down the shaft. "What we goin' to do now, Buddy?"

"Now," Buddy said, straightening and brushing his clothes, "you are going to take a look at the top man and tell us the name you know him by."

"Is that wise?" Ahmed questioned. "How far is it to your place? You said there was an army here, perhaps we should get away while we can."

"Too far to walk in this rough terrain. I'm going to try to get to my car. You stay with Orville. Be sure he gets a good look at The Mouth, then be prepared to run quick. I've still got this," Buddy produced the .25-caliber Beretta automatic. "When I get to the car I'll yell. Come as fast as you can. I'll cover you." Buddy set off down an overgrown path at a steady pace, pushing Orville ahead of him.

"I'm getting too old for this," Ahmed complained for the hundredth time.

"Yeah," Buddy joked, "but ain't it fun."

From their vantage point on the hillside, Orville and Ahmed could see both the farmhouse and the red barn. According to Orville, the barn was used for both a barracks and mess hall when exercises were held for the New Reich Army. Ahmed asked how many men were in the army? Orville didn't know, but there were girls and women, too. Some of them meaner than the men, Orville solemnly reported. Ahmed did not doubt that he was correct, thinking of some of the female agents he had known. Only a few men were in the yard, milling around as though they were waiting for something. Buddy's car sat farther away to the side of the barn under the apple tree where they had left it. Buddy should be behind the barn now, having climbed over the hill that topped the entrance to the coal chute. The men in the yard were on the blind side. Ahmed and Orville should be making their move toward the barn. One problem remained. The man Orville was to identify had not made an appearance.

The only signal Ahmed and Buddy had set up was the run to the car. Like all the assignments Ahmed had ever taken on, timing was crucial. He had to think of something to slow Buddy down. Then they saw Ray came loping from the coal chute and run to the house. A few moments later, the courtyard was filled with yelling men. The absence of the detainee's from the coal chute had been discovered.

A tall man with dark hair, graying at the temples and neatly dressed in a fashionable business suit, marched authoritatively to the middle of the yard. With a bull horn, he shouted for the men to assemble around him, then began to issue orders.

Orville punched Ahmed's shoulder, nodded his head and indicated the direction toward the barn. Ahmed swept a hand that way and the two began the climb over the hill, keeping behind as much underbrush as possible.

Once behind the barn they skittered down the grade, knocking dirt and rocks with them.

Buddy was at the car. He slipped inside as the men in the yard began to fan out, Ray and Myron handing out rifles from the front porch of the house. The car started and Buddy leaned out the window and yelled at the top of his lungs. "Yaaaaaaw Hoooooooo!

He fishtailed the big Plymouth around in the dirt yard, presenting the passenger door to Ahmed and Orville. They sprinted from the protection of the barn and Ahmed shoved Orville in ahead of him. One more lunge and he would have made it. Instead, hands grabbed him from behind. Buddy floor boarded the accelerator. The car lurched against a man, knocking him away, then plowed up dirt as it gained speed. "Get down!" Buddy yelled as a rifle bullet smashed the back window. Another bullet came through the window to crack the windshield. Buddy kept driving, leaving the running men behind, but the steel gate loomed ahead. Without slacking off on the gas, he aimed straight at the gate. He heard Orville yell, "Jeeze," as the car rammed the steel, shuddered for a moment, then wrenched the gate from the wooden posts. The shriek of metal on metal had Orville covering his ears, as the boy cowered on the floor. More bullets smashed into the solid steel body of the big automobile, and Buddy kept driving. The car tilted dangerously as they hit the rutted gravel road and skidded around a curve out of gunshot range. Finally under the protection of the rock outcrop, he slowed.

Orville climbed back into the seat. "Ain't you going back for the Mex?"

Buddy was sweating profusely. He reached behind the seats and pulled a towel up to wipe his face and hands that were not as steady as usual. A strange half-grimace tugged Buddy's lips and he said sadly, "What do you think this is Orville? Fun and games? Do you kids see so much violence on movies and TV, you can't recognize the real thing? Look at the windows. That was real bullets, not special effects. One bullet and you're dead. This is life, kid, not make believe." Buddy shook his head, "A short climb up a ladder scares the shit out of you, but live bullets are a game? That's it?"

Orville looked down at the laceless tennis shoes he had worm from the jail. "Yeah," he said, "I guess you're right. Does that mean we won't go help Miguel?"

"If you really want to help Miguel, tell me who the head man is," Buddy stated.

Orville quit picking at his shoe and looked up. "I heard Myron call him Jim, and another man say Mr. Orson. Honest, that's all I know."

"That's enough," Buddy said, and the old car picked up speed.

CHAPTER TWENTY

David waited as long as he could at the entrance, then made his way to the assigned courtroom. Bobbie must be having trouble finding a parking place, he thought. Fortunately court was still in session, the other hearings taking longer than expected, so he was not late after all. He could go looking for Jeff, but did not think there would be enough time. He knew Jeff planned to plead "not guilty", and because of the serious nature of the crime, the grand jury had specified no bail with the probably cause warrant. David would handle the issue of requesting a bail review at a preliminary hearing when it came up. He waited, keeping an eye out for Bobbie, until the hearing now under way was dismissed and the door opened by the uniformed guard.

Josh Petry met him as he approached the table for the defendant. "I've been trying to reach you. Where have you been?"

"At the hospital," David answered softly as the judge re-entered the courtroom for the case saved to be last on his docket this date. David wasn't the least disappointed to see it was an elderly man.

"My God," Petry uttered, "someone tried..."

"No," David cut him off. "I did it myself. I fell. Concussion." he indicated the new bandage Bobbie had taped over the stitches on his head. "Hell of a headache."

Petry started to ask more, then quieted when pierced by a look from the judge. "Would either of you gentlemen care to move for a postponement?" the judge glared over the top of his spectacles at the two them.

David heard Josh whisper one last comment as he moved to the prosecutors table. "Word has it that your client was picked up last night by the FBI."

David had been blaming himself for Jeff's failure to be present in the courtroom. If he had arrived in time, they would have been allowed to speak in a private room to insure that the accused, had he not already been instructed, knew what today's proceedings would entail. David would have entered the courtroom as Jeff was led in by his guards, to meet at the table. Until the judge made his entrance, they would have been able to converse. Now David stood by the table alone as the bailiff announced that court was again in session, Judge Louis Atwood, presiding.

"Please be seated." Judge Atwood found his own chair. He pulled a microphone toward him, fumbled with it, then called the bailiff to turn it off. After listening to whispered instructions, the bailiff went first to the prosecutor, then David, and asked them to approach the bench.

Petry, accompanied by another assistant D.A. and David went forward. "Sir," David began, "my client has not been presented to the court..."

"Young man," the judge interrupted, glaring at David, "do not speak until you hear what I have to say. I have been informed that Alan Jeffery Charles was transferred to a Federal Detention Center to stand Federal charges for the alleged murder of one Dr. Karen Fielding, an Israeli citizen. This would indeed be their jurisdiction as she was in the United States at the invitation of our government. In other words, it has been taken out of our hands."

David opened his mouth to protest, then snapped it closed when censured by a stern look from Judge Atwood. The judge continued, "However, there is one problem. No one seems to know where, or which detention center was designated, and the local FBI office knows nothing of any such orders to transfer the prisoner. Would you," he consulted a piece of paper, "Mr. Middleton, have knowledge of your clients whereabouts?"

David was as stunned as anyone else by this turn of events. "No, your honor."

The judge held David's gaze. "You know that if I find that statement untrue, I will hold you in contempt." David kept his eyes straight on the watery blue of the older man's eyes, but said nothing. Judge Atwood finally looked away. "It appears, gentlemen, the accused is missing."

David was speechless, and the judge's smug smile made him feel like he just had his wrists slapped by a grade school teacher. Josh Petry's look of astonishment matched David's. "So," the judge spoke again, "my request for a postponement was not an idle question."

Josh found his voice first. "Uh, your honor, on behalf of the prosecution I request a postponement until Alan Jeffery Charles can be located."

The judge turned to David again. "Do you wish to enter a plea for your client at this time?" Once again, David simply said, "No, your honor."

"Then this hearing is postponed until one month from today, or until papers are received by this court relieving the State of Tennessee, the County of Knox, and the City of Knoxville from this case." The gavel fell sharply on the block, and the judge started to rise.

David spoke up. "Thank you, your honor. I would like to be allowed to speak to the jailer that handled the transfer and see the paperwork used for the release of my client into Federal authority."

"Of course, young man. Anything pertaining to your client is available to you." Judge Atwood, turned, then stopped. With a conspiratorial wink, he whispered to David, "If you want to be a damn good trial lawyer, don't let the judge intimidate you." David stood silent as Judge Atwood left the courtroom, his black judicial robe swirling around him.

Petry was in consultation with his cohort, so David shouldered his briefcase and turned to find Bobbie. The spectators were filing out of the courtroom. He did not see Bobbie waiting for him and started to follow a knot of people toward the exit.

Josh Petry saw him move and called for him to wait. Briefly introducing the other lawyer, he urged David through a door to the back that exited from the building by a side hall. Josh took up their conversation where it was left off. "Concussion, you say? You do look a bit green around the gills. Surely your aren't driving?"

"No," David answered, wishing his head would quit hurting, "my fiancée came with me today. She let me out at the front and went to park the car. I better go around front and find her, she'll wonder what happened to me."

The men headed in the direction of the main entrance. "I did leave you a voice mail message, Josh. We were cutting it close getting here." David spied the blue Park Avenue in a row just to the side of the courthouse. "There's her car. She must be waiting for me at the door."

The men shook hands and the two Assistant D.A.'s headed into the parking lot while David turned to the courthouse steps. Negotiating the shallow steps again with the briefcase on his shoulder throwing off his balance, he gratefully accepted an open door, courteously held by a departing man. The hallway was virtually empty, a guard lounging by a courtroom still in session. Several people ascended and descended the steps without paying any attention to David, and Bobbie was no where in sight. Puzzled, David had no idea where to look for her, then he saw a woman come in and approach the guard at the courtroom door. She showed him a handbag very similar to the one Bobbie carried. David could hear her asking where she should turn in her find, holding the handbag out toward the guard. The man pointed down the hall to a sign over the County Clerk's office.

David swung in front of her as she walked across the entrance lobby to the hall. "Excuse me, please. Did you find the purse outside?"

The woman clutched the leather bag to her bosom, like he might grab it and run. "I found this, young man, and I have every intention of turning it in," she proclaimed indignantly.

"Yes, of course. The right thing to do. My friend carries one like it and I just wanted to ask where you found it. She is supposed to meet me here, but I haven't seen her."

"Humph," the woman said, still eyeing him like he would turn into a purse snatcher. She pushed past him and he had no choice but to follow in her wake. She let the door to the Clerk's office swing shut behind her, catching his arm in a bruising grip. David extracted himself from the door in time to hear her say she found the purse on the pavement beside a blue Buick. A rush of adrenaline brought sudden sweat to David's armpits.

David pushed to the counter beside the woman, whose malevolent look could have turned him to stone. The young woman behind the counter was opening the bag, and emptied the contents on the counter. The purse-finder sneered at David, "I found it. I'm the one who turned it in. If the owner does not claim it, the contents are rightfully mine."

David stifled the urge to hit the greedy do-gooder. He spoke to the young clerk behind the counter. "The bag looks like one my fiancée carries. She was parking the car and should have met me in the courtroom. Would you look at the driver's license, please? The name is Roberta Foster, of Smithville, Tennessee. I have not been able to find her and I'm worried something may have happened to her." While the clerk went through the contents of the purse, David was silently praying. He knew Bobbie had left her gun at home. No weapon could be carried into the courthouse, even by a bona fide law enforcement officer unless they were on duty. Without a doubt the bag belonged to Bobbie, it was her compact, her lipstick, her billfold, the girl laid on the counter.

The billfold opened to Bobbie's picture on the drivers license and only a few dollars. David realized he was holding his breath. The girl turned the picture to him. "Yes," he nodded to her, and reached for the bag.

"Oh no you don't," Mrs. Do-Right caught his arm. "I found it."

The counter girl came to his rescue. "Thank you madam, for turning this in. Please leave your name and telephone number. If the owner does not claim it in thirty days, I'll give you a call."

The woman looked from the girl to David, said "Humph," again and scribbled on the paper put before her. "I expect to hear from you," she iterated, and retreated rather ungraciously through the door.

The girl turned back to David. "Could your girl friend have dropped this?"

"I don't think so. She's a deputy sheriff and usually carries a gun in it." David's face registered his concern. "Do you think you might let me have it?"

The clerk was interested in the handbag. "I knew something about it was different. This side pocket, it's a holster, isn't it?"

David was beginning to be aware of a deep fear building in his chest. "Yes," he answered, "could I at least have the car keys? I don't have any other transportation. I need to go look for Bobbie and this is wasting time."

"Oh, yes, of course, but I have to keep all the contents with the bag if you think foul play may be involved. Is that what you think?"

David knew the girl thought it was a rhetorical question, but the truth of it hit him like a sledge hammer. Someone, maybe the same someone who destroyed his office and killed Pete Stryker, had harmed Bobbie. He knew it like he knew his name. There was no way an experienced police officer like Bobbie would drop her bag when she was used to putting her hand on the gun concealed there. She almost always wore the strap across her body, not only on her shoulder. Only if she needed to maneuver, would she drop the bag. David suddenly felt ill.

A man filling out an application for a vehicle license at the other end of the counter came over to them. "Mister, you better sit down. You're white as a ghost." The girl at the counter picked up a phone. David sidled backwards to a chair with the help of the young man. Almost before she hung up the phone, a Knox County Deputy was beside David.

Ashamed that he had reacted with weakness, David lowered his head to over his knee until the queasy feeling in his stomach passed. "Dear God! Bobbie! If anything had happened to her, he would not be responsible for his actions. Finally words began to enter his consciousness. The deputy wanted to know if he should call the paramedics. The girl wanted to know who she could call, and the young man stood helpless by David's shoulder.

David roused himself. "No, no, I'm okay. I, ah, I had a fall last night, stitches in my head," he indicated the bandage. "I'm okay now, just felt faint for a moment." He felt like a fool when the young man and deputy helped him stand.

"You're the lawyer from the Charles case, aren't you?" the deputy questioned. When David nodded, the man picked up the briefcase. "There is a lounge right around the corner. You better rest a minute before you try to go anywhere. You got somebody to pick you up?"

David gripped his crutches when the young man handed them to him and stumbled after the deputy, giving a brief smile to the concerned girl behind the counter. He turned to thank the man who had come to his aid, but the swinging door told him it was too late.

The deputy settled him in a leather chair, with the briefcase at his feet. David declined the offer of coffee and the man seemed content to leave him alone. David fished his phone from the briefcase then sat with it in his hand. Who should he call? He could reach Petry, but if Jeff's case should go forward it might compromise the proceedings if the prosecuting and defense attorneys spent too much time together. Reluctantly, he dialed Steve's number. When the Dekalb County Sheriff found out David had led his niece into danger, there would be hell to pay, and David was the one in debt. The phone on the other end rang, and David asked for the sheriff before his courage ran out.

* * * * *

Ahmed, his hands firmly held behind his back by handcuffs, was led into the presence of the leader of a Neo-Nazi army, the size of which would have startled the unbelievers in Washington, D. C. The man, whom he had known only briefly as an Embassy security officer in Berlin, looked at him with undisguised curiosity.

"Dr. Faziz," he said, "Funny how you always seem to turn up in the strangest places. Seems your luck has run out this time, old man. You aren't worth enough for a contract, but there are several of your former colleagues who will gladly honor a sanction. They hate your guts!" A malevolent gleam in Jim Orson's eyes included him in that group.

Ahmed shrugged, like the words meant nothing to him. "It is nice to see old friends," he added an innocent smile. "You've come up in the world, I'd say. When last we met, you were pulling guard duty for an under-secretary." Ahmed kept a half amused, cynical expression, never blinking an eye.

Orson understood the slur. He grabbed Ray by the shirt front. "Take this man and lock him up. This time stay where you can see him." To Ahmed he said. "We will have a trial. These men need to see what happens to a man who fails to carry out his assignment. It will be a democratic process to let everyone know that the New Reich is a just and benevolent government. In the New Order, Doctor, you will yet serve my purpose."

Ahmed stood straight, holding his shoulders back with a bravado that was only part bluff. He watched as the men respectfully parted for their leader to make his way inside the farmhouse. Ray yanked on the handcuffs, pulling Ahmed's attention to him. The stocky man then grabbed Ahmed's thin tee shirt to turn him around. The material ripped in the man's grip. He shoved Ahmed in the direction of the barn.

Once inside Ahmed was thrown through the door of a walk-in pantry and heard the lock click. He smoothed the tatters of material still covering his shoulders, aware that unlike the coal chute, no drafts entered this prison, but neither did much light. He squatted down in a position learned from the tribesmen of his African desert home. It brought rest, without restriction of quick action. Orson, if that was his correct name, would not wait long for the farce of a trial. Ahmed had escaped once, and his two companions made a clean get-a-way. At least Ahmed hoped they had. With Zero you never knew how things would go.

Ahmed cleared his mind to consider his position. The trial would be quick, the penalty death. A quick death, he was certain. Orson wanted to impress his followers of his ability to mete out justice with mercy. A firing squad probably, or maybe hanging. Something public, of course, with all the men ordered to witness the so-called justice. With a start, he realized that tomorrow was the day Ahmed Faziz would cease to exist, here, or anywhere else for that matter. He had not made, did not intend to make, the coded contact with his man in Zurich.

Outside the pantry Ray, with a rifle across his lap, sat in a straight chair tilted back on two legs. What the hell, now? What could be so funny that his prisoner was laughing his head off?

*   *   *   *   *

Bobbie was roughly shoved through a steel door set in the solid concrete basement wall. Her quick glance around when she was pulled from the automobile gave her no clue as to her whereabouts, except the knowledge that it was an underground parking garage. The distance they had traveled did not take more than a few minutes, so she must still be in Knoxville. She didn't have time to wonder where in Knoxville, as the narrow faced man pushed her inside the room.

Her eyes adjusting to the brighter lights, she was surprised to see the room was a large, windowless area, furnished in a lavish style more suited to a pent-house apartment. A curvaceous blonde woman occupied a chair midway into the room. Bobbie stepped forward as the man behind her pressed his hand into her back.

The woman rose gracefully from the chair. She came to scrutinize Bobbie while she spoke to the man in the same strange language he had used with the chauffeur. Before their conversation ended another man stepped from a door on the far side of the room.

Bobbie did a double-take, and her heart speeded up a notch. She moved forward, into the center of the room, her hand going out to the man she considered a friend. "Jeff, thank God you're here. What's going on? I left David at the courthouse," she stammered. "Aren't you supposed to be there?" Bobbie stopped, looking from one to the other of the three people in the room with her. Jeff did not respond to her greeting or questions, and then it hit her. She was completely wrong about him. Something David had realized and told her this morning. In horror and revulsion she began to back up in the direction of the entrance door.

Finally Jeff's eyes made contact with her. "Sorry for the rough invitation, Bobbie. I can see a bruise on your jaw. Ibrahim should have been more tactful. But then, would you have come if I only asked?" He smiled a familiar little lost puppy smile, as though pleading with her to understand. His eyes hardened as they followed hers to the door. He shook his head, "It won't open from this side without the combination."

Bobbie was still unable to grasp her situation. Her mind didn't want to accept the fact that she had been forcibly kidnapped. She kept wanting to shake her head clear of the ringing in her ears. She gathered up her courage. "What's this about, Jeff? Why aren't you in jail?"

"Time for questions and answers later. Right now I have things to do. I trust you will be comfortable here. Nadja will take good care of you." He approached the woman and spoke to her in the foreign tongue, then slipping an arm around the thin man's shoulders like the best of friends, left when a buzzer sounded to open the door.

"Why don't you sit down?" the woman rounded a counter to a mini-kitchen. "I'll fix us something to drink."

Bobbie sat on the curved end of a sectional sofa and pulled her feet under her, trying to get her jumping nerves under control. The thin man had taken her shoes in the car. Bobbie remembered catching his kneecap with one of the hard heels before the driver hit her. She watched the blonde woman put ice in two plastic glasses. In one she poured two fingers of vodka, then held the bottle over the second glass like a question mark. "No, thank you," Bobbie told her. "Just a soft drink if you have it." Bobbie decided that for the moment it would help her cause if she used honey, not vinegar. She wanted to know who the woman was and why they both were in this velvet dungeon. Tales of white slavers who kidnapped blonde women to sell to Arabs went through her head. No, she told herself. It's not me they want, it's David. She had to find a way out!

Bobbie had traveled to France one summer with her 4-H Club. They had spent the summer learning to prune and graft grapevines. She remembered a good time with the kids from her school and not paying much attention to living in a foreign country. Now she wished she could place the faint accent she heard from the other woman when she spoke English. It wasn't any French she had heard, maybe Eastern Europe, like what she heard on TV now and then. She smiled when the blonde brought her drink.

Nadja did not return the smile. She looked at the girl through slitted eyes. Why did Fischer think this painfully provincial creature would bring the lawyer, or his brother to heel? She was pretty enough, Nadja granted, and not cowering in a corner like a frightened mouse. It would be interesting to see what Fischer would do with her.

Bobbie sipped her drink, then reached to where her handbag should have been. Uh, oh, not there. She remembered the driver dropping it in the street by her aunt's car. She glanced at her watch. By now David should be out of court and would be looking for her. If he saw the car he would find her purse and know she was in trouble. Oh lord, she thought, he would go ballistic and after this morning there was no telling what he would do. She had never felt in fear of any man, but this morning David had emanated a dangerous strength that gave her goose pimples. If David was angry with

Jeff then, now he would likely kill him. And she had no doubt David was capable of it.

Bobbie made herself stop chewing on a nail, and got up to go over to the kitchen where the woman was sitting on a bar stool. "Would you have any aspirin? My jaw is really sore."

Without answering, Nadja went to a cabinet and handed Bobbie a bottle of the pain relievers. Bobbie helped herself to another canned cola and ice from a bucket, while the blonde poured more vodka in her own glass. Bobbie returned to the sofa, and the silence seemed to solidify around them. "Don't you have a TV or radio or something?" The woman pushed her long hair behind her ear. Instead of answering Bobbie she lit a cigarette and ignored her.

Bobbie tried again, "Some music, or something? Maybe we could talk. I'd really like to know where I am. This place is like a tomb. Must be all concrete for no sounds to come through. I don't even hear any cars, but I know several were parked outside the door." Apparently that subject didn't interest the blonde. She continued to sip her drink in silence.

After checking her watch, the woman went to the refrigerator and began preparing food. Bobbie wondered if her offer to help would be rejected. She decided not to risk it and instead began to explore what was a small apartment in itself. A half wall partitioned the bedroom area with a bath behind. Bobbie went into the bath and closed the door, noting the absence of a lock. The space was windowless, fresh air coming from a ceiling vent. She admired the luxurious fittings and expensive towels. She availed herself of the facilities, then opened the cabinets to find feminine as well as male grooming articles. Combs, hairbrush, lipstick and pressed powder, an electric razor, but no razor blades. A small linen closet was stocked with more towels, new toothbrushes still in their packaging, along with a popular brand of toothpaste and mouthwash. The soap and shower gel in the enclosed tub was an expensive brand. What place was this, she wondered. No expense had been spared to make the occupants comfortable.

She checked her own watch. I've got to get out of here before David comes looking for me. Now, with the men gone is my best chance, she thought. She picked up the brush and tried to tame her tousled hair, then gave up and walked back into the room. The woman was setting food on the counter that served as an eating bar. It looked good. A seafood salad on greens with tomato crescents.

Bobbie sat on a bar stool as the blonde put hot brown and serve rolls in a basket. Coffee, with a delicious fresh aroma dripped in a pot. "Won't you at least tell me your name?" Bobbie smiled.

"Nadja," the woman relented enough to say.

"Oh," Bobbie gushed, "That is so exotic. You must be from Hungary, or maybe Romania. I've always wanted to see that part of Europe."

Bobbie's friendly overture didn't work. Nadja just shook her head," without explaining. The two women ate in silence as Bobbie despaired over the paper plates, cups and plastic utensils. Nothing at all to use to escape. She could just see herself holding a plastic knife to the thin man's throat. Then again…, she slipped one into the pocket of her slacks.

CHAPTER TWENTY-ONE

Bobbie was beginning to feel drowsy. True, she and David didn't get any sleep last night, but this was different. She could feel her mind begin to relax and numbness creep up her limbs in spite of knowing she had to stay alert. Couldn't be, she thought. I checked the pills Nadja gave me. Aspirin was stamped on each one, and I poured my soda from the can myself. But not the first one, her brain reminded her, and then she ate the food at lunch. Nadja had handed her the drink and fixed the food. She got up and paced the width of the room, feeling more and more groggy. Nadja's eyes followed her, but the woman did not stir from her bar stool and cigarette. Now Bobbie's vision was beginning to blur. She ground her fists into her eye sockets, determined to fight whatever drug Nadja had given her. She made it back to the sofa in time to softly collapse on the cushions.

Nadja looked at the sleeping girl, smiled slightly and went to the door. She keyed in the necessary code, standing back while the door swung open. Stepping to the threshold where she could still keep an eye on her charge, she motioned for the big man who had chauffeured the sedan that abducted Bobbie. Together they checked their watches, agreed on the time, then the man scooped Bobbie up in his arms and carried her to the car. While the chauffeur stayed along side the sedan, Nadja did a thorough search of the apartment, making sure no trace of Bobbie's presence lingered. She removed the bag of garbage that included the lunch paper plates and utensils, made sure the plastic cup Bobbie drank from was among the trash. She checked the bath and found hairs from Bobbie's curly head in the hairbrush. She picked up all other evidence that she and Jeff Fischer had occupied the room, even the bed sheets. Bundling all the items together, she carried them out of the apartment to an incinerator chute in the building service area. Satisfied everything went down the chute, she nodded to the man, who removed a powerful shop vacuum cleaner from the trunk of the vehicle, put on rubber gloves and completed sanitizing the apartment.

Nadja watched from the doorway, smiling her approval as he methodically went over every surface of the room and furniture. When the vacuum cleaner was again in the trunk, she got into the front of the sedan with him. Fischer had left strict instructions. He was not yet ready to reveal his plans, but Nadja was sure it would not be long before he would use the information from Karen Fielding to gain what he wanted. She would go along with him for the present, to make sure she was one of the things he wanted. Not even Ben Abdu Hammad would be as rich as Fischer. Fischer was weak, but to gain the new technology she would make sure he did not falter. Nadja checked to make sure the girl was still soundly asleep before she told the driver to raise the black shield between the seats.

The car made it's way through Knoxville's rush hour traffic on the interstate heading west. Approximately thirty-five miles later, it took an exit that led to a northbound route skirting the ridge of the Cumberland Plateau. Another turn and the road narrowed and began to ascend. Winding back and forth in hairpin turns, it went higher and higher into the rugged, heavily forested mountains.

* * * * *

Steve Milloy, the Dekalb County Sheriff was kept waiting, the same as any one with complaints at the Knoxville Police Headquarters. David sat silent beside the Sheriff. Steve had not exploded as David expected when he told the Sheriff his situation over the phone. Instead, the only words Steve uttered were for David to sit tight and wait for him. The receiver crashed down before David could explain.

The Sheriff arrived so quickly David was sure the blue lights and sirens had not been spared. With professional calm Steve listened to David, inspected Ellen's car, and called an acquaintance, the Knoxville Chief of Police. Now they were kept waiting. Though Steve had not spoken two words to David since he picked him up at the courthouse, David knew the Sheriff was very, very angry.

Finally a police lieutenant led them into the Chief's office. Steve and the Chief shook hands while Steve told him the problem without bothering to introduce David. Left standing to himself while the men conversed, David reached in his jacket pocket for a handkerchief. His hand came out with a business card that had been left there the last time he wore the coat. He looked at the printed name. Senator Edgar Charles. With sudden inspiration, David knew what he had to do.

Neither Steve nor the Chief paid attention as David made his way out the door. He continued past the office staff to the outside doors, only a few curious faces turned in his direction. At the side of the building, where the traffic noise was less, he dialed the number from the card. A receptionist answered, passed him to an aide, who on hearing David's name immediately asked him to hold. David was beginning to wonder if he had bought enough minutes on his mobile phone contract when the Senator came on.

"This better be important," Charles snarled. "The Senate is in session, I left a bill I sponsor on the floor."

"Thank you, Senator. It is important. Why did you have the FBI pick up your brother?"

Silence on the other end, then Charles choked out, "I don't think I understand what you're asking. Where is my brother?"

David didn't want to play cat and mouse with the Senator. "He did not appear in court this morning for the arraignment hearing. The judge received information that Jeff was being held at a Federal Detention Center for due process in Federal courts. The FBI removed him from the Knoxville jail during the night. I need to know where you are holding him."

"Wait a minute," the Senator ordered, and David heard voices as the man spoke to someone else. He came back with another order, "Meet me at the airport General Aviation hangars. I can be there in," hesitation again while voices conferred, "three hours."

"Senator," the urgency in David's voice came through, "there is more. My fiancée is missing. I have reason to believe someone kidnapped her."

David couldn't tell what was happening on the other end of this telephone conversation. Finally Charles came back to him, "I'll do what I can. Meet me at the airport." The call went dead.

David looked at the phone in his hand, hoping he had made the right choice. He had been wrong about Jeff and why he had decided to trust Jeff's brother, David didn't have the slightest notion. Still it was going right to the top. If any one had the information he needed it would be the Senator.

It took some doing, but David finally talked the Sheriff into taking him to the Knoxville airport. Steve was still not speaking, did not tell David what the Police Chief and he discussed, and made no effort to keep his anger to himself. David took this as his just due. Worse, David blamed himself. If Bobbie was in trouble, he was the one to blame. Why had he been so dense that he had not picked up on the obvious falsehoods Jeff had fed him? Once he opened his mind to Kuwait, he could see the flaws in Jeff's story. Whether Jeff had deliberately baited him, or actually made a slip, it didn't matter. Jeff had used a name he would have had no way of knowing, unless... The code name for the secret, sensitive mission only a very few of the top echelon would recognize. A mission that failed. David was part of that mission, an Army sharp shooter, expert enough to use a specially designed sniper rifle on Saddam Hussein. Somehow Hussein knew in advance and was prepared for the three men who had infiltrated his guard to attempt his assassination.

Taking control of a guard shack at a crossroads close to the Imperial Palace in Karbala, David, with another American and an Iraqi civilian were to wait for Saddam's motorcade, then both Americans would target the Iraqi leader. One of them should get him. David knew the risks when he took the assignment. Only the fact that the rifles were accurate at an extremely long range gave them any chance at all. The civilian would get them away before Hussein's bodyguards could get to the outpost, hide them until an Army reconnaissance helicopter could pick them up. It could work, with a lot of luck and accurate marksmanship.

Everything went according to plan at first. David hadn't liked cutting a man's throat when they commandeered the mud hut, but their success meant no prisoners. The Iraqui citizen had been able to come up with the correct passwords for the daily check. The guards were changed every third day, so it had to be before then. Word came that Hussein would return to Bagdad via this road the next day.

David and his cohort, a Lieutenant named Roy, moved into position on the flat roof of the mud hut. A jeep appeared in the distance, but it was not the usual entourage of vehicles that accompanied the dictator, and far too early to be the motorcade. It stopped at the hut, then the Iraqui civilian started screaming for them to get out. They were found out! All was lost! David had seen only four men in the jeep, and knew they could defend their position, until he saw several more vehicles, including armored cars come over the hill. Roy and David looked at each other, went to the windowless side of the hut and jumped from the roof. David's ankle twisted, but he ignored the pain and ran, following Roy out into the desert where the rocks could give them cover. Suddenly Roy stopped. David stopped too when he realized they were in a minefield. The mines were covered with sand, but the prevailing breeze had half exposed the windward side of the field. Old, but deadly compression mines. One wrong step, and KABOOM! Horror crept into his brain as he watched Roy gingerly take a step, then two, then again. The fourth step lifted the man into the air with an explosion that rocked the ground. David gritted his teeth and waited for his own death. When the debris around him settled, he could see parts of Roy's body scattered over the sand. Revulsion choked his throat as he gagged. He looked back and saw the Iraqui soldiers standing at the edge of the mine field. One of them lifted a rifle aimed in his direction. It was run, or die where he stood. He ran blindly, made it past Roy's remains and in another instant would have been safe behind the rocks when he felt something hit his hip from behind. With superhuman effort he dove for the safety of the rocks. The noise and shock waves drove him even farther toward his goal. Funny, there was no pain. He looked around him, seeing parts of bone and flesh amid blood soaking into the sand. Detached, he wondered who had been injured. Then he reached down to his twisted ankle. It was not there. A wave of nausea caught him and he passed out.

David had relived this nightmare over and over again. He had not fully regained his senses until he was safely away from the region, hospitalized in Germany. Only after three emergency surgeries was he alert enough to know the real extent of the damage he had suffered. By then the splintered bone of what was left of his hip had been removed, one kidney gone, intestines repaired, and the first of many skin grafts begun. He lived, and wondered why. Roy had a wife who would never welcome her husband home.

He found later the Iraqui who would have taken he and Roy into hiding had come for him only a few minutes after the soldiers left. The man and his woman had managed to cauterize the main arteries with lighted cigarettes to stop the bleeding long enough to transport the wounded man to the arranged pick up point after dark.

He also was told that Saddam had used the incident for his propaganda, citing that all three men were dead. The superiority of the Iraqui army would protect the country's leader. No assassination attempt would ever succeed, was the message broadcast to the Iraqui people.

His superiors had assured David the combined governments working together in the Persian Gulf War would never admit such a mission ever took place. There could be no retribution for something that never happened.

Thoroughly debriefed during his hospital stay, he knew they were betrayed by someone who passed along the information to Saddam. David thought it ironic that Roy was the one who paid the ultimate price for that treason, and David's own life inevitably altered, but no one would ever know why.

The nightmares had lessened after a time, but he had buried Kuwait so far back in his memory that he had not only missed the reference to the war, he had actually believed Jeff. Now, he could put together the Washington reports, Jeff's lies, and the Senator's warning. But that was only part of the equation. How did the aborted assassination on the Vice President fit in? He could see what it might have to do with Oak Ridge and all the money and power ownership of the invention would bring, but why Jeff Fischer, when he had thirty million dollars waiting when he took the name Jeff Charles again? Why kill Karen Fielding? I'm going around in circles, David thought, his mind refusing to calm down so he could think straight.

There was one thing with no room for error. Bobbie. Whatever it took, whatever was required of him, she came first. He knew he would gladly pay with his life for Bobbie's safety. The life she had so recently given back to him.

With commendable restraint Steve spoke to him. "David, you know I'm angry. If you weren't so dammed stubborn you could have asked for my help. I should have locked the two of you up!"

David remained silent, as Steve maneuvered the Patrol car through the traffic. There really wasn't much he could say.

"Look, David, we need to work together. I love Bobbie, too, she's my sister's child. When her mother died, I gave her a job, then let her talk me into the academy. She's as stubborn as you are, but strong and smart, too. If some one is detaining her against her will they might be sorry. Let's not take this out on each other."

David was grateful for Steve's words. He wasn't above taking all the help he could get. "Thanks, Steve. You know I trust you, but believe me, this isn't just a local man mad at me. We've stumbled onto international espionage. These people are terrorist who hold no value on human life. I know. I was there in that part of the world. It's greed and power, plain, but not so simple."

Steve grudgingly gave David a grim smile. "Well, you convinced me when you have a U. S. Senator at your beck and call."

* * * * *

Ahmed heard a commotion in the barn adjoining his improvised cell. From what he could tell, it was a call to mobilize. He banged on the door of the pantry but with so much going on, men rushing to get their gear and yelling to each other, no one paid any attention. He settled down again and waited until the noises diminished. On his feet, he pounded on the door, calling to Ray as loudly as he could. No answer. Surely not everyone left the barn. Orson had ordered Ray to personally guard the prisoner.

Taking the few steps to the back of the closet to gain space, he hit the door with his shoulder, once, then again. It didn't budge. The almost dark interior of the closet made searching through the contents difficult. Surely there was something he could use to batter the door open. Feeling with his hands as much as looking, he began to explore the objects on the storage shelves. About to give up he came to a stack of iron skillets. He picked out a medium size pan, positioned himself and swung it at the door knob. The metal pan, vibrating in his hand sent shock waves up his arm. He staggered upright, clutching his arm while numbing pain loosened his grip on the skillet. He shoved the door again with his shoulder, but the lock held. Stripping out of the remains of his tee shirt, he wrapped the handle of the heavy skillet and swung again. This time there was a satisfying screech as the wooden frame gave way. One more swing with the skillet, and he was out.

Flexing his still numb fingers, he made his way out of the closet, holding the iron skillet at ready like a weapon. The barn was empty. He checked from one end to the other, no one inside, no one outside. Whatever had caused the sudden evacuation, it appeared he was the only occupant. He brazenly walked into the sunshine, blinking until he could look around. Only a few chickens scratched for bugs in the yard. Deserted! The house was the same, not a soul in sight, upstairs or down, the signs of a hasty exit apparent in the scattered clothing and personal effects left behind. The yard was vacant of the trucks and vans of this morning. Ahmed had a grin on his face. Obviously his execution had been stayed, at least for a time.

The unmistakable "wop, wop" of helicopter blades broke into the silence. A bullhorn called for all weapons to be put down and all personnel to assemble in the yard. Ahmed ran out, shaded his eyes to watch a fully armed Marine Cobra Helicopter touch down in front of the barn. He wasn't a bit surprised when Buddy Adams jumped from the open door.

"You can put the skillet down now, friend, but don't you dare hug my neck." The toothy smile told Ahmed Buddy was genuinely glad to see him alive. Buddy turned to give some orders to the men fanning out to search the compound.

Ahmed hugged the iron skillet to his chest like it was his old friend. "What did you do with the boy?"

"Took him back to jail. Don't worry, I'll put in a good word for him, but he has to learn breaking the law isn't fun and games." Buddy looked at Ahmed, "You okay? Feel like going down the coal chute again?"

Ahmed shivered at the thought, but Buddy just grinned. "Come here, son," Buddy beckoned to a young marine. "We need your jacket."

Without question the young man shucked the camouflage jacket and handed it to Buddy, then addressed him as a military officer even though Buddy wore jeans and a plaid shirt. "Yes sir, Colonel. Is that all Colonel?"

"Proceed as before, Corporal," Buddy replied, and returned the man's smart salute. The marine left them, his muscled chest proudly proclaiming U. S. Marine stamped on his undershirt.

"So it's Colonel," Ahmed said thoughtfully, buttoning the jacket over his own chest. "I wondered where you got the pull for a helicopter. What else is going on that I don't know about?

"Well, right about now the ATF, with some help from the Federal Marshals, is rounding up Jim Orson's Nazi army. They had agents surrounding this compound since I contacted them last night. Let's go see what's hiding in that mountain vault. You are okay, aren't you?"

Ahmed assured Buddy that the only thing Orson had done was set his execution date, then locked him up again. They jogged over to the coal chute, where Buddy returned another salute. "All clear, sir," the young private said as they entered the shaft.

Ahmed had to shiver again, trotting behind Buddy through the black walled passage. Signs of hasty use were all about them as shredded paper bits littered the floor. Even if they were able to enter the vaulted area, all evidence would probably be destroyed. He glanced up briefly as they crossed under the air vent. The screened top was missing. The escape route had been well used this day. At the vault door Buddy came up short.

"Okay, Miguel, open it."

"Open it yourself, Colonel."

"Not your specialty, huh?" Buddy grimaced. Ahmed only wagged his head. "Guess we'll have to blow it."

"No," Ahmed said with emphasis. "Look at these side walls. This was a coal mine, remember? This looks to be bituminous coal. Soft coal. A blast powerful enough to open that door would bring the entire mountain down on us."

"Well," Buddy ran his fingers over the wall and came away with black grit, "what do you propose we do?"

"Why don't we just open the door," Ahmed said as he grasped the lever and pulled down. The huge vault door silently glided out to reveal an electrically lighted room. Like the chute, evidence of a quick exit made the room look like the computers were featured in a demolition derby.

"We're too late," Buddy observed. "How'd you know the door was open?"

"A matter of deduction, dear sir," Ahmed quipped, "Actually, I once found myself in a similar situation in Russia. I destroyed what I could of my equipment, shredded all the documents and got out of there. I didn't wait around to lock up. Let's see where this tunnel leads."

"Wait," Buddy touched a device so small Ahmed had not noticed it hooked over his ear. To Ahmed's surprise, a voice came out of thin air and said, "Yes, Colonel?" Buddy gave orders for a guard to be stationed at the vault, and nothing touched until the demolition and electronic experts got there. His orders were acknowledged by the same voice, then Buddy touched the device at his ear again. Ahmed pointedly stared. The tiny, thin wafer appeared not to be attached to any wires or transmit to any kind of radio he could see on Buddy's person.

Buddy saw the puzzled expression on Ahmed's face and pointed to his ear. "New technology. Glad to see it works down here in a coal mine." He reached into a pocket and handed Ahmed one of the tiny devices. "Hook it over your ear, then if we get separated all you have to do is touch it and speak my name. Mine is monitored by control, so if we get into trouble they can send someone after us."

Ahmed curved the flexible hook to his ear, then said "Buddy".

"Not so loud," Buddy winced. "The volume control is on the backside. Slide the control all the way and I'll be the only one who hears you."

The two men headed to the arch in the coal wall Ahmed had indicated at the back of the room. They entered another horizontal shaft lit with light bulbs strung along the ceiling. Several chutes branched off the lighted passage, honeycombing the mountain. A quick look in one showed rifles and ammunition, along with boxes of dynamite. They didn't take time to search all the side offshoots, but continued following the main tunnel. It was hard to know how far they had walked when daylight filtered through an opening to the hillside. They came out in a meadow, forming a flat ledge on the hill. No road was visible in the rugged rocks and heavy forest ringed the area, then they heard the buzz of an All Terrain Vehicle in the distance.

The unseen voice spoke again, this time with urgency. "Colonel, where are you?" Buddy touched his ear. "Miguel Rios and I are on the other side of the mountain. The tunnel goes straight through. On our way back now. Have any of the ATF personnel reported in?"

"NO, er, no sir! I have warned them away," the voice shouted. "The demolition specialist checked the vault. That whole room is wired. Enough explosive to bring down the hillside, and the mountain with it. We don't know if there is time to search for the detonator. Get as far away as you can. It's going to blow!"

"Control," Buddy commanded, "Evacuate now. Get the men and get that bird airborne NOW! Do you read me?"

"Yes sir, Colonel. And Colonel,"

"WHAT?" Buddy shouted back.

"Colonel, YOU get the hell out of there!"

Buddy pointed in the direction they heard the ATV, and ran. Ahmed followed on his heels.

CHAPTER TWENTY-TWO

Something hit the side of the car. It swerved, then straightened out. Bobby grabbed at the armrest and tried to sit up. Eyes burning and throat raw with thirst, she made another effort to raise herself. Still groggy, she felt a hand on her arm help her to a sitting position. She scrubbed at her eyes, trying to see who was in the automobile with her.

It took a moment, but she finally found enough spit to wet her tongue and asked the classic question. "Where am I?"

"Why don't you go back to sleep?" the man sitting next to her said softly. "Here, lean on me." He drew her back against him. She snuggled to him for a moment, then jerked erect.

Bobbie blinked, trying to clear her vision. She was so thirsty she wondered if she had slept for days. "Water," she croaked. "I need water."

The man knocked on the dividing panel and it lowered slightly. He spoke to whoever was in the front and bottled water was passed through. He broke the seal and handed it to Bobbie. She gratefully drank in large gulps, until his hand slowed her intake. "Careful," he said in that same soft, calm voice, "take it easy. There's more." He released the bottle and Bobbie drank again, this time slower, swishing the water around her dry mouth. Nothing had ever tasted so good. She tipped the empty bottle up to let the last drops trickle on her fingers, then wet her eyes. Her vision began to clear.

The man still had one arm around her, steadying her in the car. She tried to see out the windows, but they were too dark. That's when she remembered her abduction, the underground apartment, Nadja, and Jeff Fischer. She turned to her companion, then froze.

Jim Orson felt Bobbie flinch. He smiled, and withdrew his arm. "It's okay, Miss Foster, I won't let anything happen to you."

Bobbie leaned back in the seat. It was the same sedan. The window on her side was cracked. She met Orson's eye. "You're one of them."

"If you mean one of the Hammaddi, no, not like Fischer. I want no part of that terrorist sect, but they have proved very useful." Orson lapsed into silence.

"But..., but you're here," Bobbie sputtered. "I thought,--I thought...," she trailed off.

Orson's lips pressed together. "You thought I was one of the good guys, so what am I doing in this car?" Bobbie closed her mouth and nodded. "Well, you see, everyone has their own idea of what's good, or what's bad. I happen to think it's bad when our meddling government shuts down enterprise for the sake of their botched environmental agenda. Sure, let the coal burning power plants spew pollutants into the air, let the oil tankers poison the oceans with their sludge, but no, we must not use the technology of broadcast electricity to power vehicles."

There was a passion to Orson's speech that made Bobbie take notice. "You mean the Vice President, don't you? You," she hesitated accusingly, "You planned the assassination?"

"Not alone, but yes, I had a hand in it. Too bad Ibrahim Hassim picked the wrong man for the job, but there is always next time." He let out a long sigh, "There I was, expected to put my life on the line, when all those Washington asses aren't fit to govern this great nation. More and more of us are getting fed up with them. One day soon, the New Order, the New Reich, will take over. Then you'll see what happens to all the niggers and jews , and the rest of the illegal aliens who're taking over our country. You'll see what happens to those pansy lawmakers who want to take away our guns."

Bobbie shuddered to think this was going on in her state, much less the nation. Maybe if she kept quiet, he would quit preaching his hate message to her.

Silence didn't help. Orson continued, fired up to fever pitch. "The explosion that shook the car and woke you up blasted our Tennessee headquarters to hell and back, but it won't stop us. We set that charge and I hope we sent all those dammed marines to hell with it. We paid with a few of our men, but we got more of those ATF bastards sniffing around our place. Nothing like a good Tennessee redneck when it comes to mountain warfare. Soon as we catch up with that no good Fischer, I'm going to get myself to Houston, collect my payoff, and it's the Wyoming mountains for a while." Orson slipped his arm around Bobbie again. His voice calmed, again soft and seductive. "I had eyes for you back in Carthage. You need me, too, not some sorry one-legged cripple like that lawyer. Come with me, baby. You and I would make a great team. Why, with our genes I bet we can produce some superior New World citizens."

Bobbie sat motionless for a moment, like she was thinking over his invitation. She even looked up at him with a crooked little smile. Then she reached behind her and brought his arm over her head and laid his hand, palm up, in her lap.

He smiled back at her, wondering what she was going to do. He left his arm where she placed it, feeling her fingers massage their way up to his shoulder through his shirt sleeve. He felt himself becoming aroused when suddenly she clamped down hard, finding an acupressure point and his arm went numb.

She threw the useless hand back in his lap. "Don't touch me again."

Enraged, he slapped her with his other hand, then grabbed her hair, pulling her to him. Bobbie screamed. The sliding window came down and Nadja pointed an automatic at Orson. "Do not," she threatened. "Fischer wants her unharmed." Orson dropped Bobbie and she fell back against the car seat.

* * * * *

David and Steve arrived at the Fixed Base Operations Terminal on the general aviation side of Magee Tyson Airport just as the white Lear cut its engines. Linemen swarmed to the aircraft, placing the chocks and securing it. David waited at the door of the terminal as first a bodyguard descended from the Lear, then the two pilots. When Senator Charles appeared, he went out to greet the man.

Edgar Charles was angry. It was obvious when he ignored David's outstretched hand. Now we're even, David thought of his rudeness when they first met, but keeping score on each other doesn't help a bit. "Please come inside, Senator. There is someone you should meet."

Charles looked surprised, but continued to walk with David. "I thought you said you were alone. We have to keep a lid on this."

David swung on his crutches into the terminal as the bodyguard held the door. "Senator, this is Steve Milloy, Sheriff of Dekalb County, Tennessee. Steve, The Honorable Senator from Illinois, Edgar Charles. Sir," David addressed Charles, "Steve has been in on this from the beginning, but only recently was told the serious nature of the problem. He is someone you can trust with your life, as I do. He is also my fiancée's uncle."

Charles looked from David to Steve, then extended his hand. "A law enforcement officer is always a good friend to have," he said. "Now tell me where my brother is," he turned to David.

"That is what I was hoping you could tell me," David responded. "I only know what I was told in court."

The bodyguard came and whispered in Charles ear. Charles swept a hand toward the rear of the building. "Come," he said, "I have arranged to have a conference room available. It is ready now." He spoke privately to the guard, who nodded agreement to the instructions, then the three of them made their way into a room occupied by a large conference table and upholstered chairs. A lineman, clad in white overalls emblazoned with the FBO logo, arrived carrying a tray with a coffee carafe and water pitchers, cups and glasses. He filled the water glasses and placed them in front of each chair.

"Please be seated, gentlemen. I expect the Atlanta Division FBI Chief to be here momentarily. While we wait, fill me in again on what occurred at the courthouse this morning."

When the lineman finished dispensing water and disappeared through the door, David recited the whole episode of the delayed hearing and the judges instructions. Then he explained why he thought Bobbie had been kidnapped. Steve did not interrupt until David got to Bobbie's handbag. He spoke up when David concluded.

"The Knoxville police chief and I have known each other since our academy days. He will release the automobile and handbag to me as soon as they have been printed and cataloged. I have permission to work across jurisdiction lines to look for my niece."

The Senator sat with his fingers steepled together and pursed mouth. He put his hands down and looked at Steve, but addressed David. "I thought you said he understood this is Federal business. National security is threatened. The NSA is involved. The FBI is involved. The Vice President is involved. Dammit, the President is involved!" he finished in a crescendo.

Steve's face turned a shade near crimson. David could almost hear him grinding his teeth. That's all I need, David thought, two angry men fighting each other. "Sir," David addressed the Senator again, "the Sheriff is well aware of what interference in a federal investigation could mean. He is simply as worried about Bobbie as I am. Please, let's hear what the FBI has to say before we argue." David, spread his hands in supplication.

Charles glared at him, but turned his friendly smile back on as the Atlanta Bureau Chief greeted him from the door. Three men came into the room, one remaining standing while the other two joined the group at the table.

Introductions made, Charles got down to business. The FBI men looked at each other, then the Chief cleared his throat. "The Knoxville Field Office has already received a call from a Judge Louis Atwood, demanding an explanation for information sent him concerning Alan Jeffrey Charles." He looked apologetically to the Senator. "My answer to you is the same as we gave the judge. We have no record of any orders from Washington, written or verbal, to take custody of the prisoner. In other words, we didn't do it."

David and Charles were both trying to talk at once. David rose, holding on to the table for balance. For the moment Charles gave David the floor. "Have you questioned all your men?"

The look David got was the second time he knew the FBI didn't think much of small town lawyers. "We are taking steps to find the fugitive."

"You have of course checked the Federal Prison in Atlanta," David heard the in drawn breath, "or the center at Lexington, Kentucky. How about the minimum security facility at Maxwell Air Force Base in Alabama? Fort Knox?"

"That's enough," Charles snapped. "These men know how to do their job. Gentlemen, we are all upset, but let's put our heads together and pool our information. Proceed, George," he addressed the senior man.

David sat down, the wedge of concerns getting bigger by the minute. Would they be required to take a vote to accomplish anything? Maybe a good old fashioned all out fight was what it would take. He should have let Steve go at the Senator.

The Chief gave David a conciliatory look, "We have ascertained the transfer documents are fakes, as is the information relayed to the court. I have notified the state and local authorities to put out an APB on Alan Jeffery Charles, alias Jeffery A. Fischer. We have done as much nationwide. Sorry, Senator, but it seems your brother is missing, <u>again</u>." Emphasis on the last word.

Charles sagged against the table. The man standing brought a mug of coffee and put it before the Senator. He rallied and sipped the hot liquid while you could have heard a pin drop on the surface of the conference table. His audience waited with baited breath for his next words.

Charles spoke, seemingly to no one in particular. "I thought it would work. I thought I had him this time. I would have kept my bargain, all thirty million dollars of it."

David was sympathetic, but this wasn't finding Bobbie. He stood again to be sure Charles would pay attention to him. "Senator, I realized this morning that what Jeff told me happened in Saudi Arabia was sheer fabrication. Fiction, worthy of his writing talent. He spun a tale and I was fool enough to believe it. Now I think you need to tell us the real story."

Edgar Charles head was bowed, eyes staring into the mug of coffee as he stirred the brown liquid. Gently he set the cup away from him and looked up at David. "You're right," he said, "but I'm the bigger fool. I thought I could control my brother. I thought I could keep everything neatly tucked away in the archives, buried under tons of paperwork. Most of it would go to the incinerator soon."

The Senator pushed away from the table and walked to the door. "Gentlemen, there are only two of us in this room that my information concerns. George, please take your men and leave. You know I work closely with the FBI. I'll come to the Knoxville Field Office as soon as possible and file a formal complaint. Don't worry, I can square things in Washington. It's your case, for now, so do all you can to locate my brother and the missing girl."

The Bureau Chief looked stunned. "But--," he stuttered, "I know what you're doing Edgar. You can't protect him forever. I'll give you twenty-four hours, then we move full force with the National Security boys. Understood?"

Edgar Charles continued to hold the door to the conference room open after the FBI agents left. "Sheriff?"

Steve stubbornly refused to budge from his chair. David leaned over and told him, "Go on, Steve, the FBI will need a good description of Bobbie. I gave one to the police downtown, tell the FBI that, and anything else you can think of."

Steve pulled back, glared at David and snarled, "I'll go, but you better start getting your priorities in order, or you'll answer to me." He left the room like a thundercloud ready to send lightning bolts at both David and the Senator.

Charles resumed his seat at the table. David moved to a chair opposite the Senator. Without preamble Charles began. "I know who you are Middleton, and how you fit into this. I had you checked out after our conversation aboard my plane. Before then I had never seen you, so I didn't know the nature of your handicap. While we talked that evening, things began to fall into place. You're the surviving rifleman from Operation Sureshot. Except it wasn't sure, and no shots were fired. Saddam knew of the attempt almost as soon as you crossed the border between Iraq and Kuwait. There was a traitor. I'm afraid at last it will have to come out. The traitor's name is Alan Jeffery Charles."

David sat silent, mesmerized by the words. What did Charles want him to say? A name for the treason was the only thing David had not known during his hospital stay in Germany.

Charles spoke softly. "Saying I'm sorry wouldn't begin to be enough, so I'll not even try. I'm no psychiatrist so I can't even tell you why he did it. The drugs, of course, maybe money, who knows, but more to get back at our father."

Charles had David's attention now. The father was dead now, so how could Jeff hurt him this time, David wondered. What was all this now?

Charles continued his monologue. "I was the one who was born with the golden gavel. Oh, Jeff had the silver spoon all right, money, education, and a distinguished name, but I was the one who went into the family business and Jeff had to go to work. I, the first son, was the one with junior after my name. I was the one who would inherit the power, run the businesses, chair the boards, make the decisions. I knew Jeff hated father, and probably me, too, but I never dreamed he would go this far. When he got into that mess in Saudi, I simply couldn't believe he would deliberately commit treason." Charles paused, looking at David. There was no sympathy on the young man's face, but Charles hoped David believed what he was hearing.

"I don't expect you to understand, but our father was not an unkind man. He made his fortune from his ability to read people, to know who to trust and who would falter. He loved us both. He knew Jeff was weak, but he could not sit by and let Jeff be tried and possibly executed for treason. He had the power and the money to save both his sons and himself, maybe even our nation. If this had come out we would have been ruined. A proud name that has served our country since colonial days would be dragged through the mud. Our financial standings and banking institutions would fail. Our holdings are so extensive there would be a backlash in the economy. It could have triggered a recession. He did what he thought was right. I know you have suffered, others too, but my father did not escape. The worry and the torment he went through brought about his death."

Charles was beginning to look haggard as he continued. "I thought it was over when I was told Jeff died in Denver. I could relax. They say don't speak of the devil, but it's happening again. This time it's going to be different. I swear that to you. I can't live with it anymore. I can guess where you got most of your information about Jeff. There is only one person who is bulldog enough to never let go. That's Lt.Col. Frank Barger. How long have you known him?"

David took a moment to reply. "I don't know a Frank Barger. I got the reports off the Internet." David hesitated, the Internet wasn't exactly a lie. "Who is Col. Barger?"

"Col. Barger is the liaison officer Jeff tried to blame for the treason. He's a Special Forces officer who was a courier between the U. N. and the allied headquarters. No one believed any of the accusations, but it ruined his career. He wants his name cleared of even a hint of suspicion."

"Sorry, I don't know any Barger," David said as another piece of the puzzle fell into place. "I told you, Jeff and I talked for a long time."

"Okay, play it your way right now, but you might as well know that what can be pulled up from archives on a computer is not accurate. What went into those reports was only the outline of the evidence. My father saw to that, and God knows I've done my part."

"Senator," David kept his voice even and emotionless. "Thank you for what you have told me. Can we agree that what is past is past? There is no point digging up useless dirt. What is important now, is what we make of the present. I take it you do believe Jeff to be dangerous, and possibly unbalanced. I need to find Bobbie. My gut feeling is that she's in danger. Can you help me there?"

Charles nodded slowly, "One more thing. It may help us locate your girl and my brother. You need to know what it is Jeff is after. The Oak Ridge technology for sure, but do you have any idea what that has unleashed?"

David shrugged, "I don't suppose the oil cartel is too happy, but I haven't considered anything other than greed and power."

"How about world domination?"

"Oh, come on now. Even the automobile didn't bring that about. I don't see how..."

Charles cut David off. "The revolutionary engine is powered by magnets that are attracted or repulsed to a beam of static electricity. The engine creates the power to turn the driveshaft the same way a generator creates the power to turn over an internal combustion engine. No one before has harnessed the electricity in the air all around us. Now, somewhat like the towers that transmit cell phone signals, it is possible to send beams of electricity to receivers through the atmosphere. Unfortunately, not very practical. The range of transmission is very short, but nothing can come between the broadcast tower and the receivers. To use it on the highways, all vegetation would have to be cleared, and any animal, including man, unfortunate enough to be caught in the magnetized fields would be instantly fried to a crisp. Are you beginning to get the picture? The technology is promising, but a lot of research still needs to be done."

Charles took a sip from his water glass while he let David digest the information. "Of course the Vice President got involved when he learned the effects on the environment. Bad as that could be, it gets worse. Here at ground level the weight of the air limits the beams range, but in space---," Charles heard David gasp as he drew in air. "In space, pure sunshine to generate electricity with no atmosphere to cut through, it becomes just what the Starwars boys are looking for. Now, do you understand what I have been trying to tell you?" Charles drank more water, waiting for David to say something.

"How, how--," David started, then shut his mouth before saying, "I think I understand, hard as it is to grasp the magnitude. I have questions, but now's not the time for most of them. There is something else. Something I need to know, if you can tell me. Who is it that wants me dead, and what do they think kidnapping Bobbie can do for them?" Even as David asked, he knew the answers to his questions.

If the Senator could place David from his knowledge of what happened in the Gulf War, someone who was actually there could, too. Jeff could have recognized David as the Sureshot survivor. He couldn't take the chance that David would remember who had been in the room when the operative team was briefed. Even if David only suspected who sabotaged his mission, Jeff could be in trouble. Jeff wouldn't take the chance that anything would keep him from owning the--. David's brain didn't want to accept what he was thinking. It sounded too much like science fiction. A Death Ray Machine? Bobbie?. David's heart was thudding. Holding Bobbie would insure David played ball, in Jeff's ball park, with Jeff making the rules. Lord in heaven, David prayed silently, what do I do now? Help me, Lord, or she doesn't have a chance.

Senator Charles spoke again. "Jeff will contact you, you can be sure of that. Not personally, he will send a message by some means. Where are you staying?"

David flinched but told the truth. "Bobbie's apartment." He pulled a scratch pad across the table and scribbled the phone number, his mobile number, and Bobbie's address.

"Good," Charles was regaining his take command authority. "Collect your Sheriff and wait there. I'll go visit with George and the FBI. I'll stay in touch. Call me the minute you hear anything. You've got my numbers."

David nodded, feeling like he had just been hit by a freight train. "I can't just sit and wait!"

"Use your head, man. Let the Sheriff do the searching, you stick by the phone." Charles was at the door, the bodyguard waiting. Before he disappeared he turned back. "Good luck, then again, maybe I'd better say good hunting." With that he was gone.

David could have put his head down and cried.

* * * * *

The blast scorched a path across the meadow that would have seared Ahmed and Buddy to well-done on a meat thermometer. The woods hadn't offered enough protection to escape the flying rock and dirt spewing from the mouth of the tunnel. Percussion waves blew leaves and twigs off the trees, leaving stinging cuts and bruises on the two men's exposed skin surfaces.

Buddy wiped blood from his cheek with a well used handkerchief. "Enough coal left in that mine to burn for years. If all the ammunition and dynamite we saw didn't go with the first blast, we better keep going. This whole hillside will be an inferno. No way to investigate this site now. Shit!"

Ahmed settled for the sleeve of the jacket to wipe his face. "This wasn't their main headquarters. We know who to look for now, if he got away."

"Yeah, Orson will turn up again. I'd bet my pay check on it. I've put a year of my life in this gig. I'm tired of getting all the piss ant assignments they throw me. I'm not getting any younger, maybe I'll go ahead and take my retirement."

Ahmed shook his head wearily. "You wouldn't like it. It doesn't work. I know, I tried."

A voice in the air made both men jump. "Colonel, are you okay?"

Buddy touched his ear. "Control, you just scared the livin' daylights out of me. Where are you?"

"Airborne, sir. Fifteen air miles north. We're helping the ATF mop up. Some casualties here, but none at the site, if you and your partner aren't hurt."

"Both Rios and I are uninjured. Can you swing back this way and pick us up?

"Not at your location, sir. There's a road one mile due north. We can collect you there if you can make it fast. Our fuel is near critical, estimate half an hour air time, and we need fifteen minutes to take us home."

"We'll make it, son." Buddy touched the earpiece again and motioned to Ahmed. "Well, partner, what you waiting for?"

CHAPTER TWENTY-THREE

David paced back and forth, a difficult thing to do on crutches and one leg. There were times when the frustration of his physical limitations seemed insurmountable. This was one of them. His need for action was so strong he could taste it in his mouth. He simply could not remain here, sitting by the telephone waiting for a message that might, or might not come. A bitterness for his handicap he had not felt for a long time was simmering just beneath the surface of his emotions. He wanted to be with Steve, who was working with the law enforcement of the area to set up road blocks and scour the area for any one who might have seen anything in the courthouse parking lot this morning. He wanted to be anywhere but Bobbie's apartment where everything reminded him she was in danger.

By the time a courtesy car from the airport FBO had dropped him back at the courthouse, Steve had arranged for the Buick and Bobbie's handbag to be released to David. He was instructed to drive the automobile to Bobbie's apartment in Smithville and stay there until Steve got back to him. David had to wonder if Senator Charles and Sheriff Milloy had joined forces, since both seemed to think waiting and worrying was the thing for him to do. Since he had no brilliant plan to ride gallantly to Bobbie's rescue in his shining armor, he did just that. Now the waiting was getting to him.

The waiting was bad enough without his head splitting down the middle. He had forgotten about the headache for a while, now it was hammering away at his skull in full force. He realized his head wasn't the only thing wrong. He hadn't eaten since breakfast. Maybe the headache would ease off if he ate something, and a cup of good, strong coffee might help.

The coffee was ready and he had just built a monster of a sandwich when the door buzzer sounded. He went to the door and used the peephole. A woman was standing so close to the door, he could not really get a good look. He opened the door.

The tall blonde pushed her hair behind her ear and smiled. "Please, may I come in?"

David was hungry, his head hurt, and he had better things to do. "I'm not buying anything you're selling." He started to shut the door.

"Mr. Middleton," her voice was soft and seductive, "I have a message for you. I believe you will be interested in buying what I have to sell."

David opened the door wide and the woman walked into the living room. Walked was the wrong name for the way she moved. It should have been set to music. He couldn't quite place her accent, nor take his eyes away from her. "Do I know you?"

"We have never met," Nadja replied with a smile that would have most men falling on their knees at her feet. "May I?, she gestured to a chair. Sitting gracefully, she shrugged her shoulders, giving David a clear view of her cleavage.

David sank down in another chair, gripping his crutches with white knuckled hands. "You have a message?"

Nadja seemed in no hurry. She reached in her purse and brought out a pack of Camel cigarettes. "Mind if I smoke?" she asked with a hint of amusement. The lighter was in her hand when David cleared his throat. He was staring at the pack of Camel Straights.

He whispered to keep from shouting. "You're from Fischer or Charles, or whoever the hell he calls himself now."

The cigarette went back in the pack unlighted. "Listen closely. I will say this only once. Tonight there will be a houseboat on the water--, what you call your lake? Oh yes, Center Hill. A houseboat will be at a place called Holmes Creek after full dark. It will tie up on the island across the channel. Do not come unless you are alone. Do not approach the boat. Stay on the opposite shore, you will be told what to do. Do not notify the authorities. Do not try to follow me when I leave. That is the message. I see no need to make threats. You know the consequences if you try to be a hero." Nadja's seductive smile swept over David from head to toe. "Do not sacrifice yourself, when you know you can't win. Your sweetheart is fine. I have seen to her myself. Fischer is enjoying her company until I return."

Something about the blonde's cold dark eyes gave David chills. She was beautiful in the esthetic sense. She would numb you before inflicting pain. The thought of Bobbie with Jeff Fischer was definitely painful. "I know the place, and I understand what you are saying". David levered himself up with his crutches. "It gets dark early this time of year. Shall we say 8:00pm?"

Nadja rose with the same grace she had entered the room. She crossed to him and tucked the pack of cigarettes in his shirt pocket, taking the opportunity to leave her hand on his chest. "You are a very attractive man, you know. It is a shame you lost your leg. Don't lose more than that." Brushing her hair over her shoulder, she made her way out of the apartment. David pulled the pack of cigarettes from his shirt pocket and viciously flung them at the closing door.

The thought of food forgotten, David franticly searched for Buddy's telephone number. He knew Buddy had left it with Bobbie. The Sheriff's office would have it for Orville, but if he went there or called it might be construed as informing the authorities. Was someone watching the apartment? Was the phone tapped? Could they monitor his cell phone? All of this went through his head, knowing it was possible, but not likely.

Buddy was the only one he could call. A government agent no one knew was a government agent.

Calm down, David told himself, now I'm making up riddles. He finally drank the coffee and ate part of the sandwich to quiet his rebelling stomach. He checked his watch. 4:00pm. That gave him exactly four hours to come up with a plan to free Bobbie, put Jeff under wraps and settle this whole mess once and for all. While drinking the coffee, he remembered how he could reach Buddy. Buddy had told him the first day they met that he worked at an auto dealership in Sparta and if he needed to reach him he could call there. The pages of the Regional Telephone Book literally flew from the book as David tore through to the yellow section. He dialed with record speed. "Come on, come on," he drummed his fingers as he counted the rings. One, two, three, four, on the fifth ring a receptionist answered. No, Adams was not there, but if David would leave a message, she would see that he got it. Yes, he was very good at calling in for his messages. Briefly David told her he needed to reach Adams immediately. It was urgent that he speak to him in person. He left Bobbie's number.

* * * * * *

The number listed in the telephone directory as Sparta, Tennessee, was actually answered in a Washington D.C. office building. The 'receptionist', a highly trained voice recognition technician, immediately dialed another number. In minutes she was speaking to Lt. Col. Frank Barger.

"I think your hunch paid off, Colonel. The caller identified himself as David Middleton. Said the matter was urgent. Here is the number.

Buddy Adams acknowledged the call as the helicopter landed safely at the National Guard Armory. Buddy, with Ahmed, retrieved his Plymouth and immediately left the Armory compound. Obliging guardsmen had knocked the broken glass from the windows, so with the wind rushing through the vehicle it was impossible to carry on a conversation. Neither man said anything until Buddy pulled up in front of his cabin.

Ahmed still wore the camouflage jacket, now as stained and bloody as his shirt had been. Buddy's plaid shirt wasn't much better. Both men looked exhausted.

Ahmed voiced his concern. "Is this place safe now?"

"Doesn't matter," Buddy answered. "We won't stay long. Come on, I need your help."

After checking his perimeter monitors, Buddy led the way inside. "I've got the feeling we'll need all the firepower I have on hand. Help me load it in the car."

The men carried the weapons from the cabin to the trunk of the old muscle car. Ahmed would have loved to inspect the hardware, but agreed with Buddy their time was limited. Orson might have seen enough to recognize Buddy when he escaped from the compound. Rounds of ammunition, grenades, and explosives were loaded with the guns. He did ask, when Buddy carried out an M47 anti-tank rocket launcher, what kind of trouble Buddy expected.

Buddy did not favor him with an answer. Instead, still using the tiny earpiece, he called for help. "Control, I want a team in here immediately to clean up the equipment and dismantle the cabin." His order was acknowledged, stating a team would be there in less than twenty minutes. Buddy warned them to be careful, then motioned Ahmed into the car.

"Can you tell me where we are going?" Ahmed was more than weary.

"Yep," Buddy rubbed his stomach. "Little joint I know right out of Smithville. I was there the other night. Great steaks! You hungry?"

Ahmed smiled ruefully. When was it he had last eaten? He didn't remember. "Are you going to call the lawyer?" he recalled the handicapped man at the big house on the lake.

"Uh huh, soon as we eat. I'm pretty sure I know what he wants, and that might take some time. I don't know about you, but I'm plumb out of get up and go. Give us a chance to rest up. I haven't done a ten minute mile over mountain terrain since boot camp. How about you?"

Ahmed expended the energy to laugh. "The desert is harsh. I had to keep fit so I could work with the Bedouin tribesmen. They would not have allowed me to live in their midst if I had shown any sign of weakness. Weakness is unforgivable. It makes you less a man."

"I'll quit feeling sorry for you then," Buddy grinned. He tromped down on the accelerator and the big car shot forward.

Over steaks so rare they could have been Tartare, Ahmed eyed his former adversary. "I have a need to know," he began, "why you have not turned me in. We were never friends. Why have you taken my word for what has occurred?"

Buddy continued to chew his meat. He returned Ahmed's gaze. "Where were you in '91?"

"Niger, I told you. I was out of the game."

"Well, I wasn't. My cover was an assignment to courier service between the U. N. and Allied Headquarters in Saudi Arabia. I got wind of something coming up, but couldn't put a finger on it. Security was so tight the President couldn't have squeezed in. Then everything went to hell. It was still hush, hush, but I got a glimmer. A team had been sent in to assassinate Saddam. Smart bombs didn't find him, so they would try a different tactic. Then everything broke loose. Only one survivor came out of Iraq. Saddam had our intelligence almost before we had it. I jumped into it with both feet. It wasn't hard to trace it to the Hamaddi. You remember Ben Abdu Hamad? Yeah, of course you do. Well, that bastard found an American he could use, and Abdu and Saddam were close. The American, assigned to Headquarters as an aide, gave the Hamaddi information, and of course the intelligence found its way to Saddam. I don't know the whole story because just about then, I found myself on the defensive. I--me," Buddy pointed to his own chest, "I was the one accused of treason! I couldn't reveal some of my sources and it was close, whether I would stand court martial or just plain get shot. Some of my superiors came forward to vouch for me, and all charges were dropped. Except I've been relegated to the scrap heap now. Nothing has been the same since. I was re-assigned to JOTT. That's short for Joint Operations Tactical Team. I haven't been out of the states, but I did get command of a great bunch of guys, specialist from all branches of the military. We've done Waco, and a lot of behind the scenes work, now the Sparta gig. I know it's important. Heaven help us if we let this New Reich get a foothold, but it's not the same. I want my record exonerated. I want to retire without the black marks."

Ahmed knew what Buddy was saying. A clean record might help, but it was the soul that was damaged beyond repair. Loyalty was a fleeting thing. Buddy would pay with loneliness one day, the same as Ahmed. He didn't voice this thought, and Buddy continued with his story.

"I took up with Orville and met Middleton after the kid stole the truck. I didn't pick up on it right away, then after he got involved with this Fischer case, I did some research. Middleton is the lone survivor of that sabotaged mission. And guess who's paying the bills for the Sparta Hunting Club? A Houston corporation, listed as oil brokers, one of many under a holding company controlled by none other than Ben Abdu Hamad, himself."

Buddy finished his meal, and called for coffee. Ahmed had said nothing. The coffee was served, and Buddy resumed his tale. "When the fingerprints of Middleton's client matched the file prints for the younger Charles, I knew heaven had sent me my answers. I've kept plugging away at what evidence is archived. There is more I need to know to trap that traitor. Now I've got a chance. Orson was in Saudi at the same time as the younger Charles, assigned to the American Embassy. He always did toady up to the big shots, and got handed the security assignment for the senior Charles when the Senator came to investigate the charges against his son. Do you see where I'm going?"

Ahmed nodded sagely, "I see how the bombing of the National Laboratory and the research are involved. Obviously this man Fischer, as you call him, used his connection to bring in the Hamaddi, and they have used the Neo Nazi's, but why assassinate the Vice President? And, why bring me in to do it?"

"Hey, who knows. Maybe its politics, but you know the way they work. You're the scapegoat. A known assassin, a lone gunman, out of sight for years, now with who knows what connections? You were perfect. It would take the law weeks to come up with anything since you were clean for ten years. Time for all their other plans to work. No wonder they want you dead. Dead men don't talk." Buddy had a grimace on his face.

Ahmed considered. It made sense. "Still, you have not answered my question. Why have you decided to trust me?"

Buddy grinned his familiar toothy smile without a trace of humor. "You have reason to hate the Hamaddi as much as I do. How long ago has it been since your wife was killed in that car bombing? Thirty years? No, I don't think you have forgotten it was the Hamaddi who took credit for that act of terror."

Ahmed did not let Buddy's insight show on his face. What the man said was true, but much had transpired in the years that followed the tragedy. "Very astute, er..., what should I call you, Colonel?"

"I like Buddy. Think I'll stick with it." Buddy motioned to the waiter for the check. "Ready to go, partner?"

Ahmed leaned back, relaxed. "No." Buddy sat down again, the surprise clear on his face. Ahmed spoke again, "I see what you will get from this, but what do I get if I aid you?"

"Do you want money? Is that it? I already told you I would help clear you. Suppose you tell me?"

"I, too, want to be exonerated. I will take responsibility for my actions only to a degree. Ibrahim Hassim contacted me. He was never connected to the Hamaddi before. We were comrades in the beginning. How do I know the Hamaddi are running this set?"

Buddy straightened in his chair and looked Ahmed in the eyes. "You don't. Neither do I. We're in the same boat. You got another plan? Feel free to do it your way. Me, I'll give you odds Fischer is still tied in with them. Middleton is who he will contact. I get my hands on Fischer and I get my answers. You--, you might get to live a while longer."

"There's another kicker. What's been scaring Orville scares me, too. The kid was on his way to tell me about the National Laboratory, when he got picked up. He opened up after I made it clear those were real bullets breaking the windows in the car. Several of the dams that belong to TVA are juiced, along with the nuclear plants at Watts Bar and Soddy Daisy. They've got the explosives and suicide squads in place. Oklahoma will look like a playground if those dams and plants blow. Trouble is, we don't know which dams or if other nuclear plants may be wired. Whoever set the charge at the compound today knows what they're doing. I didn't see anything obvious when we went through there, did you?"

Buddy got up and went to the counter to pay their bill. Ahmed sat for a moment longer, then he resolutely followed Buddy out the door.

* * * * *

Bobbie knew exactly where she was. This was her beat. For a month at a time several Dekalb County deputies rotated making the rounds of the campgrounds, marinas, and access areas on Center Hill Lake. Orson kept her locked in the car as supplies were loaded aboard a large houseboat, while Nadja left them, driving a small white sedan. As soon as Bobbie saw the boat she knew which marina rented this line. It was as luxurious as the underground suite in Knoxville. Whoever was putting up the money for Jeff didn't mind spending it.

She recognized the remote access area where the boat and white car were waiting for them. Somehow, she needed to get word to David, or Steve. There were no fishermen on the bank, and no one else in sight. She dug her bare feet in the dirt, but Orson simply twisted her arm and pushed her up the gangplank onto the boat ahead of him. She pulled loose, wrenching her arm in the process. Before she could climb the railing and jump into the lake, he grabbed her close up to him.

"You're trying my patience, my dear," he said grinding his hips against her. "I think you need to know who is in charge here."

Oh, God, Bobbie thought, not one of those. The more I fight, the more I attract him. She stopped struggling.

"That's more like it," he said and started to bend his head to her.

"Bobbie," the hesitant voice and timid smile of Jeff Fischer loomed over Orson's shoulder. "I'll take care of her now, Jim. Bobbie, come this way. These staterooms are very nice. Beautiful weather for a cruise, don't you think?"

Bobbie grasped at anything that might help her, even begging. "Jeff, I haven't done anything to you. I don't even know what this is all about. Can't you let me go?"

Jeff just smiled sadly and took her arm, as Orson reluctantly released her. "Just a minute," before they moved away, Orson snarled at Jeff, "who said you were running this show? What happened to that Hassim character?"

Jeff bristled, the hang dog look gone as he straightened his shoulders. "It's my show now. You have a choice. Take the car and go to Houston, or get in the cabin and wait."

"Not so fast," Orson snarled. "You and your buddies need my men. How do you think you can pull this off without us?"

236

Jeff laughed in the man's face. "Everything is arranged. A model of the vehicle was put together in Houston two days ago. It works. Karen had her uses."

"You're lying! If the dammed thing worked you wouldn't have picked up this bitch." Orson eyed Bobbie who was edging closer to the gangplank. He went over and grabbed her by the arm. "I say I take care of her. She's going to like it and beg for more."

"Uh, uh," Jeff wagged his finger at Orson, like he was talking to a naughty child. "I have other plans for her. You were in Saudi Arabia and in on that deal with me. Did you recognize the man she will marry? No, I suppose not, or you would be very respectful now. Maybe you never knew his name. I didn't until lately. It's Middleton. Lieutenant David Middleton. He can blow this whole operation if he's put some things together. He's talked to my brother, too. That's double jeopardy. Big brother would love to have a reason to be rid of me permanently, and you are very expendable to him." Jeff actually laughed. "You and Edgar's so called friend in Houston are so greedy you would let me take the rap for Karen's murder. I suppose I should thank you for setting her up the night you took her home from the bar. Made it easy for Ibrahim to…, shall we say, put her out of her misery. You didn't have to do that. She was becoming difficult, but I could control her. What about me? Weren't you afraid I'd talk? Would I have hung myself in my cell rather than go to trial? Well, you didn't get rid of me. So, where do we stand now?"

Orson's fingers were digging into Bobbie's arm. She could feel the anger in him. Maybe she could make him mad enough to jump Jeff. "You're just a low down pervert. How'd you ever get on a detail with the Vice President? Must have bribed your way to him. I know his family. He wouldn't have anything to do with the likes of you. Jeff's the one in charge. He can let me go, if he wants to."

Jeff watched the color on Orson's face go from florid to blood red. He moved toward Bobbie. "I really don't think she likes you. Let go of her now, and get out of here. You're finished. I am running the show now. Not you or your Houston corporate friend. He's got the plans for the car, so he doesn't need you either. That was all he wanted. The rest of this operation is mine. Get out while I'm in the mood to let you."

Orson released Bobbie and reached for his sock and the small gun holstered there. She shoved him and made for the gang plank.

Jeff watched the small white car turn into the ramp, as Orson pulled the small pistol. As the man straightened, a gunshot rang out, slicing through the afternoon sun. Orson looked toward the shore where the shot came from, then down as a red blossom appeared on his white shirt. The gun dropped into the lake from his lifeless hand. Disbelief smoothed his face and with a soft gurgle bringing blood from his mouth, he pitched overboard into the shallow water.

Bobbie was stunned, holding her hand to her mouth as the body splashed into the water. She collected her wits and sprinted down the gangplank, right into Nadja's smoking automatic. It wasn't the weapon, but what was in the woman's eyes that stopped Bobbie on the spot. She docilely turned around and walked back up the gangplank.

Fischer's voice was mild as he berated Nadja. "Did you have to kill him?"

The woman acted as though she had only disposed of some trash. "He was no longer of any use. You would bargain with damaged goods? Were you going to stand by and let him rape her?" she indicated Bobbie. "Perhaps you were afraid of the man. He had a gun. He would have killed her and you. I don't understand you. There are times you appeal to me, then times when I abhor your weakness. I did what you should have done." Nadja tossed her hair back, took Bobbie by the arm and went to the main cabin. She called back through the door. "I saw Middleton. Your message is delivered. Eight o'clock tonight."

Bobbie was quaking inside, still shocked by the bullet that killed the man beside her. She knew she had to think of some way to head off David. She didn't understand all they had said about Saudi Arabia. David was wounded and lost his leg there, she knew. What could they want with him now? Hadn't he suffered enough? She had until eight o'clock to figure out what the message was.

Nadja led her to the lower deck and shoved her in a cabin. She heard the click of a lock and immediately surveyed her prison. One of the smaller cabins, it contained a double bunk, small chest, and one chair, all firmly fastened to the boat. A locker was built into the bulkhead. It was absolutely empty, not even a coat hangar. A small sliding window let air and light in above the top bunk. Bobbie climbed up and tried the window. It opened, but would never be big enough for her to squeeze through. At least she would be able to call for help if they got near any of the usually heavy marine traffic on the lake.

* * * * *

"I understand, friend, just calm down. No, not there. Somewhere we can be alone."

Ahmed listened to the one sided telephone conversation, as Buddy talked to Middleton. They were at a pay phone, on the outskirts of Smithville. Ahmed was keeping a low profile, as one of the posters with his pictures was plastered to the wall by the telephone.

The conversation went on. "No, don't say any more. Remember where the truck tried to run us off the road? Okay? Right. Yeah, that deserted farm house. Pull your car around back. I'll be waiting." Buddy hung up.

"That kid's so nervous he'll rattle when he walks," he told Ahmed. "They got Bobbie. Meeting tonight at 8:00, the Holmes Creek Campground. You know the place?"

Ahmed huffed out his breath. He knew it, and wished he had never seen the place. Now he knew why he was wanted for questioning. The murder of the black girl. Even if he was pardoned in the assassination attempt, he had that hanging over his head. "Yes," he answered Buddy, "I used a cabin on that road. The campground is deserted now, closed for the winter, but a boat launching ramp is open."

"Good," Buddy said, "Now lets go meet Middleton and he can fill in the details."

CHAPTER TWENTY-FOUR

The Buick jolted over the ruts of what used to be a gravel driveway. David hated to think what Ellen would say when she got the mud splattered automobile back. He turned behind what was left of the abandoned house. The roof was partially collapsed on one side, rusted tin almost on the ground. Paint had long since peeled from the wood clapboards. A kitchen porch, still outfitted with a dented washtub, offered some shelter to the rear of the house. The small yard was barely big enough to park two cars before trees closed in. David didn't like the looks of it, but would keep the vehicles from being seen from the road.

Where was Buddy? David sat in the car with the windows down. The yard was as muddy as the ruts in the driveway from a recent rain. He kept his mind focused on the old house. I don't know who lived here, he thought. Having grown up in Smithville, he knew almost as many of Dekalb County's residents as Ellen. Now let me see, there was Jimmy Orr, went to school with me, lived out this way. Then there was…, "Oh hell," David said out loud. He wasn't doing a very good job keeping his mind off Bobbie. If they hurt her, he thought, making silent threats. No matter how he searched his mind for answers, he simply did not see any reason for anyone to kidnap Bobbie. Okay, David theorized, so Fischer would know I have discovered his lies. If all he wants is me dead, why take Bobbie? Why not send that blonde to just shoot me? She would probably enjoy it. He hadn't liked it when the woman undressed him with her eyes. He got the feeling she looked at him like a wounded animal and wanted to be in on the kill.

Come on, come on Buddy. You said you'd be here. David couldn't sit still any longer. He got out of the car and went to the back porch of the house, careful to keep his crutches out of the holes in the rotted wood.

Finally he heard another car round the house. The old muscle car was riddled with bullet holes, and only one window held glass. Somehow it was still running and Buddy parked beside the Buick. David saw a second man in the car. It was Faziz. He didn't have time to wonder why, when Buddy stepped out of the car.

"Evenin', friend," Buddy hailed.

David decided on the spot there was no way Buddy could be the man Senator Charles had named as involved in the Saudi espionage. Who would think Buddy was a military officer, much less a Colonel? He looked like he had spent the day in a coal chute. Faziz didn't look much better, and the car was on its last leg; make that tire. Neither man looked fresh, but he had called and they were here to help him. Maybe he could get some ideas.

240

Buddy plopped down on what was left of the steps and Ahmed stood a little apart. "Hey, Miguel, come on over here. You, too, Middleton. We got us some planning to do."

David lowered himself to a step and Ahmed moved closer, but continued to stand. "Don't mind him," Buddy pointed a finger at Ahmed. "He thinks it's a sin to be tired. Now, tell me all of the message, then describe the messenger."

David recounted those few moments in Bobbie's apartment, then gave a description of Nadja. When he got to her cold, dark eyes he heard Ahmed hiss through his teeth. He looked at Buddy to see the man give a thumbs up sign to Ahmed.

Ahmed's deep voice caught David's attention. "Was there a man with her? A tall, thin man with a narrow face and deep set eyes?"

David shook his head. "Not in the building. She said not to follow her and I didn't. Could be someone else was in her car. Bobbie's apartment is on the back side of the building. You can't see the parking lot."

"I know her," Ahmed said, and David had the feeling that was not good news.

"Now here's what we're going to do," Buddy spoke up. "Follow orders to a tee. You go alone, Middleton. Miguel and I will be in the background. Don't worry, we're good at hiding. Ain't that so, amigo?" Buddy pointed to his ear without touching the small device still attached. "Give me your earpiece, Miguel and we'll fix the boy right up."

Ahmed took his device from a jacket pocket and handed it to Buddy. Buddy examined the reverse side and set the volume. He then handed it to David.

"What's this?" David asked.

"I don't know what they call it, but it's the handiest gadget control has come up with in a long time. Put it over your ear like this." Buddy showed him the one on his own ear. "Now get it comfortable and listen." Buddy walked out in the yard beyond the cars. "Can you hear me?"

David jumped as it seemed the voice came from inside his head. "Yes," he said very tentatively. "Okay," the voice said, "now touch it." David did, but nothing happened. Buddy walked back. "Did you hear what I just said?"

"You said touch it," David replied.

Ahmed broke into the conversation. "He said you're a pain in the--, never mind. It is a communication device. Only Buddy can hear you, but his is programmed to communicate with his team as well as you. Have I got that right, amigo?" he finished for Buddy.

"Yeah," Buddy checked his watch. "Touching it turns it off and on, but you leave it on all the time. That way Miguel and I can keep up with you and I'll hear everything you hear and say. Okay? Now, listen to me and listen good. No matter what they say to you, don't let them rile you. Keep calm, and keep them talking. Don't make threats and don't argue, just go along with what they tell you. You got that?"

David wanted to argue with Buddy right this minute, but nodded agreement.

"Now, go." Buddy gave David a confident grin. "We'll be along. Relax, friend. Take it easy. This is going to be a piece of cake."

David drove off wondering whose cake?

* * * * *

The big Buick stopped at the metal gates padlocked across the campground road. When David passed the dock and launching ramp only one truck and boat trailer waited for a late fisherman. The cabins along the road were deserted again; the fishing tournament won and celebrated.

David switched on the flashlight suspended by a strap from his shoulder and uncuffed his crutches to put them through the gate while he used his arms to swing himself over the metal bars. He had stopped at the apartment long enough to change into cut off blue jeans and a black pocket tee shirt. He found the pack of Camel cigarettes Nadja had left him and transferred them to the tee shirt. The blonde would not have left them without reason, he thought. They had identified her as Fischer's messenger, so they might be important now, like a password maybe. On the inside of the gate he settled himself back between his sticks, and started the uphill climb.

An additional pair of gates on each side of the gatehouse were closed but not locked. This area was under open skies, easy to see the small structure as David's night vision improved. He wanted to limit the use of the flash, but he did briefly switch it on to insure no one waited in the shadows.

He lifted the pin and let the heavy gate swing open, using its slow, creaking progress to softly say, "Buddy?" There was no answer and he stopped himself before he touched the tiny device at his ear. In the dark, surely no one would notice the thin, flesh colored wire over his ear. The communication wafer lay flat just behind his earlobe, almost invisible. He remembered he had not noticed the one on Buddy until it was pointed out to him. This wasn't a hearing aid to be worn inside the ear. It picked up voices, both David's and anyone within twenty feet of him and was programmed by a computer chip to transmit to a similar devise. It received sound from its twin, transferring the voice to David's hearing via his skull bone behind the ear. The range was approximately two hundred yards. Buddy had briefed David on the technology as they drove the distance to the campground. Somewhere on the five miles of road into the campground the Plymouth and

Buddy's voice had disappeared. Since Buddy did not now answer to his name, David hoped he was not too far behind.

No one lurked just inside the campground. The huge southern oaks and cedars that shaded the campsites threw a ghostly pattern into the dark skies. Night insects calling through the still air set up a buzzing that reminded David his hurting head thrummed in tune with their cadence. Tonight there would be very little moonlight. The waning moon would offer small help, and moonrise was an hour away. David could imagine mist rising from the damp grass. A small animal scurrying in the fallen leaves made him jump. Calming his active imagination, he reminded himself Bobbie might very well be here. He kept to the main road as it began descending to the lake.

He had seen no one as he entered the campground. Now a feeling crawled across the back of his neck. David stopped and listened. Nothing in his head, nothing except a gentle breeze in the treetops. The feeling grew stronger as he moved his crutches forward and followed the road. Each tree hid the unknown; each campsite a trap. There was no way he could search the large twenty-one acre park. Was it his imagination, or was someone tracking his progress? He softly said "Buddy?" No answer.

He reached the campground boat ramp, where the road ended in the lake. To his left, probably a hundred yards away across the channel, lights blazed aboard a large houseboat, David wondered how he was to hail the craft. He moved through the lakeside campsites until he was opposite the boat. The water of the lake was only a few feet below the rocks lining the shore. Remembering some of his Boy Scout Morse code he used the flashlight to blink an on off, on off, hello. He could see movement on the boat, but no one acknowledged his presence. He was beginning to feel frustration build up. If Bobbie was being held aboard that craft, he could swim the distance easy. Fischer had arranged this meeting. He had one more chance, then David would peel his clothes and take matters in his own hands. About to do that, a voice inside his head said, "Don't let them rattle you. They know you're here. They're making you wait. Someone tailed you from the time you left the car. He's coming toward you now."

David stood stock still until the man was almost on him, then turned to find a tall, thin man slipping through the shadows.

The man came close and peered into David's face. "Could I have a cigarette, please?"

David was momentarily confused. "I don't smoke--," he said, then remembered the pack the blonde had tucked in his shirt pocket. He threw them down on a picnic table beside the man's hand. Without taking his eyes from David, the man inserted his finger in the cigarette pack and drew out a small tracking device, holding it up between his fingers for David to see.

With only the word, "Pardon," he ran his hand familiarly over David's torso. When he got to the cut off jeans David had donned, he swept his hand along David's bare leg to the sock above the athletic shoe. At the empty pants leg he stopped and drew back, apparently satisfied David was neither armed nor wired. He moved to lean against the picnic table. David could feel every nerve in his body coming alive while he submitted to the search. His Army training had lain dormant for nine years; now once again he could be the highly skilled, finely tuned killer they had made of him. Knowing Bobbie's life depended on him, he let the man live. "I have done what you asked. It is time you do as I ask. I want to know why I am here, and why are you holding Bobbie Foster?"

The thin man seemed unaware of the change in David's demeanor . "Miss Foster is well and comfortable. There is something you can do for us that will insure she stays healthy. An errand Fischer would ask of you."

"David," the inside voice said, "talk, make Fischer come to you. This man is Ibrahim Hassim. Make a deal with him. Tell him you'll agree to speak to Fischer if he will tell you about the dams."

"What?" David said out loud, but the man facing David thought he was asking what errand. "I am merely the messenger," Hassim answered. "Come, I have a boat at the dock. Fischer would see you and give you the instructions."

"No, David," the inside voice was urgent, "make a deal. Tell him you know the Center Hill Dam is loaded with explosives. Get him to admit it." David wanted to put his hand to his head and stop everything. His need to get to Bobbie was overwhelming. What did Buddy mean about the dam?

"Sorry," David told the Arab, reverting to courtroom tactics. "I need a few questions answered before I agree to anything. For one thing, why blow up this dam?"

The man before David hesitated, giving a slight shrug. "What we do next does not concern you."

"I think it does." David's voice remained strong and confident, even as the unspoken admission hit home. If the dam went--, he didn't want to think of the consequences. "Is Miss Foster aboard that houseboat? Everything on this lake would be swept down river if the dam goes."

Hassim thought he had the advantage again. "Ah, then you will cooperate. Come with me. I will take you to Fischer."

David grabbed at another admission. Bobbie was aboard the boat! His insides lurched with an urge to throttle Hassim. He listened, but this time there was no voice inside his head telling him what to do. He followed the thin man to the back side of the Park down a steep hill to the launching dock and ramp.

The hill was difficult to navigate on crutches and he fell behind. He whispered, "Did you get that? Bobbie is on the boat." Buddy's voice came through again. "David, stall again. Go with him, if you have to, but give me time to swim to the island." Swim Buddy, David was thinking. but this is my show now. I'll be there, too.

David calmed himself, tamping back his need for violence. All of today's frustrations were clogging his thinking. At the loading dock by the boat ramp, Hassim waited as a metal rowboat glided to the dock from the shadows on the lake. David took his time climbing down the hill and through the parking lot. His rubber tipped crutches made no sound as he swung onto the small dock. He stayed back from the boat. Hassim displayed a small revolver, for some reason now in a hurry. "Leave your supports here on the dock." He motioned for David to drop his crutches. "Now get in the boat."

"I thought this was a friendly meeting," David played for time. "I've come alone. I have obeyed your instructions. Why do you need to hold a gun on me?" The man remained impassive. David tried again. "I need my sticks to walk. I can't leave them here."

Hassim said something in Arabic, then motioned for the big man at the oars of the rowboat to help. The inside voice chuckled, "He said you talk too much." This time the voice was Ahmed Faziz. Buddy must have left the communication device with him to swim the channel. David would like to know where the little man was now.

Hassim motioned again with the gun, and David clambered into the rowboat, reaching back to leave his crutches on the dock as directed. The boat moved out into the lake.

The rowboat approached the houseboat, oars steadily dipping in the water. A rope was thrown and the rowboat pulled along side the craft. David started to rise, then stayed down as Hassim pushed the automatic in his side. "We wait here," the man said.

David recognized the figure ambling toward the rail. Even the little half smile that made the man look apathetic was familiar. The voice was every bit as apologetic as before. David could have thrown up.

"So sorry it had to come to this, David. I had better plans, but they just didn't work out." Jeff Fischer, or the name he was born with, Alan Jeffrey Charles leaned over the rail to talk.

"Jeff," David said evenly, keeping his voice calm, "there has to be a better way. Go get Bobbie and come with us. I give you my word I'll do everything I can to help you."

"An enticing offer, David," Jeff lolled against the rail, looking relaxed. "Maybe I only thought you put two and two together. Guess you don't know what's at stake. Odds are you wouldn't believe me if I told you."

David felt a helplessness invade his body. The real odds were that Bobbie would be in danger if he tried anything now. He had no choice but to listen. Wait, he told himself. Jeff had just given him an opening.

"Are you talking about the Oak Ridge vehicle and the military application, Jeff. Not much I don't know. I had a nice long chat with the Senator today.

Jeff stood still, languidly letting his arms dangle over the rail of the houseboat. He stared down at David, with no sign of emotion. His voice betrayed the only hint that David had got to him. "Nice try, but my esteemed brother doesn't have the answers. Where is he, by the way? Lurking around on the fringe of things as usual? No matter. What I want you to do will not take long."

David broke in. "I'm not going to do anything without Bobbie. I know she's aboard. Let her go with me and I'll run your errand for you."

Jeff's laugh gave David chills. He withdrew from the rail and entered the lighted cabin. David was tensing to jump at Hassim when Ahmed's voice spoke again. "Sit still. Fischer is not through with you yet."

Jeff, with Bobbie between he and Nadja, appeared at the sliding glass doors. The light was behind them, but Bobbie seemed to be all right. David felt his fingers curl around the slat seat of the rowboat. It was all he could do to control his anger.

"See for yourself," he called to David. "Bobbie, tell him we haven't hurt you. Tell him to be a good boy and I'll let you go when he does as I ask."

It tore into David's heart to see Bobbie stiff and silent. She looked to be okay, but somehow she seemed almost inert. Finally, she tried to move forward, but Nadja had a painful grip on her arm. When she spoke her voice was dull and lifeless. "I'm okay, David. Go on and do what you need to. I'll wait for you here." Bobbie twisted away from Nadja and retreated into the cabin.

The knife in his heart stabbed deeper. David knew Bobbie would sacrifice herself for him, telling him to leave. He got a grip on his jangling nerves. Nadja had disappeared with Bobbie, and Fischer leaned against the rail again.

Jeff's voice interrupted his thoughts. "Go to Knoxville to the newspaper office. In the bottom right hand drawer of my desk there is a box of used computer disks. Bring it to me and I'll make all your dreams come true."

"That's all?" David replied, unbelievingly. "You just want some old computer disks?"

"That's it," Jeff said airily, waving a hand. I must have them by first light. I will send Hassim to this location again at, let's say 4:00am. That should give you plenty of time if you hurry. But then you know all about the time change between here and there. Better go. If anything where to happen to me, I have left Bobbie to Nadja, if you fail to return on time."

The mocking tone to Jeff's voice only served to fuel David's rage at how stupid he had been. He used a finger to poke the oarsman, and the boat moved back into the channel. David sat mesmerized as Bobbie's clear, alto voice could be heard slowly singing an old country hymn. *"He will keep me till the river rolls its waters at my feet; then He'll bear me safely over, where the loved ones I shall meet."* Her message was clear. Go, David. Get away! Save yourself!

The rowboat was almost to the loading dock when the silence of the night was broken by blaring sirens. Whirling lights could be seen tearing down the winding road to the campground. What looked like a parade of law enforcement vehicles advanced on the campground. With a curse the oarsman turned the boat back into the lake. David launched himself at Hassim. Distracted by the police, Hassim barely raised his gun. David made a grab at his arm, violently rocking the flat bottomed boat. He made contact, surprised at the wiry strength of the thin man. The oarsman shouted something and swung one of the heavy poles, missed David's leg and struck Hassim a glancing blow. The Arab yelped, but held his position. David, blew out his breath and used arms and shoulders that lifted over two hundred pounds in the gym. Slowly the gun turned in the man's hand. The rowboat tipped dangerously as the man in the back dropped the oars and moved forward. David twisted his body on his one leg and pivoted in time to block a blow. A hammer like fist slammed into his shoulder and the recoil reaction fired the weapon. David didn't have to wonder who was hit. Hassim sagged in his arms, the gun dropped into the waters of the lake. He released the Arab to grapple with the big man aiming another sledge-hammer fist at him. He ducked, then tackled his adversary at waist level. They both went over the gunnel into the chilling water. On land David would be no opponent for the man who displayed the moves of a professional wrestler. In the water, where a missing leg and no balance problem held him back, David let the black rage envelope him. He gulped air, then dragged the flailing man down to the mud and rock bottom of the lake bed. Underwater the big man was no match for David. Arms kept powerful by daily lifting his own body weight with every step he took, pounded the man into the rocks until David felt him go limp. He released the body, and shot to the surface for air. Suddenly his mind cleared, the rage exhausted. He breathed deep again, turned and dived. The lack of daylight turned the murky water black as the disturbed sediment from the bottom rose to the surface. David found what he was looking for and hauled the heavy man to the surface. For a moment it looked like it was too late, then first a cough, then a sputter as

David's victim took a breath. The fight was gone out of his captive. David towed him to the shoreline.

Steve was standing there to give him a hand. David shook himself, splattering everyone with drops of cold water as he grasped Steve's shoulder for support. The Sheriff called to Scottie and Jim Ed, both with flak vests over their deputies uniforms, and ordered the arrest of the recovering man.

David tugged on Steve's arm. "Bobbie," he said between ragged breaths. "Steve, Bobbie's on that boat." The houseboat, lights out, was rapidly untying from its mooring. The rumble of the engines could be heard. "Steve, please. My sticks are on the dock. Help me to the water. I can swim to the boat.!"

"No," the inside voice came. "Wait, I am coming!" David shook his head, surprised the communication device had survived the dousing. "Bobbie's on that boat!" David screamed. "Wait," the voice said again. "You can't catch them. Go to the dock. I'm almost there."

Steve looked confused by David's outburst. "I heard you the first time," he yelled back.

"To the dock," David said more calmly, and hopped with his hand on Steve's shoulder for balance. Ahmed was running along the shore from the trees. He caught them as they made the dock.

"They have the girl on the deck so no one will fire on them." He pitched David one of the special sniper's rifles from Buddy's cache. David grabbed the gun with remembered intimacy. He threw himself down on his stomach as the floating dock swayed with the weight of the men. Ahmed stretched out beside him with a twin of the rifle. Through the sight David could see the boat in the green glow of night vision. Jeff was standing on the fore deck holding Bobbie in front of him. Nadja was to their side. The houseboat began to slide from its mooring. Without a word Steve backed from the dock and ordered his men away from the shoreline.

"I'll take the woman. You get Fischer. On the count of three." Ahmed's calm voice did little to reassure David. Bobbie--, Bobbie was all David could think. Jeff's face, visible behind Bobbie's shoulder was the only target area that would insure Bobbie's release. An impossibly small, moving target from this distance.

"I can't take the chance. I can't do it." David's breathing was short and rapid.

"I know who you are, Lieutenant. You are Special Forces, the best of the lot," Ahmed's emotionless voice took David back to his Army instructor. "Buddy knows, too. He is waiting with a rocket launcher. If you want Bobbie to live, take the shot."

David sighted the gun as the houseboat began a slow turn to the deeper water. Once more he put the rifle down. Ahmed said nothing. On his stomach, rifle braced on its own tripod, David dried his hands and again took aim.

Bobbie, standing in the bow of the boat saw the men on the dock as the sliver of moon came from behind the clouds. Fischer shoved her around more in front of him as the boat turned. She slumped, supported only by Jeff's arm, causing him to lean forward. Through the scope his face looked white in the scant light.

David blanked his mind, shutting out all thought. There was nothing in this night except the rifle and the mark. All sounds were silent. All movement stilled. Nothing. Nothing but the gun in his hands, sights aligned. He quietly called the numbers. "One, two, three."

To those intently watching this drama, it seemed only one gunshot echoed over the water. David had yet to breathe. It seemed to take forever for Fischer to fall, then he seemed to simply crumple at Bobbie's feet. Nadja was nowhere in sight. Bobbie staggered to the rail and tumbled over into the water, surfaced and floundered safely away from the churning propellers of the houseboat.

David sighted again, but there was no other movement on the boat. He pushed the rifle behind him and rolled his body into the water, swimming to Bobbie. He reached her and her arms went around his neck. She clung to him as he pulled her farther from the boat, then kicked off again to swim toward the shore.

What looked like all the fireworks on the planet lighted the skies, then sound caught up, blasting eardrums. Waves of lake water washed over the heads of the swimmers and pieces of metal rained down. The force separated Bobbie from David's grasp, and she went under. David was coughing up water, but grabbed at Bobbie when she surfaced again. He missed, trying to avoid hot metal turning the lake water to steam. She seemed to revive somewhat, and paddled on her own toward the nearest rocky shoreline.

What was left of the hull of the houseboat began to settle below the surface of the water, again sending water surging from the site. The momentum pushed Bobbie and David closer to the shore. Bobbie clung to a rock as David made his way to her.

Chunks of flaming debris floated around them. David found purchase on a rock and pulled Bobbie to him. She was shaking, crying and laughing all at the same time. David was emotionally drained, unable to believe what had just occurred. He held Bobbie tight against him and quietly went to pieces.

CHAPTER TWENTY-FIVE

Never had as many Tennessee law enforcement officers gathered in one place since the Martin Luther King, Jr. assassination. Search lights from Tennessee Wildlife Resource and Corp of Engineer boats roved over the now quiet waters of the lake looking for survivors and examining every piece of flotsam. Spotlights on patrol cars from the State Police were covering every inch of the campground. Jim Ed waded into the lake and took Bobbie from David, handing her to Scott while he helped David to the bank. Blankets were thrown over the shivering swimmers and Steve handed David his crutches. Someone had turned on the heater in one of the police cruisers and both Bobbie and David were deposited in the warmth.

When her teeth stopped chattering, Bobbie's slurred words touched David's heart. "I knew you would never leave without me."

"Your faith in me made that shot, not me." David pushed back his blanket as he warmed.

"I wasn't scared," Bobbie lied, "well, maybe a little."

David's grin was made for the big screen. "You know, lil'bit, you're really something. Brave, beautiful, smart, too. I'm so sorry you had to go through this. I don't think Steve will ever forgive me for getting you into this mess."

Bobbie pulled back. "What's this, mister? I thought it was the other way around. I was the one with the Vice President, remember? I'm the one who got in trouble first. You're always trying to steal the spotlight."

David groaned through his smile. "I won't ever get the last word with you, will I?"

"You might if you keep trying. Sometime in the next hundred years." Bobbie yawned widely. "I think they were giving me something to keep me quiet. All I drank was water I was so thirsty. Something could have been in the water. I just want to go to sleep, now that it's over. It is over, isn't it?" Before David could answer, Bobbie surrendered to the lull after the storm and went sound asleep in David's arms.

After a few minutes of catching his breath and letting his racing heart slow, David gently lowered Bobbie to the seat and exited the vehicle. EMT's had arrived, ready for casualties. He refused to go in the ambulance with Bobbie, telling them she thought she had been given drugs. More groggy than awake, she didn't make a fuss after David promised he would go get the stitches in his head dressed. When the ambulance left, he went looking for Buddy.

He found Steve and Ahmed together by the Sheriff's car. Ahmed extended his hand. "Congratulations, that was beautiful work." When the hand was withdrawn David held the tiny communication device Ahmed had worn.

"Have you seen Buddy?" David glanced around again. "Who?" Ahmed asked, his voice and face conveying only curiosity. David understood. The spook was still undercover. Seeming to rub his head, he removed the other device and circumspectly slipped both into his pocket.

David decided Buddy could stay a ghost for all he cared. If Fischer was really dead, this should end it, but a lot of loose ends needed tying up. He spoke to Ahmed, "I'm not the only one who knows the drill. Great shot you made."

Ahmed merely shrugged. "Nadja will not bother you again."

"I wish you'd tell me who blew that boat to smithereens," Steve joined the conversation. "No survivors have been found, so that only leaves you to tell me what the hell is going on now. I'm getting sick and tired of trying to be the law in this part of the world when I'm the last one to know anything." He turned on David. "Son, if you ever put my niece through anything like that again--, Oh hell, David." Steve grabbed David in a bear hug. "I knew I should have locked the two of you up, for my own sanity."

David returned the hug, genuinely happy to be part of Steve's family. "By the way, Steve, how did you know we were here at the campground?"

"Good, honest police work. A traffic officer remembered giving Bobbie a ticket for parking in a reserved space this morning. Then another witness came forward. He saw her forced into a car. He got the license plate number. The car belonged to a rental agency who uses a satellite service to track their vehicles. It is sitting down the creek at the marina where a man matching the description of the man you almost drowned rented a boat. This was the most logical place to look for you. So here we are."

David grinned again. "I wouldn't say that's too shabby for a backwoods sheriff." He gestured to Ahmed. "Is Dr. Faziz in your custody?" Steve indicated that was so. "I have agreed to represent him in any necessary legal proceedings. Just for the record, but let's wait until morning. I do need to speak to my client now."

Steve's mouth quirked, but he moved away and began organizing his men. "Thank you," Ahmed said. "For more than you know. Buddy sacrificed his career for you tonight, whether you know it or not. With Fischer gone, he has no way of clearing his name. I thank you for not giving him away. I'm sure his team has retrieved him by now. A man and a woman who ran a Neo-Nazi compound were captured and have confirmed the dams in this vicinity have been wired for sabotage. The JOTT team will take care of it. No need to alert the public. Wouldn't want to create panic. By the way, he sent you this message. He said to tell you it's been a hoot, and that he'll see you again soon."

David only nodded to acknowledge the message, but he was thinking who on earth is JOTT? Was it possible that Buddy really was Lt. Col. Frank Barger?. If not, where had the communication device come from? Easy, David told himself. One puzzle at a time. He turned his attention back to Faziz. "If you are as tired as I am, we'll talk in the morning. Go with the Sheriff. The County jail's not too bad. You can get some sleep there. I want to contact Senator Charles." Ahmed agreed that was probably the best course.

Before they could make their way to the cars, more men and vehicles poured through the open campground gates. David reached Steve as Edgar Charles himself walked up.

The Senator was rumpled and disheveled. He looked like time had fast-forwarded and he aged ten years. Running a hand through his standing hair, his voice was as rough as his appearance. "Did you get Jeff? Did you get my brother? Is he dead?"

David was the obvious one to answer. "Yes," David had the grace to look the man in the eye. "I shot him. I know I hit him, but they haven't found the body yet. The houseboat sank, it might be weeks before all the bodies are recovered."

Charles collapsed in on himself. His bodyguard stood by in case he was unable to stand, but the man was made of sterner stuff. He took a deep breath. "It's over, then. Thank God." He turned away before he could display any more emotion.

David had a moments regret. After all, traitor or not, Jeff was the man's brother. David's thoughts went back nine years to the day he left the Army Hospital in Germany. He had sworn to himself never to kill again. He had broken his own vow. In his heart and mind he knew Jeff would never let Bobbie go alive. She would die, if not by his hand, by the ice cold blonde woman. When Bobbie's life hung in the balance there was no other choice. He had hesitated pulling the trigger. The target area was so small, any slight shift or movement and it would be Bobbie who would take the hit. Why did he have to use the rifle when his skill with the weapon had caused him so much agony? That was the irony of it. What he wanted was to get his hands on the man, but at that moment it was only Bobbie who mattered. The rifle was his only option and he took the shot. God must have heard his prayers. Bobbie was unhurt. And David knew he would do it again. He hoped God would forgive him.

The Senator regained his composure and asked David to walk with him. Out of earshot from the crowd, he spoke. "Thank you, Middleton. You have ended a nightmare that went on far too long. Please let me know when his body is recovered. I'll pay all expenses for cremation and ask you to dispose of the ashes without ceremony. The public and his children believe, as I did, that my brother died in Denver and is buried there. I'd like to keep it that way."

David supposed he should feel honored with the Senator's trust, but hoped he had seen the last of Fischer forever. Then again, maybe scattering the ashes would put a closure on Operation Sureshot for him. "I will see to it," David told Charles, and turned back to the gathering crowd.

Charles was not finished. "If you ever need anything or whatever I can do, it is yours for the asking. I hope you will come to Washington. We could use a good, honest lawyer. I heard you might run for the House."

David's grin was grudging. "That rumor was started by the press. I'm going to marry Bobbie and settle down right here. Thanks for your offer, though." Both men started back down the hill.

More men were milling around the campground. When David and Senator Charles passed the gatehouse the Atlanta FBI Division Chief, wearing a lettered FBI jacket squared off at the Senator. "Edgar Charles, I am placing you under arrest for conspiracy to illicitly steal secrets from the National Laboratory in Oak Ridge, Tennessee and treason for aiding and abetting a known terrorist organization in gaining that information. You have the right--," the Chief took malicious pleasure in making the charge.

Charles cut him off. "George, what are you saying?" Sincere shock colored his face. "You knew I wanted to put an end to Jeff's activities by permanently committing him to mental facilities. I never had any dealings with him for any other reason."

David could feel the tension in the air as the FBI Chief went in for the kill. David had his own reasons for doubting the Senator. Anyone with as much power and money would always be suspect, and the unanswered question of why have Jeff report on Karen Fielding was sticking in David's mind.

The smug response from the FBI grabbed David's undivided attention. "We got a tip that your Houston oil brokerage was financing some terrorist activities right here in Tennessee. I asked the Director to confiscate their records. Your brother was routinely sending technical information to that location. We got it in black and white. You can't get out of this one, Edgar. I knew you were protecting your brother, but I never dreamed you were in on it."

David interrupted. "Don't say anything, Senator." Charles gratefully let David take over. "Please present the warrant for this arrest," he told the Chief. The paper was handed to him. He read without looking up. The air fairly crackled around him. Finally he raised his head and let the paper flutter in his finger tips as he addressed the Senator. "This is only an order to detain you, with reasonable suspicion for questioning. There is no probable cause listed. You can take care of it now, or wait until morning when I can be there."

Charles grasped at the offer like a drowning man. He turned on the Chief. "Sorry, George. I really don't know what you are talking about. I'll make a statement when my attorney is present. I'm staying aboard my plane at the Smithville Airport. Give me a call in the morning."

One of the FBI Agents accompanying the Chief whispered something, and the man backed off. "All right, Edgar, but you better be there in the morning. File a flight plan and I've got you. We set up a command post at the Dekalb County Sheriff's office. Be there at 9:00am, or I will have probably cause," this last aimed at David. The man turned on his heel and marched to his vehicle followed by his retinue.

David was wondering just how much trouble one man could get in. Less than two weeks ago his life was so placid he might as well been comatose. His mama always told him trouble came in bunches. He was beginning to believe old wives sayings were often rooted in truth. Whatever possessed him to offer to represent Faziz and Charles? Faziz, yes, the man had helped him, but he had never expected Charles to accept his offer. Yeah, okay, probably only until some Washington hotshot could get here. David huffed with the thought, then it hit him. 9:00am was not the only deadline given him tonight. Jeff had told him he needed some computer disks by 4:00am. What time was it anyway?

He found Steve as the Sheriff was preparing to leave with Faziz. Someone had brought in the floating rowboat. Hassim was not in the little craft. David told them one of the terrorists was wounded in a struggle, so if no one was in the boat, he couldn't have gone far. No bodies had been pulled from the wreckage and no survivors found in the water, or on land. The search was called off until morning. The Corp of Engineers would post guards and man the campground as long as necessary. The Sheriff was glad to retreat to town and maybe his bed sometime before dawn.

"What time is it?" David asked. Steve checked his watch. "Almost midnight," he responded. David moaned the prospect of no sleep. More than twenty-four hours sleep deprivation didn't lead to a clear head. He needed all his faculties and a level head to greet the new day. "Steve, can you lend me someone to drive me to Knoxville. It's important, or I wouldn't ask."

Steve muttered something under his breath. "Don't you ever give up? David, one of your clients is dead. You shot him! Another was on the run until this mysterious Buddy Adams turned him in. Now you represent an accused murderer and assassin, who also just shot a woman on a boat. A U.S. Senator, possibly guilty of treason, will meet with you to answer questions for the FBI at 9:00am. Not to mention you promised to petition Judge Jenkins in a case of cow rustling, and for permission to release a dead girl for burial. To top it all off, your head is bleeding again. That bandage is soaked with lake water and dripping down on your shirt, which is also soaking wet. What in God's name is so important in Knoxville?"

"I don't know," David replied honestly. "It was the only thing Jeff Fischer asked me to do in exchange for Bobbie. I was to go fetch some computer disks from his newspaper desk. I was to have them back here at the park and meet Ibrahim Hassim by a 4:00am deadline. The timing seemed very important to him. It might be worth the drive to see what's on those disks."

Steve made an instant decision. He checked his watch again. "You go with Scott to the Hospital and get that head fixed. Ask them for some caffeine pills, they got 'em, then come to my office. That'll give me time to take Faziz with me. We'll leave for Knoxville from town. Now, move!"

Startled by Steve's sudden capitulation, David did just that.

* * * * *

The trip to Knoxville was uneventful. Ahmed had talked Steve into allowing him to accompany them to the newspaper office, citing that if part of the information on the disks was in Arabic he could translate. David had refused the caffeine pills and crawled in the rear seat of the Sheriff's cruiser, while the two older men occupied the front. While his busy mind didn't turn off, he was able to doze, then sleep deeply for part of the trip. It was almost 2:00am CDT when a security guard called Ben Parry and got permission for them to retrieve the things from Jeff's desk. David asked for a box and they cleaned out the cubical. Parry arrived before they finished, still wearing his pajama top. He offered his office and computer, hovering over the desk like any good news hound. The first disk was loaded. ACCESS DENIED, the screen told them. Disappointed, David asked if the editor knew Jeff's password. No, he was told. Reporters forwarded their bylines to him electronically, but no password was needed.

David's hunch wouldn't give up. His gut feeling about the information contained on the disks was telling him it was important they know the contents of the files. Inspiration hit him. "Wait," he said, "let me try." When the request for a password came up again, he tapped in the day's date, the time of 4:00am and *AJC,* the initials for Alan Jeffery Charles. This time the loading light blinked and signaled done.

It was all there. Everything. All the correspondence with the terrorist organization, naming Ben Abdu Hamad and the Hamaddi. It outlined his supposed partnership with Jim Orson, who had instigated the elimination of the vice-president. Ahmed Faziz was named as coerced to perform, and expendable, intended to die in the assassination attempt by Secret Service bullets. The enlistment of the New Reich Army for manpower and their explosive experts, exposed Jim Orson's secret life. The jewel of the lot was a disk with all the technical information on the magno-electronic propulsion system. Specifications and plans were complete to build the vehicle. Even the military application plans were there.

Jeff had left records of his agreement with his brother. David bludgeoned himself with the knowledge Jeff had lied even more than he had previously realized. My brain kept trying to tell me not to believe the man. I guess my pride, thinking I had finally got the chance to practice big time law got in the way. What a fool I've been. David was stricken with remorse. His stupidity had almost killed Bobbie. I should back out right now, and go back to defending indigents and cow rustlers.

"Wow," was all Steve had to say, beginning to understand the enormity of the treason. Ahmed was drinking in everything he was reading on the computer screen, translating correspondence and affirming most of the terrorist activities as true.

Not only were all the recent events recorded, Jeff had the enormous ego to have begun an autobiography, spanning from Operation Sureshot to the present. How much was fiction, how much true David didn't have a clue, but it explained and answered the remaining questions in David's mind. There was no doubt that Lt. Col. Frank Barger was not only innocent of any charges in the matter of Sureshot, but getting too close to the truth for Jeff's liking. Jeff had deliberately tried to rid himself of the Colonel.

Reporting on Karen Fielding was Jeff's idea, too. His brother, the Senator, had no notion that Jeff was setting her up to take his place as the traitor if their plot was discovered prematurely. He had played on her former relationship with Ibrahim Hassim to trick her into the espionage, making her believe Jeff was the dupe. She not only knew of the military application of the technology she helped develop in Oak Ridge, but by the time Jeff finished brain-washing her, she was certain it was Ibrahim's true cause, and would lead to peace between Israel and the Palestinians.

If this unfinished autobiography was anywhere close to the truth, Jeff's purpose was only to destroy his brother. In his script, he was the poor relation in the family, mistreated and ignored. Jeff didn't give a fig for world politics. Ben Abdu Hamad and the Hamaddi, along with Saddam Hussein could have all of that. What Jeff wanted was to humiliate his brother, and ruin the family business until his brother was forced into bankruptcy. He wanted Edgar to come begging to HIM. Everything was there, from the smallest slight to every misunderstood intention his brother had ever made.

When Jeff started recounting the supposed evils of their father, David had read enough. It was plain that Edgar Charles was right. His brother was more than unbalanced. Had Jeff agreed to David's last entreaty when they bargained over Bobbie and accepted David's help, the only plea he could have presented to the court was insanity. *I hope his body is recovered quick,* David prayed. *I don't think I will sleep until I have sprinkled his ashes where they will never be found.*

David checked his watch and reminded the men they had a deadline to keep. Steve used his identification as a law officer to confiscate all of the records and Fischer's possessions, with the aid and approval of Fischer's Attorney of Record, David Middleton. He promised to call Ben Parry with the story, or better yet Parry could send a reporter to the Center Hill campground to get the information from the Corp of Engineers. Parry enthusiastically pumped his hand and said he would go himself.

There was no sleep for David or any of the three on the ride back to Smithville. Sirens and lights cleared any traffic on the interstate, and they pulled into the campground on the dot of 4:00am. Clearing them with the Rangers left on duty, Steve led the way to the lakefront.

"Jeff told me to meet Hassim back here." David pointed to the ground beneath him. "If there was to be a rendezvous with another party, I suppose word got out and it was called off."

Ahmed gave his stoical shrug, in the middle-eastern manner. "It may depend on how vital any of that information is to them."

"Well, nothing earth shaking is happening, and I'm tired. If anyone is around I don't see them. Let's call it a night. Steve, you will wait until morning to hand over the disks to the FBI, won't you?

"I plan to do that. I may be just a poor county sheriff, ignorant of proper procedure. Nobody tells me a thing, so how do I know if it's important?"

"Steve," David grinned. "If I told you all I know, you still won't know a thing, but my hunch is that we may want to go over those disks when our heads are clear. Besides, my client is dead. I expect he posthumously will get all the publicity he had in mind when he made those computer files. Mind dropping me at Bobbie's apartment? I need to clean up for the meeting this morning."

Steve shook his head in mock disgust. "Might as well, You smell like a dead fish and look worse. Your taxi awaits," Steve grimaced and started down the hill.

What the men did not see was a lone man with a superficial gunshot wound in his shoulder standing in the trees behind the campsite. Ibrahim Hassim slipped silently through the trees and rounded the hill and fence that marked the campground boundaries. Almost at the end of his strength, he continued across the boulders and deep crevices that lined the original creek bed. The small boat with a trolling motor was tied behind a fallen tree trunk. Less than a mile farther up the creek was the marina.

* * * * *

David didn't exactly look sharp when he met Senator Edgar Charles outside the Dekalb County Sheriff's office in Smithville. He was making do with his few clothing purchases from Knoxville. At least he was clean and shaved. Again the news media was making the most of the latest string of events bombarding the rural peace of Tennessee. David was shouting "NO COMMENT," over the noise and confusion of questions and strobe lights, while making an effort to keep Charles away from the video cameras. Charles bodyguard and spokesperson used sheer muscle to clear a path to the door of the building. Once inside the door was locked by a Deputy. The Sheriff was waiting for them.

"David, I need a word with you." Without a glance at the Senator, Steve stepped into the tiny break room. David followed. Steve began without preamble. "It's bad, David. I've been here since seven. I have been informed all of us, including the Senator will face charges of obstructing justice, and conspiracy with intent for treason. Are you sure the Senator can be trusted? Everyone in the country knows his reputation. Always in the news or the cover of some magazine with some international big shot. I have to say I got my suspicions, what with terrorist here in my home town. The FBI's got some pretty convincing proof against that Houston company. Those computer disks shed a lot of light, but still don't prove the Charles brothers weren't working together."

"Steve, I learning that my gut feelings are better at reading people than my so called intellect. Let me talk to them before we panic."

"I sure hope you can talk your way out of this one." Steve mopped his face with a handkerchief, "You've got your work cut out for you, son." He bolted out the door of the room without waiting for David to respond.

David negotiated the break room door on his crutches, cursing his handicap for making him slow. Steve was out of sight. David needed to know where Steve had put the computer disks.

Charles bodyguard stood in the hall holding the door to the office open for David. Edgar Charles was seated before the FBI Chief who was seated behind the desk. David controlled his expression as he spotted last nights computer disks neatly stacked on the corner of the desk. Several agents, recognizable from yesterday were crowding the small room.

Charles was his usual well-groomed image in immaculate attire, unless you looked at the dark circles under his eyes. David took the chair beside him. "I had hoped for a word with you this morning. Sorry, but what Steve told me was important."

"Glad you're here, Middleton. Let's get this over." He took a sheaf of papers from a briefcase and leaned forward to put them on the desk.

"George, if you will examine those papers you will find as of three years ago, I have had no connection with the Optima Oil Corporation. I divested my portfolio of them and some other unprofitable investments. Later the corporation was sold to Tri-World Oil. The sale was approved by the Federal Trade Commission. At that time I thought my brother dead and buried in Denver. It wasn't until last year I learned he was alive and living in Tennessee. I had to do something. Members of my political party have been urging me to run for the Presidency. I offered him money to simply disappear again and he laughed in my face. He told me he knew what the Oak Ridge Laboratory was developing and he would make his own money by using that technology for himself. At that time I knew little of the project. I went to the Vice President and he briefed me on the research. It was only later that the VP and I both learned of the military application of the technology. I never dreamed Jeff knew of that potential. I came to Tennessee to question him on what he knew. He convinced me it was Karen Fielding who was stealing information on the new propulsion system for industrial espionage. I came up with the scheme to have him report to me to make sure he didn't go off the deep end again."

"I sold my stock in Opt Oil, but not my interest. By that I mean I still had good friends that elected to stay with the corporation during their transfer to Tri-World. One of them, his name is on that top letter," Charles pointed to the stack of papers, "agreed to use the e-mail address at his office for my contact with my brother. Stupid idea now, but at the time I was trying to keep several projects going, and didn't want to take the time to worry about Jeff. I didn't know this so called friend would turn on me and side with Jeff when he got wind of the project. I do dumb things from time to time, and trying to bribe my brother was one of them. The whole thing was a scheme to trap Jeff into doing something that I could use to commit him to the sanitarium again."

Charles fell silent while the FBI Chief glanced through the paperwork. Grudgingly he admitted the documents were legitimate. "You're not off the hook, yet Edgar. Those records in Houston are incriminating. Now, I suppose you are going to tell me you and the FTC didn't know Tri-World Oil has mid-east connections? I'll warn you that new evidence has surfaced that confirm a holding company owned by none other than Ben Abdu Hamad has control of Tri-World."

David couldn't keep quiet. "I have no idea what you are looking for, but if you do have evidence, I need to see it. Please make it available at once. I would like to review it before you make more accusations."

One of the men in the background stifled a laugh. His boss laughed out loud. "Edgar, are you sure you want this Public Defender representing you?"

His smug expression made David want to puke.

CHAPTER TWENTY-SIX

Charles pace left David ten feet behind. "Wait," David called, and swung on his crutches to the open door of the sedan. "One minute, Senator."

Charles motioned him into the car. David uncuffed his sticks as the vehicle gained speed. "Sir, I understand if you want other counsel to represent you. I never thought you would want me to handle the whole case."

"How do you know that?" Charles snapped. "Middleton, I've confided more to you about my family than I have my wife. I have law firms on retainer, if you want their help, fine. Right now you're stuck with me."

"I could have ended this today, but I wanted a chance to talk with you. Last night Sheriff Milloy and I went to Knoxville and brought the contents of Jeff's desk back with us. There is some very interesting information on computer disks. I know the FBI has not accessed the information yet. In fact, when they do they will owe you an apology."

Charles rubbed a finger across his neatly trimmed mustache in a gesture that David was beginning to recognize as thought. "You have looked at it?"

"Yes, last night."

"How can you be sure the FBI doesn't already know what's on them?"

"If they had reviewed them there would have been no meeting this morning,. I have the disks in my pocket."

"What?" Charles looked at David like he was either daft, or the biggest liar in creation.

"A little slight of hand, when I stumbled into the desk. Sometimes I use my disability for something besides sympathy."

Charles didn't perk up. "What good does that do? We'll be accused of tampering with evidence."

"No," David said, "We will make copies and I will slip these back to Steve. He has not yet officially turned over what we brought from Knoxville. I only happened to recognize them sitting on Steve's desk. My gut is telling me it is important you look at them. All of us are late comers to this story except you. You're one of the key players. I think we missed something going over them last night." David wasn't really sure of anything except he needed to view the disks again himself. There was something still on the edge of his mind.

Charles leaned over to tap the driver on the shoulder. "To my plane."

* * * * *

David made a quick visit to the jail. Orville was to be transferred to a juvenile boot camp facility. Seems a Federal Judge had taken an interest in his case, and recommended clemency. Six months of military type training and discipline, then a foster home. Maggie and John Lewis had already volunteered and would be considered as Orville's foster parents. David wanted to say goodbye to the boy.

He found Orville in his favorite position, hanging on the bars of his cell. "Hey, kid. Heard you got a break. Make the most of it, will you? The Army's not a bad life. I know. I might have been a career officer if I had two legs."

Orville just shrugged. "Guess I can't complain. Some of the guys here tell me it's a good camp. Glad you didn't stay in the Army, 'cause you wouldn't be here now. Guess you're a pretty good lawyer, huh?"

David ruffled the jet black hair growing on Orville's head. "Mr. and Mrs. Lewis have put in a bid for you. Do your time and stay out of trouble and they'll be waiting for you."

"I know," Orville nodded, "Mrs. Lewis said they'll visit and bring me anything I need. She already brought me a new pair of boots and new shirt and jeans to wear when I leave here. I'll make them proud, don't you worry."

"You make me proud now, Orville. Goodbye, kid." David pushed open the unlocked cell door.

Orville came to stand in the opening. "Mr. Middleton, if you see Buddy again, tell him I said Hey."

David nodded his head yes, reluctant to leave the youth, but hoping he never had to lay eyes on Buddy Adams again.

He spent a few minutes with Ahmed Faziz, going over his account of what happened the night the black girl was murdered. David had sent Ellen and Mamie to Lebanon to talk to the motel manager. They now knew another man was behind bars, accused of a similar murder at the same motel. The DNA reports were not in yet, but David knew without a doubt Dr. Ahmed Faziz would be cleared. Faziz had elected to remain in jail rather than ask for bail. David knew the man had no where else to go. He would try to hurry the laboratory reports.

David left Ahmed, headed for the hospital to pick up Bobbie, when two FBI Agents asked very politely for a minute of his time.

David was ushered into the Sheriff's office to face the Atlanta Bureau Chief. "Middleton, you must live a charmed life. I don't know how you do it, but everything on the disks you turned over to us verifies what Edgar Charles has been claiming. I guess we owe you an apology. No hard feelings?"

David accepted the extended hand. "No hard feelings. Are you about to wrap up your operation here, now that Fischer's body has been recovered?"

"Charles said you will make the arrangements for his brother, so I guess we might as well. One more thing, though. Like I said, you must have providence on your side. How did you get the State Department to vouch of Ahmed Faziz? Turns out he was working for the government all along. The Vice President was in on the set up from the beginning. Anyway, it will be a long time before the Hamaddi will try anything here in the U.S. again. We're closing up shop today, be gone by tomorrow. If you ever need anything, give me a call. I'm in the Atlanta phone book."

David, sincerely hoping he would never need an Atlanta phone book, said goodbye, and excused himself to leave the office. He knew the cover for Faziz was a fabrication, not sure why the Vice President had gone along with it. Even with Jeff's body at the mortuary it seemed like this case would never end. Not that he was complaining for the moment. Senator Charles had left him with a fat retainer check, the FBI was leaving town, and Bobbie was waiting at the hospital.

David arrived at her room to hear words not fit for a lady coming out of his fiancée's beautiful mouth. What now? David's nerves still had a long way to go before he quit jumping at noise and shadow. Swinging through the door, he drew up short when he saw her before a mirror, trying to subdue her hair. Wild curls were trying to escape as she pushed pins to hold them down.

Taking a calming breath he said, "Why don't you leave it down?"

Bobbie spun around, her eyes clear and sparkling. She had spent three days in the bed before her doctor would certify her detoxified of the drugs she had been given. "I swear, I think I'll have it all cut off. How would you like me with short hair?"

David cocked his head. "Humm. Might do. Come here." She came to him holding out hairpins in her hand. David turned her around and made a single thick braid of her hair. She looked in the mirror, laughed and took the braid to twist it around against her nape and pinned it there.

"Not bad," she admired herself. "Maybe you should take up dressing hair. Might be safer than the law."

"I doubt that," David helped her slip a jacket over the modest dress she wore. "Ready to go? You know you can stay home if you want."

"I know," Bobbie looked up at him with a tear clinging to her lashes. "I want to go."

David squeezed her hand and they went out to the Buick. With David driving, Bobbie beside him, Ellen and Mamie in the rear seat, they made their way to Nashville and Mt. Olivet Cemetery. The open grave was waiting, and a simple ceremony laid Shemisha to rest beside her father. On the other side of her son, a space waited for Mamie. For the time being, Mamie would continue to stay with Ellen.

The ride home was somber with little conversation. At Ellen's house, David and Bobbie transferred to her car. Tommy, when he came to cut the grass, had found Bobbie's car in the shed. A gallon of gas from the lawnmower can got them to the market where David filled the tank. They made another stop at the mortuary. The previous evening David had viewed Jeff's body go into the crematorium furnace. Now a small box was handed to him. He returned to the car and he and Bobbie drove north into a remote part of a wildlife refuge. Just as the sun was setting, David stood on a cliff's edge, Bobbie beside him, and let the breeze scatter Jeff's ashes to the rocks below. The few kernels of bone that did not burn were dropped into the stream far below. David knelt on the rocky lip and fanned the flame from a match to set fire to the cardboard box that had contained Jeff's earthly remains. When it too, was reduced to ashes, he pushed them from the ledge. Nothing remained of the man who could have had so much, but ended with nothing. For a moment David and Bobbie stood hand in hand, watching the sun sink from view behind the hills.

* * * * *

In Nashville a tall, thin man with deep set eyes spoke into the telephone with the reverence due an elder. He spoke Arabic with all the customary courtesy due a Sheik of the ruling class. He spoke each word with care. "Honored one, I was there to meet the man who would bring the missing information. I would not dishonor you by failing. He never appeared. The coward did not return to keep his promise to our brother, Fischer. Yes, yes, I will try again. No, by the Holy one, I will see that you are revenged in the death of our brother.

When he hung up the telephone, he wiped the sweat from his face. Fischer was dead, Nadja was dead, but Faziz lived, and I live. I, Ibrahim Hassim live. I need to leave this place, Ben Abdu has long arms. I would have been safer with the Mossaad in Israel. He looked at his swollen hand and arm. The gunshot wound in his shoulder had not healed well. Now red streaks lined his arm and neck. He made up his mind to seek a doctor. What better doctor could he find than Ahmed Faziz?

* * * * *

Bobbie waited nervously as Aunt Ellen fussed with her bridal veil. The strains of the music started and Bobbie's brother Michel, looking quite debonair in a rented tuxedo offered Aunt Ellen his arm and they followed

Paula and Lorna Jane down the aisle of the church. Bobbie placed her hand on Uncle Steve's arm and they entered the sanctuary.

David waited for her at the altar. David, standing on two legs, straight and tall and ever so handsome in his formal morning coat. His smile had enough candle power to light the room. To his side, Jim Ed, looking all the world like a Hollywood star himself, was the best man. As many of Bobbie's brothers and sisters who could come on such short notice lined the front row pew. The groom's side of the church was occupied by Senator Edgar Charles and enough Washington press corp to fill six pews. The whole church overflowed with friends and well-wishers. Bobbie had a brief moment to wonder how Aunt Ellen and Mamie could have arranged a formal wedding so quickly, then Uncle Steve was handing her to David.

The ceremony was mercifully short. Both Bobbie and David said the traditional vows in clear voices. Aunt Ellen cried. So did Mamie and most of the other females in the church. One brother was video taping, another snapping pictures. Then the organ rang out the Wedding March and David walked his bride to the church door. If his gait was a bit strange, rolling like a sailor, no one commented. Later, after the wedding luncheon, the bride and groom circled the dance floor to the strains of The Tennessee Waltz. No one seemed to notice that Bobbie shortened her steps to match David's halting stride, they could only see two beautiful people very much in love.

Even later, at the door of Bobbie's apartment David swept Bobbie up in his arms and carried her inside. He even managed to kick the door closed behind them.

* * * * *

November 1999

David looked up from his desk as Ellen escorted Cal Snead into his office. The man was carrying a bundle wrapped in newspaper, the size of a small child.

"Hello, Cal," David swiveled around in his new chair. "What can I do for you today?"

"Come to pay my bill." The spare man continued to stand and hold the package.

"You don't owe me anything. The County paid your bill." David was curious about the package that was beginning to show grease spots through the paper while a salty aroma invaded the room.

"I pay what I owe," Cal said. "The Missus says you went to the judge for me and got old man Clemmons told to keep his animals fenced in." He deposited the bulky item in the middle of David's paperwork. A corner of the paper tore, and a country ham showed through. Cal Snead smiled thinly at David. "Hope you and your new missus like ham. I put it up last year. Plenty of salt and smoke let it cure real good." The man ducked his head, wiping his hand on the front of his overalls. "Well, I be seeing you'ns."

David sighed and looked at the greasy mess on his desk as Snead backed out the door. Cal Snead did say last year, didn't he? At least that pig was paid for. David had seen to it out of his own pocket. He did like country ham.

* * * * *

The phone rang. "Don't answer that," David growled. Bobbie gently rolled from his side and reached for the dratted thing. She poked David on his shoulder and extended the phone to him. She yawned widely, then turned over again.

Still half asleep, David hadn't caught the name of the caller. Suddenly he sat straight up, and exclaimed, "What? You don't mean it? The President, too? Well, I don't know. Can I call you back? Yeah, it's only seven, here. Okay, I'll call then."

"Go away, David," Bobbie muttered when David gently shook her.

"Can't, honey, I live here. Would you mind telling me where you put the coffee? I used all that was in the canister."

"Umph," was all Bobbie said.

"Mrs. Middleton, your husband wants his breakfast." Seeing he was making no headway, David crawled over her legs to his side of the bed. They needed a bigger place, he thought. While the repairs were being made to my office, I should have remodeled the whole third floor into a master suite. He pulled Bobbie's sleeping form to him. It was late when they went to bed last night, but the news he had for her was too good to wait. He liked her new haircut. Short, springy curls wrapped themselves around his fingers as he toyed with them. When he looked down, her eyes were open.

She smiled, pulled away and sat up. "Okay, you know where the coffee is, so why do I have to get up?"

"Well, I couldn't very well ask you if you need a new dress when you're asleep."

Bobbie grabbed a pillow and stuffed it down on David's chest. "Why do I need a new dress?"

"Oh," David said off handed, throwing the pillow back at her. "We have an invitation to visit the White House."

"The one in Washington?"

"Is there more than one?"

"I can think of several, right here in Smithville."

"Yes, Washington." David tried to make his voice condescending, but couldn't help laughing. Life would never be dull again.

Bobbie threw herself at him on the bed. "You bet I want a new dress. When?"

David blocked an elbow from attacking his stomach on Bobbie's enthusiastic approach. "Senator Charles will send his plane for us at three this afternoon. I need to call and confirm that we can make it."

"Yes, yes, yes," Bobbie bounced out of the bed. "Call and say yes! I told you a month ago to accept that D. C. law firm's offer. I won't have time to get a dress today. Actually," she swung around to the door. "I'm going to need several new dresses."

"We'll fly up this afternoon, and home tonight. Won't one dress do?" David thought he knew the answer, but wanted to let her tell him.

Bobbie sat on the edge of the bed again and looked at her husband. "I hope he looks just like his father," she said.

David grasped her hand and kissed the palm. "I hope she looks just like her mother."

"You knew." Bobbie sounded disappointed. "How? I just went to the doctor yesterday."

"Well, when I saw Miguel out at the Tidwell's yesterday, I asked him why my always hungry wife had suddenly lost her appetite. Bobbie, is it okay with you? I'm so happy I could burst." David never lost an opportunity to thank God for this woman. He did so now, in silent prayer. She would be a wonderful mother.

Bobbie's eyes misted over. She swiped a hand across her face, then matched his brilliant smile. "You know it is, Mr. Middleton."

* * * * *

Miguel Rios sat at his desk finishing his notes from today's clinic. Ahmed Faziz had formally adopted the Mexican name when the papers from Washington had come through, granting him the option of remaining in the United States. He was offered the Witness Protection Program and was seriously considering that move. Buddy Adams had disappeared the same time Washington had cleared Faziz of any charges in the assassination attempt. Of course Ahmed would have to spend several months with the CIA, NSA, and FBI, naming names and places. He owed the Colonel for making that deal for him.

Ahmed had no regrets. That part of his life was over, and he knew his information on the Hamaddi and other terrorist sects would help the U. S. to format plans, if they would take him seriously, to protect against future terrorism. What he could tell them would have to be followed up with extreme measures around the world, and he hoped politics would not get in the way. The American public's arrogance in thinking nothing could happen in this country made that thinking far from true. The shores and boundaries of this nation no longer protected its citizens from invasion. Daily, hundreds of illegal aliens came into the United States, some with fake papers, and some with no papers at all. Even he, as Dr. Ahmed Faziz with a legitimate visa, had unwillingly participated in what would have been an act of terrorism if carried to completion as planned. Now, he knew of a way he could repay Frank Barger for arranging his pardon. He had gotten the idea from an old friend.

When he was released from the jail, he refused David Middleton's offer to stay with him and his new bride. He was thinking of just disappearing again, but needed to work to save some money. He had gone back to the farm.

He spent his time in jail studying American methods and passed the tests for EMT. He went to Carlos, asking to be allowed to care for the Mexican workers in the area. He held a small clinic each day, then worked in the fields, the same as any of the migrant workers.

It was there Ibrahim Hassim found him. The man was sick. More than sick, he was dying. Streaks of poisoned blood were reaching vital organs from the untended gunshot wound in the shoulder of the man who once had been his friend. Ibrahim knew he was dying. He had waited too long to come for help.

Ahmed had done what he could, telling Carlos the man was his brother. He used the antibiotics from the clinic, but it was too late. Ibrahim was semi-conscious and ranting with fever most of the time, but in his lucid moments answered Ahmed's questions. It was easy for Ahmed to get him to talk about the Gulf War, and the man Ibrahim knew only as Fischer here in the states. It was enough. Lt. Colonel Frank Barger, alias Buddy Adams, would be exonerated.

Even with a new name and identity, Ahmed knew he would never be safe. Ibrahim had found him, others could, too. He would go to Washington, repay his debt and disappear on his own.

When the time came, Ahmed gave his friend the name of Pablo Rios, and Carlos made arrangements for the burial in the Potter's Field section of the County cemetery.

* * * * *

David was surprised to see Miguel Rios join them for the flight to D. C. Miguel told him the Senator's aide had called and requested his presence, too. Other than that, neither of them knew what prompted the occasion.

The flight was smooth and a limo was waiting to slip them through the Washington evening traffic. David was dressed in a dark suit, wearing his prosthesis and Bobbie had chosen a dress suitable for day or evening. Even Miguel had squandered some of his hard earned nest egg on new clothes.

Clearing the gates of the grounds, the limo circled to the north entrance portico of the magnificent mansion. Bobbie was holding her breath, as the uniformed chauffeur handed her down from the vehicle. The Vice President was there to kiss her cheek and shake David's hand. They thanked him for the beautiful silver tea service he sent for a wedding gift. After inquiring about Ellen he led them into the house that is the symbol of American royalty. Senator Charles greeted Bobbie and David and escorted them into the formal reception Blue Room where uniformed servers were pouring cocktails and wine. They were soon surrounded by celebrities from all walks of life. Everyone seemed to already know who they were. David found himself fending off questions about his missing leg to a young Hollywood starlet while Bobbie was holding court with the Vice President in attendance. He heard them laughing about the time the Vice President had rescued her cat from a tree on her family's farm. Miguel Rios had disappeared at the door, and so far no one had said why they were invited.

With all the usual Pomp and Circumstance, the President made an appearance with his wife at his side. The First Lady stayed to join the party, but the Chief Executive begged off, claiming a desk loaded with work. Both Bobbie and David were introduced and thanked for their part in keeping a deadly terrorist attack from the U.S.

The party progressed to dinner, presided over by the First Lady. So many courses were served David lost count. He was seated by a stout matron whose name he had forgotten and a man he had never met before. The conversation was stilted, David not conversant on Washington gossip and his dinner companions not interested in Tennessee. Bobbie was having the time of her life. Seated by the Vice President she had just told his wife that she and David were expecting. She would not be drinking the wine. Congratulations made the rounds and their talk centered on baby health and care.

David finished his desert of cherry tart with ice cream and tried to catch Edgar Charles eye across the long table. When the diners pushed back their chairs, Charles made his way to David. "Do you think your wife would mind if I spirit you away for a while?"

David looked at Bobbie, still immersed in conversation. "What did you have in mind?"

"I want you to meet some people. We'll need to go to my downtown office. Its not far, won't take long." He clapped David on the back.

"Actually, this is why you were invited." He spoke to a young marine in the hall, asking that his car be brought around.

David excused himself and went to speak to Bobbie. Ensconced in the East Room among her admirers, David took a moment to admire her himself. The ladies with her graciously retreated to give them some privacy. Bobbie noted David limping badly. "Is it time to go?" she asked.

"No." David wagged his head and gave her an apologetic smile. "I came to tell you the Senator and I will be discussing some business. I didn't want you to worry if you couldn't find me. I won't be long, and I will ask him for transportation back to the airport. I'll be glad to get home. This brace is heavy and hot to wear. Wish I'd listened to you and stayed on my crutches. You'll be okay?"

"Sure. I've known the Vice President's family all my life. The surroundings are a bit intimidating, but I'll manage. Go make it quick. I'm getting tired, too."

David quickly kissed the tip of her nose, then joined the Senator at the door. Charles was correct about the distance. Less than ten minutes in the car saw them to an all glass edifice across from the Pentagon. They stepped off the elevator on an upper floor. Discreet gold leaf lettering on double glass doors named a prestigious law firm.

Though no one was at the reception desk, Charles seemed to know where he was going. Leading the way through a warren of offices he came to a large conference room situated in the middle of the suite. Tastefully done with artifact filled bookcases and beautifully framed paintings by Monet and Renoir, the room had no windows. Lighting came softly from behind the cornice running the perimeter of the ceiling. The large table and at least eighteen chairs were empty.

David spoke first. "Is there something I should know?"

Charles merely nodded. He stuck his hands in his pant's pockets and walked to the end of the room. From there he turned to address David. "I had a feeling about you from the start. I know you'll make a great member of the team. Have you considered my offer?"

David knew Bobbie had been encouraging him to accept. As a member of the large law firm David could give her, and now their child the security of a life she deserved. He had not made up his mind until tonight. Seeing her at ease among the elite of this nation and knowing she was never embarrassed by his handicap was the deciding vote. He started to speak, but Charles interrupted.

"Before you say anything, I want you to meet some of the members of this team." Charles gestured all around him. "This is the offices of a law firm, and the ordinary business is handled like any legitimate concern. However, there are certain duties that come with acceptance in this enterprise. As chairperson of the Senate Armed Forces Committee, I head a team of highly trained personnel from all branches of the services. We report directly to the President as Commander in Chief. We call it JOTT, Joint Operations Tactical Team. This is our headquarters."

David broke in. "With all due respect, I am a lawyer, but what would that have to do with a military operation? I have never heard of JOTT."

"No, and you never will. Officially, we don't exist. Don't get me wrong, but all of our so-called security agencies are so bound up in bureaucracy it limits their effectiveness. It is not our purpose to interfere with any of the agencies. We only assist as needed, then only with the approval of the President. You might think we are moving in on the Secret Service. Not so, again, we only assist when called on by the President. We are adding to the team personnel who are exceptional in surveillance. If you had kept your gut feeling about Jeff to yourself, we may have never known that Jeff was backing up his plans for his own use. Thanks to your swiping those computer disks before the FBI got to them, I could interpret some of his correspondence and reports to Houston. Without that I could not prove my so called friend with Tri-World Oil was double crossing me and taking advantage of the situation for his own profit. He would have succeeded and built the car, except Jeff had held back one essential piece of information and Karen Fielding's plans didn't work. When Ben Abdul Hamad learned the plans were incomplete, he ordered the sabotage of the TVA to bring Jeff into line, but Jeff held out for more money. My brother made a big mistake trying to work both ends of the deal. With the information on the disks, JOTT was able to defuse the terrorist plot."

David had lowered himself in a chair as Charles talked. The hard plastic of his brace was beginning to chaff his stomach. He wished he hadn't worn the artificial leg. And he wished he was not hearing what Charles was telling him. Jeff's supposed fictional writing was not fiction at all.

Charles started to pull out a chair when the door of the room opened. Ahmed Faziz, alias Miguel Rios entered followed by a man David had hoped never to see again. Charles motioned the newcomers into the room. "Come in, gentlemen. I was about to ask Mr. Middleton his decision."

"Howdy, friend. You and your pretty lady doing okay?" Buddy Adams protruding front teeth made him look like a happy chipmunk. "Told you I'd see you again."

David rose and grasped the extended hand. "You may be sorry you do," he scowled down at the smaller man. "If Bobbie had been aboard that boat you blew up--,"

Buddy didn't let him finish. "Whoa, friend. I only made that threat to jar you to action. I saw her swim away before I fired. Just sent the rocket in to make sure none of those bastards got away. Didn't doubt you got Fischer.

You're the best there is. Nobody else could have made that shot. We need you here. Rios will work with you, but you're one damn good assassin."

"Gentlemen, let's get back to business." The Senator pounded his fist on the table like a gavel. He shoved a sheaf of papers over to David. "Take your time reading these, but they don't leave this room. I need your decision tonight. Colonel Barger, Mr. Rios and I will give you some privacy." He stepped to the door and the other men followed.

David sat for a moment, thinking of the past few months. He had felt more alive than anytime since the Gulf War. Quickly scanning the documents, his trained mind saw he was offered everything he wanted for Bobbie and their children. A disclaimer stated the work could be hazardous. Well, a small law practice in Tennessee had definitely held danger. That was life, wasn't it? He would be fully reinstated in the Army, all privileges restored and the rank of Major to start. David had to smile at that. He tapped on his hollow left leg. Would he be the first of many handicapped Army personnel? Plus he would work openly as an attorney with the large law firm here in D. C.

He thought of Buddy calling him a good assassin. Was that what he was? Could he do it again? Surveillance was easy, but if they handed him a rifle, could he do it? Not to kill needlessly, but yes, he would to save a life, or many lives, if that was what it took. David was staring off in space when the men returned to the room.

"Well?" Charles asked.

David handed the signed papers back to the Senator. He swiveled around, wishing the fake leg wouldn't get in his way. He looked at Rios and winked, then spoke to Buddy. "Orville said I should tell you Hey."

About The Author

Judy Lucas grew up in central Florida. Along with a love for writing, she enjoyed participating in summer reading and story telling programs at the local library where she could exaggerate the description of Cinderella's ball gown for the young girls, and add zip to the westerns for the boys. She now lives in Crossville, Tennessee after an active career in accounting, spending some of those years as a government employee in Europe and the Middle-East. Besides writing and travel, she enjoys cooking and collecting recipes.